JOURNAL FOR THE STUDY OF THE OLD TESTAMENT SUPPLEMENT SERIES
79

Editors
David J A Clines
Philip R Davies

JSOT Press
Sheffield

GIBEAH

The Search for a Biblical City

Patrick M. Arnold, S.J.

Journal for the Study of the Old Testament
Supplement Series 79

To Mary Jean and Allan P. Arnold

Published by JSOT Press
JSOT Press is an imprint of
Sheffield Academic Press Ltd
The University of Sheffield
343 Fulwood Road
Sheffield S10 3BP
England

Printed in Great Britain
by Billing & Sons Ltd
Worcester

British Library Cataloguing in Publication Data

Arnold, Patrick M.
   Gibeah : the search for a Biblical city.
   —(JSOT supplement series, ISSN 0309-0787; 79).
   I. Title   II. Series
   933

ISBN 1-85075-223-0

CONTENTS

ACKNOWLEDGMENTS

At the end of a long writing project, it is a humbling and happy experience to acknowledge the many people and organizations that have offered me such generous assistance.

Dr J. Maxwell Miller, my dissertation director at Emory University, first pointed me in the right direction in my 'search for Gibeah' by offering sage literary, historical, and archaeological advice. Above all, his scholarly integrity and writing craftsmanship set an example for me which I can only hope to emulate. Dr John Hayes of Emory contributed many original ideas and much good-spirited encouragement to the production of this book. Dr Martin Buss also offered wise counsel and moral support. Thanks also to Drs Gene Tucker and Oded Borowski of Emory, and Dr Israel Finkelstein of Bar-Ilan University in Israel for their helpful suggestions.

Thanks are very much in order to such colleagues as Stuart Irvine and Diana Edelman for their friendly scholarly advice, and to many of my Jesuit brothers for their encouragement, support, and good humor during this writing project.

I am very grateful to the Catholic Biblical Association for their helpful assistance in the form of a Young Scholars grant, and to the theology faculties of St Louis University, the Jesuit School of Theology in Berkeley, and the University of San Diego for various concrete kinds of help and assistance.

Finally, I am thankful to the people of Jeba in Occupied Palestine for their kind welcome and hospitality during my visits to their village.

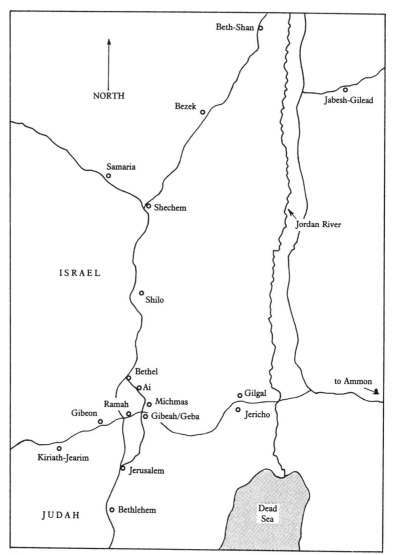

Map 1: The Location of Gibeah at Jeba

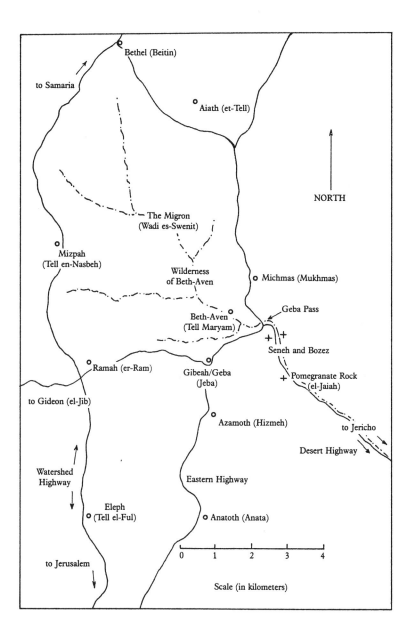

Bethel (Beitin)

to Samaria

Aiath (et-Tell)

NORTH

The Migron
(Wadi es-Swenit)

Mizpah
(Tell en-Nasbeh)

Wilderness
of Beth-Aven

Michmas (Mukhmas)

Geba Pass

Beth-Aven
(Tell Maryam)

Seneh and Bozez

Ramah (er-Ram)

Gibeah/Geba
(Jeba)

Pomegranate Rock
(el-Jaiah)

to Gideon (el-Jib)

Azamoth (Hizmeh)

to Jericho

Desert Highway

Watershed
Highway

Eastern Highway

Eleph
(Tell el-Ful)

Anatoth (Anata)

0   1   2   3   4

to Jerusalem

Scale (in kilometers)

ABBREVIATIONS

AASOR	Annual of the American Schools of Oriental Research
AB	Anchor Bible
ABD	*Anchor Bible Dictionary*
AJSL	*American Journal of Semitic Languages and Literature*
ALUOS	*Annual of the Leeds University Oriental Society*
ASTI	*Annual of the Swedish Theological Institute in Jerusalem*
ATD	Das Alte Testament Deutsch
BA	*Biblical Archaeologist*
BAR	*Biblical Archaeological Review*
BASOR	*Bulletin of the American Schools of Oriental Research*
BKAT	Biblischer Kommentar. Altes Testament
BR	*Biblical Research*
BS	*Bibliotheca Sacra*
BTAVO	Beihefte zum Tübinger Atlas der Vorderen Orients
BZ	*Biblische Zeitschrift*
BZAW	Beihefte zur Zeitschrift für die altestamentliche Wissenschaft
CBC	Cambridge Bible Commentary
CBOTS	Coniectanae Biblica: Old Testament Series
CBQ	*Catholic Biblical Quarterly*
CQ	*Critical Quarterly*
Diss.	Doctoral dissertation
DH	The Deuteronomistic History
Dtr	Deuteronomistic
E	Elohist source
EstE	*Estudios Ecclesiasticos*
ET	*Expository Times*
ETL	*Ephemerides Theologicae Lovanienses*

FRLANT	Forschungen zur Religion und Literatur des Alten und Neuen Testaments
HAIJ	J.M. Miller and J.H. Hayes, *A History of Ancient Israel and Judah* (Philadelphia: Westminster, 1986)
HAT	Handbuch zum Alten Testament
HSM	Harvard Semitic Monographs
HUCA	*Hebrew Union College Annual*
IB	Interpreter's Bible
ICC	International Critical Commentary
IDB	*Interpreter's Dictionary of the Bible*
IDBS	*Interpreter's Dictionary of the Bible Supplement*
IEJ	*Israel Exploration Journal*
IJH	J.H. Hayes and J.M. Miller, ed. *Israelite and Judean History* (Philadelphia: Westminster, 1977)
Int	*Interpretation*
J	Yahwist source
JAOS	*Journal of the American Oriental Society*
JBL	*Journal of Biblical Literature*
JSOT	*Journal for the Study of Old Testament*
JSOTSS	Journal for the Study of Old Testament Supplement Series
JSS	*Journal of Semitic Studies*
JTS	*Journal of Theological Studies*
KAT	Kommentar zum Alten Testament
KS	A. Alt, *Kleine Schriften zur Geschichte des Volkes Israel* (München: Beck, 1959)
LBC	Layman's Bible Commentary
LXX	Septuagint
MT	Masoretic Text
OrAnt	*Oriens Antiquus*
OTL	Old Testament Library
P	Priestly source
PEFQS	*Palestine Exploration Fund Quarterly Statement*
PEQ	*Palestine Exploration Quarterly*
PJB	*Palastina Jahrbuch*
RB	*Revue Biblique*
RExp	*Review and Expositor*
SBL	Society of Biblical Literature
SBT	Studies in Biblical Theology
SH	*Scripta Hierosolymitana*

SOTS	Society for Old Testament Study
ST	*Studia Theologica*
SVT	Supplements to *Vetus Testamentum*
WMANT	Wissenschaftliche Monographien zum Alten und Neuen Testament
WTJ	*Westminster Theological Journal*
WZKMU	Wissenschaftliche Zeitschrift der Karl Marx-Universität
ZAW	*Zeitschrift für die alttestamentliche Wissenschaft*
ZDPV	*Zeitschrift des Deutschen Palästina-Vereins*
ZTK	*Zeitschrift für Theologie und Kirche*

INTRODUCTION

It is well known that events in the early history of Israel are shrouded by layers of literary tradition which theological and ideological circles added to the developing biblical literature many centuries after the events their stories attempt to relate. Yet despite the daunting historical, literary, and archaeological problems which dog every attempt to peer into the ancient biblical past, the rewards of searching for history are great. The very act of imagining the real historical roots of a biblical tradition, and tracing the various political and theological uses which that tradition found in the subsequent life of Israel, is an exciting intellectual and spiritual adventure; insight comes, and moribund texts spring to life.

This book probes into one small portion of Israel's experience: the history of Gibeah, a city destined to play a key role in the life of biblical Israel. It so happens that Gibeah three different times found itself at the crossroads of events which profoundly affected the people of Israel: an intertribal massacre in the earliest days of Hebrew historical memory, Saul's uprising against the Philistines and his foundation of the Israelite nation-state, and, centuries later, the kingdom of Israel's fatally mistaken attack upon Jerusalem and Judah. Though Gibeah comprised only a tiny amount of Israel's overall territory or population, its crucial historical, geographical and literary roles in these events make it an excellent laboratory to study many of the larger forces and events that shaped Israel.

This book is a cross-disciplinary study of Gibeah approached from lexical, topographical, archaeological, historical, literary, and theological perspectives. This diverse treatment is necessary because all of these facets relating to Gibeah are so thoroughly interdependent that one cannot understand properly any single perspective on Gibeah without relating it to other approaches. Our task is to develop the study in a logical fashion so that each approach properly illuminates the other perspectives.

The first problem which concerns us is amazingly basic: it is not always clear when the biblical text even mentions Gibeah! In

Chapter 1, we will take care to determine just which stories actually tell us anything about Gibeah. Gibeah's name הגבעה means 'the hill', but in a number of texts it is not entirely clear whether an appellative form is meant ('any hill'), or whether the specific Benjaminite town of Gibeah is intended; Hebrew does not capitalize letters to distinguish proper names. To make matters more complicated, several other towns in the mountainous Benjaminite territory were also named with variants of the word for hill (גבעה), and in a number of instances it seems that copyists may have accidentally confused these toponyms. Finally, almost every important text or story about Gibeah also mentions a town named 'Geba', which also, of course, means 'hill'. We will have to discuss the strong possibility that these two toponyms are merely variant names for the same place.

A second problem relates to the whole question of historicity. Readers accustomed to biblical criticism know quite well that historians rarely take the biblical text at face value. A century of research has alerted us to the fact that a wide variety of literary works, ranging from folktales to government documents and from myths to historical reports, flowed into the traditions that were to emerge as the Bible. The authors of these sources would not have intended to convey 'historical information' as we understand this term in modernity. Historians are therefore especially concerned first to identify the *literary genre* or nature of the texts which they have before them in order that they might evaluate the historicity of a report. Moreover, since the Bible took shape over a millennium, the historian must decide whether a given passage actually originated in the period to which it is ascribed (e.g. the Conquest), or whether it is a relatively late document (e.g. postexilic) which has been editorially inserted into stories originating hundreds of years earlier.

The study of Gibeah contains exactly the same problems. We must, for example, deal with lists of towns which were purportedly compiled by Joshua, but which probably actually originated in administrative documents of Judah's monarchy, or even later. As we determine in Chapter 1 just which texts mention Gibeah, we shall also make some judgments about the genre and date of the passage in which it occurs in order to assist us in gauging the historical value of the report.

All of this very basic groundwork, tedious as it sometimes seems, is absolutely necessary in helping us solve our next problem, which at first glance also seems awfully basic: it is not at all clear exactly where Gibeah *was*. In Chapter 2 we shall review the fascinating modern 'search for Gibeah' which dates all the way back to 1838. In light of our lexical/literary study and some key topographical information given in the biblical texts, we shall see why the very first suggestion as to Gibeah's location (the village of Jeba) over a century and a half ago was probably correct. The problem here is that one of the greatest archaeologists of all time, William F. Albright, excavated a different site (Tell el-Ful) and convinced practically all of his colleagues that he had found 'Gibeah of Saul'. It will take a bit of detective work—and almost iconoclastic archaeological analysis—to see why his site, listed in most biblical atlases as Gibeah, probably served as little more than a watchtower and military fort during its career. Though archaeologists have never excavated Jeba, the sleepy little village unwittingly best fits the description as the site of Israel's first 'capital'.

Once we have determined just where Gibeah is on the ground as well as in the Bible, we can begin to look at the old stories about Gibeah in order to write its history and appreciate the traditions that grew up around it. In Chapter 3 we shall look at the awesome and baroque account of the Outrage at Gibeah (Judg. 19-21), the horrifying story of a rape-murder at Gibeah and the all-out civil war in Israel which ensued there. Abundant literary clues suggest that many of the story's details are fictional; careful readers of the Bible will realize that many of the same scenes and motifs exist elsewhere in the Bible—in the story of Sodom's destruction (Gen. 19) or of Joshua's attack on Ai (Josh. 8), for example. Moreover, the story betrays many marks of late redactional tampering by theologically tendentious editors. With so much fiction, is there anything historical in the story? It would seem so, as is confirmed by an unlikely source: the prophet Hosea. For the eighth-century BCE Hosea, the outrage which occurred at Gibeah centuries earlier was symptomatic of the whole reason Yahweh was about to destroy the kingdom of Israel forever in *another* catastrophe at Gibeah in his own day. Just what happened at Gibeah in the so-called 'days of the Judges', and how later editors attempted to cover up the story, are our principle concerns in these pages.

In Chapter 4 we shall discuss an event at Gibeah which was among the most important things that ever happened in Israel. As more and more scholars discount the historicity of the patriarchal sagas in Genesis and even the Exodus and Conquest accounts, they are left with the intriguing question: what events propelled the scattered Hebrew tribes in the hill-country of Canaan into nationhood as Israel? A growing number suggest that the answer relates to Saul's successful leadership of a Hebrew revolt against the Philistines at Gibeah, and his subsequent formation there of a monarchical government with Gibeah as its 'capital'.

Unfortunately, centuries of Judean politically inspired editorial interference have largely obscured this crucial contribution of Saul to Israel (and the role of Gibeah along with him) in our present biblical texts. While the earliest Benjaminite folk stories celebrated Saul and his Gibeah-based kingdom, his Judean rival and successor King David of Jerusalem exterminated virtually every member of the Saulide family while his literary henchmen systematically plundered the Saul story, twisting its hero into a paranoid and murderous tyrant. Later Deuteronomistic editors followed suit, portraying Saul as a king abandoned by God's spokesman Samuel. History, as they say, is written by the winners. Such literary alternatives need not deter critical historians from recovering a more objective recreation of events, however; in this case we shall glimpse something of Gibeah's proud role as the center of Israel's first kingdom.

After David's minions murdered most of the Saulide family at Gibeah, the city seems, not surprisingly, to have suffered a drastic eclipse. Indeed, the name 'Gibeah' never appears again as such in official Judean accounts or records. Did a city which played such a key role in Israel's origins now virtually disappear? Probably not. Perhaps this book's riskiest suggestion hypothesizes that, accidentally or deliberately, the name 'Gibeah of Saul' mutated within a century to 'Geba', the masculine-gendered version of the Hebrew for 'hill', as the city fell under Judean political control and linguistic influence.

After the division of the kingdoms (c. 925) and an unsuccessful Israelite attempt to seize Benjaminite territory from the Kingdom of Judah, King Asa reclaimed northern Benjamin and fortified Geba, site of ancient Gibeah of Saul. Geba and its sister fortress Mizpah now lay in Judean territory near the border with Israel, and each guarded important roads leading south toward the capital of Jerusalem.

Chapter 5 discusses Gibeah's role in events and prophecies surrounding Israel's invasion of Judah in the Syro-Ephraimite War (c. 735). After Syria's king Rezin brought Israel's puppet king Pekah under his sway, the two conspired to invade Jerusalem and replace the Davidic king Ahaz with their own choice stooge. The Israelite prophet Hosea apparently opposed this conspiracy, warning Benjamin of its imminent invasion (Hos. 5.8) while accusing Israel of a long history of bellicosity. In a stinging accusation, Hosea twice alluded to Israel's sin 'in the days of Gibeah', a vague reference that heretofore has not been satisfactorily explained. Most scholars assume the charge relates either to the rape-murder of the Levite's concubine in Judges 19, or to Saul's institution of kingship in 1 Samuel 10-15. Neither of these explanations fits the context of Hosea's oracles at all well.

Hosea probably alluded to an oral tradition in Israel that remembered the original Israelite massacre of Benjaminite Gibeah in pre-monarchical times, a memory now visible only dimly in Judges 20. Hosea seems to charge that Israel has committed war-crimes against its brother Hebrews since the earliest tribal days, and now threatens to repeat the sin as the Syro-Ephraimite forces plan to smash through the Judean border at Geba (ancient Gibeah) *en route* to Jerusalem. Only this time, Hosea says, God will punish Israel irrevocably. Israel, which has sowed violence and not justice, will reap its reward of destruction and disappear.

As the Syro-Ephraimite armies breached the border, the Judean prophet Isaiah alarmed his countrymen with an oracle of doom describing the progress of the invaders toward Jerusalem (Isa. 10.27-32). Isaiah relates that, after the forces crossed the Geba Pass, 'Gibeah of Saul' (the archaic name for the city) fled before the armies, which, incidentally, failed in their mission to replace Ahaz.

Heretofore, scholars have not related Hosea's alarm of an imminent attack on Gibeah (Hos. 5.8) to Isaiah's detailed description of the invasion's course through the city. The association of these oracles provides an excellent opportunity to view a biblical event mentioned in official documents (2 Kgs 16) from the perspective of two contemporary observers.

Geba is not mentioned again until postexilic times, when it became an important village to the resettled Jews attempting to reconstruct and restore Judean life on the land after the shock of the Babylonian Exile. In the following century as Jewish life, culture, and religion slipped into a Dark Age of Persian and Greek colonization, so too Gibeah/Geba slipped into literary obscurity.

Chapter 1

THE LITERARY SEARCH FOR GIBEAH

Searching for an ancient city is an exciting but difficult adventure; such an enterprise suggests images of Jeep caravans arduously trekking across deserts, or archaeological excavations painstakingly dissecting mysterious mounds. Vivid as these scenes may be, we rarely realize that a challenging literary search always precedes an archaeological one.

If a city is known to us only through ancient texts, we must evaluate the information those texts give to us about the city in order to determine its location.[1] This is very much the case in our search for biblical Gibeah. Compounding our difficulties, however, is the fact that not just one, but several 'Gibeahs' existed in ancient Israel, and the texts which tell us about them are frequently unclear as to which 'Gibeah' is meant. The search for Gibeah of Benjamin must therefore begin with careful textual analysis.

Textual Problems

Biblical stories relating to the traditional homeland of the tribe of Benjamin contain several place-names based on the Hebrew root גבע, the nominal stem of the word for 'hill'. This is not a surprising phenomenon in the mountainous Benjaminite area since people often name their villages after prominent natural features. Nor is the problem of topynym proliferation unique to Benjamin; dozens of place-names are duplicated throughout Palestine, though usually in widely scattered regions.[2] The presence of so many גבע-root place-names in so small an area as Benjamin, however, poses special problems for our search for Gibeah.

In the first place, it is sometimes difficult to ascertain whether a particular גבע-root word in the biblical text is to be read in an appellative sense ('a hill') or as a proper name (e.g. 'Gibeah'); Hebrew does not employ clues such as capitalization to indicate when a proper name is meant. The Greek Septuagint (LXX), for example, frequently employs the appellative 'hill' even when a proper place-name seems clearly appropriate.

Secondly, in texts certainly requiring a proper-name translation, the presence of many variant linguistic forms based on the גבע root makes it difficult to determine whether these toponyms suggest many discrete sites, or merely represent linguistic variants of a few גבע-root place-names. For example, it is crucial to this entire study whether 'Gibeah' and 'Geba' are different sites, or merely feminine and masculine toponyms referring to the same city.

Finally, the multiplicity of גבע-root toponym variants obviously created problems for ancient scribes as they transmitted and translated texts containing these place-names. In several stories, for example, copyists may have transposed 'Gibeon' for 'Gibeah' in such a fashion as to make the original reading completely mysterious.

In order to ascertain just which biblical texts refer to Gibeah of Benjamin, we must first examine each occurrence of גבע-root place-names in the Hebrew Scriptures. In the process of this survey we will also determine the literary genre and provenance of each text—a study that will liberate us from an uncritical historical acceptance of each story and aid greatly in our search for Gibeah.

At present, most scholars identify at least five גבע-root place-names in Benjaminite territory: Gibeah (also known as Gibeah of Benjamin or Gibeah of Saul), Gibeath Ha-Elohim, Gibeath Kiriath-Jearim, Geba (also known as Geba Benjamin) and Gibeon. Of these toponyms, only the name 'Gibeon' connects with certainty to a modern site: the village of el-Jib, whose Arabic name clearly retains its ancient Hebrew toponym.[3] The location of Gibeon could thus serve as a reliable reference point in our identification and location of the remaining גבע-root sites in Benjamin. Some clarification is necessary before we proceed, however.

The Unique Case of Gibeon

The excavations which definitely identified el-Jib not only produced fascinating archaeological discoveries, but also drew much scholarly attention to Gibeon, its history, and its role in early Israel. Unfortunately, the scholarly excitement over that rare event—the discovery of a clear archaeological record of an interesting and important biblical city—tended to produce a certain understandable exaggeration regarding the importance of the city. A number of studies thus commit what one might humorously call the error of 'creeping Gibeonism', that is, the tendency both (a) to find reference to the city in every obscure text, and (b) to assume that the city dominated early Israel, possessing an importance otherwise unrecorded in biblical literature. These claims need to be lightened somewhat in order to restore scholarly balance.

Regarding textual evidence, the textual/literary survey in this chapter will show only three instances of confusion between Gibeon and other גבע-root toponyms: 2 Sam. 5.25, 2 Sam. 21.6, and 2 Chron. 13.2. Each instance represents a conflict between the Masoretic text (MT), reading either 'Geba' or 'Gibeah', and the LXX (invariably reading 'Gibeon'); there can be little doubt that scribal errors caused these discrepancies. Each instance of textual confusion also requires some careful analysis to ascertain, if possible, the probable original reading. Except for these minor errors, our survey will show that Gibeon is normally clearly distinguished from the other גבע-root sites in Benjamin, most especially so from Geba, from which it is so distinctly differentiated in such a wide variety of sources[4] that there can be no question of identifying the cities with each other as A. Demsky proposed.[5] Nor is Gibeon identical with Gibeath Ha-Elohim; the only story in which this mysterious placename occurs (1 Sam. 10.5) contains no mention of Gibeon whatsoever.[6]

The other tendency of 'creeping Gibeonism', while correctly distinguishing Gibeon from other Benjaminite גבע-root sites, is to rob these towns of their historical importance; questioning, for example, whether Gibeon (and not Gibeah) served as Saul's capital,[7] or whether Gibeon possessed the only great cultic place of worship in Benjamin.[8] While we shall deal with these historical questions in some detail later, we can at least proceed on the confident assumption that Gibeon is textually and topographically identifiable and distinct from the other four גבע-root sites in Benjamin.

Let us now spell out in some detail each instance of a גבע-root site in biblical stories relating to Benjamin, and determine the literary issues and provenance of each passage.

Survey of גבע-root Toponyms

Joshua 18.21-28: The Benjaminite Town-list
Three variants of גבע-root place-names appear in Josh. 18.21-28,

which purports to be a list of towns allotted to the tribe of Benjamin by Joshua at a convocation of the Israelite tribes in Shiloh shortly after the conquest of Canaan (Josh. 18.1-10). Twelve cities are mentioned in the first half of the list, including Geba (גבע) in v. 24, while the second half cites fourteen cities including Gibeon (גבעון) in v. 25 and a site or sites in the MT known as Gibeath Kiriath Arim (גבעת קרית ערים), a term which is textually problematic. LXX here suggests 'Gibeath Jearim', Aquila's Greek translation 'Gibeath and Kiriath', and Codex Alexandrinus 'Gibeath and Kiriath Jearim'.

Several scholars identify two separate sites in the latter reading. M. Noth suggested an original 'Gibeah and Kiriath-Jearim',[9] while K. Schunck similarly proposed 'Gibeath of Saul and Kiriath-Jearim'.[10] W.F. Albright, also separating 'Gibeah' from 'Kiriath-Jearim', used his emendation to argue that the Benjaminite town list sharply distinguished 'Gibeah' from 'Geba', implying that they were two distinct sites in Benjamin.[11] Y. Aharoni also saw here two cities, a 'Gibeath-Kiriath-Jearim' and a 'Gibeah', the latter name having been eliminated through haplography.[12] Aharoni's reading thus retains the fourteen cities indicated in 18.28, but this number may itself be a secondary gloss on an already problematical text.

Since all of the textual variants are unsatisfactory, these scholars are clearly justified in seeking an emendation. The first word גבעת, as the only constant in all of the variants, should stand. However, there is no such site known simply as גבעת ('the hill of. . . '); the word in fact is the construct of גבעה, and implies a following term. The words which follow, קרית ערים (lit. 'town of cities') ought surely to be emended to read קרית יערים ('Kiriath-Jearim'—a well-known village in Benjamin), the word יערים having been omitted through haplography caused by the following word ערים. The entire phrase would thus originally have read 'the hill of Kiriath-Jearim'. In fact, such a hill is specifically mentioned in 1 Sam. 7.1 as a cultic site near Kiriath-Jearim.[13] The town-list therefore seems to name three גבע sites in Benjamin: Geba, Gibeon, and the 'hill of Kiriath-Jearim', the latter instance exemplifying the use of גבע as an appellative.

Few scholars would agree with Y. Kaufmann's claim that this list actually originated in the primitive and tumultuous events surrounding Israel's conquest of Canaan;[14] indeed, a general consensus among critics would now regard the list as a document deriving from bureaucratic court records of the Judean monarchy. A. Alt was the first to hypothesize that all of the town-lists in Joshua emerged from historical settings quite distant from that pictured in the book of

Joshua. Alt suggested plausibly that Josh. 18.21-28 was an official court document listing towns in the Benjaminite province of Judah after King Josiah expanded his border northward in a period of Assyrian decline (c. 620).[15] Noth agreed, adducing the text as evidence of this *Annexionspolitik.*[16]

Later scholars tended to date the list either much later or much earlier than Alt and Noth had suggested. S. Mowinckel proposed a postexilic Priestly setting for the list, though he admitted that it would have originated in earlier oral sources remembering the extent of tribal possessions.[17] F. Cross and G. Wright reverted to an earlier dating, claiming that the Benjaminite town-list best described Judah's political and geographical situation in the late tenth century following Abijah's attack on Jereboam of Israel (cf. 2 Chron. 13.19);[18] similarly, Z. Kallai-Kleinmann believed that the list simply represented a description of Abijah's conquests.[19]

Drawing attention to the two groupings of towns in the list (18.21-24 = 12 cities, 18.25-28 = 14 cities), Aharoni argued that the whole passage actually reflects two separate documents: a list of northern Benjaminite towns which comprised part of an Israelite record of cities within its southern 'Benjaminite district', and a Judean document from the reign of Uzziah listing the towns in Judah's Benjaminite area.[20]

Several points need to be made regarding these scholarly proposals. In the first place, there is no explicit literary evidence in the entire passage which would support Aharoni's suggestion that the list of Benjaminite towns is a composite document; literarily, the piece appears to be an original unit. Aharoni's claim was dictated by the need to explain how a monarchical list of towns in Benjamin could include both a group of cities known to have existed most of the time in the Kingdom of Israel (e.g. Bethel), and a group always clearly under Judean control (e.g. Jerusalem). The only known times in the monarchical era when Benjamin may have comprised a unified royal district were briefly after Abijah's reported victories over Jeroboam (2 Chron. 13.19) c. 900 (reflected in Cross-Wright's and Kallai—Kleinmann's theories), and Josiah's possible reconquest of formerly Israelite territory around 620 (as hypothesized by Alt-Noth). The latter theory is the most compelling since the Josian era is precisely the period when the Deuteronomistic Historian (DH), who edited the material in Joshua, apparently was active in Judah.[21] It is quite probable that DH drew lists of tribal towns from contemporary Judean records and projected them into the distant past as Joshua's 'land grants' given in the golden days of Israel's origins.

It is also by no means clear that the list of towns is divided in a north/south fashion as Aharoni claims. This assumption forced Kallai–Kleinmann to suggest that the 'Geba' of 18.24 (which is listed with so-called 'northern' towns) lay in Ephraim, while another 'Geba of Benjamin', which fails to appear in the 'southern' list, belonged to a hypothesized *third* list of Benjaminite towns, now lost as a result of homoioteleuton.[22] Yet Kallai–Kleinmann's proposed 'Geba' (Khirbet et-Tell) neither rested in Benjamin, nor apparently did it even exist in the monarchical period.[23] If the town-list's division is to be regarded as an expression of geography at all, the split is best explained by an eastern and western division of Benjamin. It appears that the towns in the first half of the list (18.21-25) lie generally east of the Palestinian watershed, while the towns in the second part (18.25-28) lie astride, and to the west of, this watershed.[24]

We may conclude that Josh. 18.21-28 lists the major inhabited towns of Judah's province of Benjamin in the last half of the seventh century (Josiah's reign), and that three גבע-root sites then existed: Geba, to the east of the Palestinian watershed, and to its west, Gibeon and the 'hill' of Kiriath Jearim.

Joshua 21: The Levitical Cities

The list of the cities ostensibly given at God's command (Num. 35.1-8) to the tribe of Levi by Joshua shortly after the Israelite invasion of Canaan mentions in Josh. 21.17 two Benjaminite גבע toponyms: Gibeon (גבעון) and Geba (גבע). The Chronicles version, however, omits Gibeon (MT: 1 Chron. 6.45, LXX: 6.60).[25]

Only fundamentalist scholars would agree today with the old suggestion that the 'Utopian' qualities of the list recommend its actual origins in the time of Joshua;[26] instead, the critics seek later historical settings for the document in a wide range of proposals. One attractive option is to see the document as evidence that the Davidic or Solomonic administration settled Levitical families in newly occupied areas as a way of gaining an Israelite foothold in foreign territories, a policy which would bear striking similarities to modern Israel's settlement of the Palestinian West Bank.[27]

Alt's proposal that the Levitical cities list derives from the same Josianic setting as the town-lists in Joshua 13–19 is unacceptable since it is unlikely that King Josiah's administration would delineate groups of priestly towns while it was in the process of eliminating their hill-shrines (including Geba; see 2 Kgs 23.8).[28] Less problematical is the suggestion that the list documents the Levitical restoration of cities in Palestine after the Jews returned from Exile.[29] The fact that all four of the Benjaminite cities in the list are mentioned in the postexilic era (Gibeon: Neh. 3.7; Geba: Neh. 12.27ff.; Anathoth: Neh. 7.27; and Almon = Alemeth: 1 Chron. 6.60) lends some weight to this proposal.

Since no convincing consensus or evidence on the dating question has yet developed, we will take a cautious approach and place the Levitical cities document very generally in monarchic or early postexilic times. We note additionally that their inclusion in this roll means that both Gibeon and Geba apparently possessed cultic significance of some kind during this era.

1 Chronicles 6–9: Genealogies

The postexilic book of 1 Chronicles contains a series of genealogies of the tribes of Israel (1 Chron. 1–9) which may include some valuable ancient material relating to גבע-root sites in Benjamin.[30] 1 Chron. 8.6-7 links the sons of the biblical judge Ehud, son of Gera the Benjaminite, with the city of Geba (גבע), though the account of Ehud's exploits in Judg. 3.12-30 makes no such mention of Geba. 1 Chron. 8.29 and 9.35 both mention Gibeon (גבעון) in the context of the patriarch Jehiel's genealogy.[31]

It is difficult to ascertain the historical reliability of these genealogies since they occur in postexilic Judean texts 600 or 700 years after the time in which the individuals supposedly lived. We will only note here that Geba and Gibeon once again appear in monarchic and postexilic records from Judah.

Judges 19–20: The Outrage of Gibeah

The last chapters of the book of Judges relate a particularly horrifying episode in the story of Israel which is often termed the 'Outrage of Gibeah'. The account begins with a gruesome narrative (Judg. 19) depicting the rape-murder of a Levite's concubine as the couple sojourned in Gibeah of Benjamin *en route* to their home in Ephraim. The next chapter details the retaliatory response of the eleven tribes of Israel against the city of Gibeah and the Benjaminite warriors who had come to its defense. Finally, Judges 21 describes how the whole congregation of Israel provided stolen virgins to the 600 surviving Benjaminite soldiers lest a whole tribe disappear from Israel.

The Hebrew text of Judges 19–20 contains 24 גבע-root variants (none occurs in Judg. 21). Most of these forms (22) are grammatically regular and textually unproblematic linguistic variants of the feminine place-name 'Gibeah' (גבעה).[32] Twice (Judg. 19.14; 20.4) this city is specially designated by the phrase 'Gibeah which is in Benjamin' (הגבעה אשר לבנימן) a narrative device evidently meant to distinguish the city from 'Gibeahs' in other tribal areas.[33] The other two גבע-root forms are variants based on the masculine toponym 'Geba'; the term 'Geba Benjamin' (גבע בנימן) occurs in 20.10, and the Hebrew expression מערה־גבע (LXX: μααραγαβέ) appears in 20.33. The former term is a designation for Geba also found in 1 Sam. 13.16, and the latter, as we shall later see, is probably a misspelling of מעבר גבע ('Geba Pass'), a locale mentioned in Isa. 10.29.[34]

The problem here of finding two גבע-root place-names closely associated in the same passage will recur again in 1 Sam. 13–14 and Isa. 10.29, and three solutions to it are possible. First, the passages could imply two separate sites. In this narrative, however, the context of 20.10 demands that 'Geba Benjamin' refer only to the site elsewhere identified in the story as 'Gibeah'. Most scholars therefore prefer a second explanation; namely, that a simple spelling or copying mistake (a dropped ה) has transformed 'Gibeah' to 'Geba' Yet a third solution, which becomes increasingly compelling as we see more instances of Gibeah/Geba entanglement, is to suppose that both toponyms refer to the same site, and that the appearance of both masculine and feminine variants is a literary phenomenon attesting to a combination of sources.

In view of its stylistic and thematic pecularities, scholars have long regarded Judges 19–21 as an 'appendix' or late addition to the main body of the book of Judges.[35] After an early tendency to deny that the chapters comprised part of the Deuteronomistic (Dtr) corpus,[36] recent critics have nuanced this judgment somewhat by suggesting that a postexilic editor included the Outrage of Gibeah narratives in a second edition of DH.[37] Other scholars have also noticed that, in addition to the presence of Dtr design and language, the narratives are laced with priestly Levitical terminology and theology.[38]

While the work of literary critics tends to focus on the late stylistic features of the story, the attention of historians converges on details in the narratives which seem to emerge from the earliest days of Israel. Hosea's references to the 'sin' at Gibeah (Hos. 9.9; 10.9) only underscore the impression that events of great antiquity lie behind the Outrage of Gibeah narratives. It is clear that this tradition, dating from the pre-monarchical era, experienced an interesting oral and literary 'life of its own' before its capture by Levitical and Dtr editors for use in their grand historical enterprises. We shall explore this long tradition in some detail in Chapter 3.

1 Samuel 9-15: The 'Rise of Saul' Stories
Samuel provides a major cluster of גבע-root toponyms within narratives relating the rise of Saul as the first King of Israel (1 Sam. 9-15). The events surrounding the establishment of the monarchy at Gibeah are among the most crucial in biblical history, for it is during this era that the scattered Hebrew tribes in the Canaanite hill-country first achieved a nascent national consciousness, unity, and mythos as 'Israel'. It is no surprise that later ideological and literary circles would compete to impose their meaning on these stories which relate the 'birth of a nation'.

At first glance, these chapters seem to present a straightforward account of God's choice of young Saul as an anointed ruler, his early successful battles against the Philistines in and around Gibeah, and his establishment there of a royal capital for his primitive Israelite kingdom. A careful critical examination of the narrative, however, reveals that editors have intertwined a number of contradictory and contrasting stories concerning Saul, thereby confusing the associated גבע-root toponyms 'Gibeah', 'Gibeath Ha-Elohim', and 'Geba' in what some scholars have regarded as a hopeless entanglement. We cannot sort out the גבע-root toponyms properly until we distinguish and identify the various stories in which these place-names occur.

A century ago, scholars began to distinguish between sections of the narratives which portrayed Saul and the institution of monarchy in a positive light (especially 9.1-10.16; 11.1-15; 13-14) and other passages (7.1-8.22; 10.17-21; 12.1-25; 15.1-34) which seemed to slight Saul (and kingship). It was assumed that the pro-Saul/pro-monarchical sources were early and historically reliable, while the later sources purveyed anti-monarchical ideology rather than history.[39] Later scholars rightly began to regard this two-source theory as too simplistic.[40]

Martin Noth's analysis of this material in his seminal study of the Deuteronomistic History provides a sound basis for our study. Noth showed that the seventh-century DH editor composed lengthy passages of the present narrative (7.2-8.22; 10.17-27a; 12.1-25) as ideological anti-monarchical commentary presupposing an earlier Saul tradition.[41] While Noth's basic analysis has won wide agreement among most scholars, others want to nuance the assumption that all anti-monarchical material is late, or that DH was purely anti-monarchical.[42] It is interesting that this late material does not mention a גבע-root toponym.[43]

Noth proposed that an old Saul tradition comprised 9.1–10.16 and 10.27b–11.15, with an expansion of related material in 13–15, and that this block of literature already contained at an early stage material unfavorable to Saul.[44] These early narratives are replete with גבע-root toponyms, and will play a key role both in our literary and archaeological search for Gibeah and our historical reconstruction of the crucial events at Israel's birth which took place there. First, we must sort out the toponyms in each story and determine the provenance of each narrative.

1 Sam. 9.1–10.16. This story describes how an unsuccessful search for his father's lost asses brought Saul to an anonymous seer for help. The Lord ordered this 'man of God', identified later in the final version of the story as Samuel the prophet, to appoint Saul prince over Israel. Despite Saul's protestations of unworthiness, Samuel anointed Saul and sent him on a secret mission which was to culminate at Gibeath Ha-Elohim, where the Philistine governor lived (10.5). There Saul was to take some unspecified action ('whatever your hand finds to do'—10.7) and proceed to Gilgal for a meeting with Samuel seven days later. On reaching Gibeah, Saul reportedly fell into the predicted prophetic rapture (10.10), but there the story abruptly ends, leaving out any mention of Saul's mysterious task or an account of the trip to Gilgal.

The goal of Saul's secret mission was Gibeath Ha-Elohim (גבעת האלהים—'hill of God'), a site with a place-name found nowhere else in the OT. Yet there should be little doubt that this unique toponymic designation refers to the well-known Benjaminite city of Gibeah since the seer's prediction is reportedly fulfilled (10.10) as Saul fell into ecstacy on his arrival at Gibeah (הגבעתה, a feminine directional form seen earlier in Judg. 20.4, 14). The notice in 10.13 that Saul then proceeded to the local 'high place' or sanctuary (MT: הבמה) suggests that the the term Gibeath Ha-Elohim designated a specific hill-shrine in or near Gibeah.[45]

Critics offer helpful solutions to two literary problems in this story that might be obvious even to a casual observer. The first is the strange permutation of an unknown 'man of God' (9.10) into the great prophet Samuel (9.15); it is now widely agreed that this metamorphosis actually represents a late editorial intrusion of

Samuel into an old piece in which the original seer was an anonymous figure.[46] The other literary oddity in the piece is even more jarring: the seer's secret and dramatic dispatch of Saul to Gibeah ends abruptly in anticlimax—Saul's conversation with an uncle (10.14-16). The lack of the story's promised climactic action by Saul, and the fact that his predicted trip to Gilgal after seven days (10.8) is reported several chapters later (13.8), leads critics naturally to suspect that editorial interference interrupted and even destroyed an originally exciting pro-Saul narrative.[47] We shall reconstruct the outlines of this old story in Chapter 4; for the moment we note only that both place-names 'Gibeah' and 'Gibeath Ha-Elohim' appeared in the earliest version of the tale, which probably originated in Saulide circles in eleventh or tenth century Benjamin.

1 Sam. 10.26–11.15. This story describes how destiny called Saul from Gibeah to save the beleagured Jabesh-Gilead community from an Ammonite attack. This heroic military rescue reportedly stampeded the grateful Israelites at Gilgal to acclaim Saul as their first king.

It is a matter of dispute where this story actually begins. Noth thought that the rescue story properly began at 10.27b and that the DH editor forged its linkage to the preceeding Mizpah story; Miller, however, would begin the story at 10.26b.[48] I would suggest that the original story began with the report (10.26) of Saul's return to his home at Gibeah (גבעתה) after the previous narratives had described his victory over the Philistines in Benjamin (now recorded in 1 Sam. 13-14). A later editor then seems to have linked the independent Mizpah story (10.17-25) with the Jabesh account by setting Saul at Gibeah when the Jabesh rescue appeal arrived. 1 Sam. 11.4 records that the Jabesh messengers came to 'Gibeah of Saul' (MT: גבעת שאול; LXX: εἰς Γαβαὰ πρὸς Σαοὺλ) with their plea for rescue. If the MT is original, this verse is the first appearance of 'Gibeah' in construct with 'Saul', but LXX's reading is preferable given the unlikelihood that an author would have intended to name Gibeah after Saul at so early a point in the story.

In unusual accord, most scholars consider the Jabesh story to be an essentially historical account since it explains the later notice that Jabeshites rescued Saul's remains from the Philistines at Beth-Shan (1 Sam. 31.11-13).[49] Such a historical connection of Jabesh-Gilead with Benjamin—and Gibeah—is also credible in the light of the tradition remembering Israel's theft of Jabesh's women as wives for the Benjaminite survivors of the Gibeah massacre (Judg. 21). We

regard this narrative as part of the old pro-Saul saga which emerged
from eleventh or tenth century Benjamin.

1 Sam. 13.1-14.23. This narrative describes the Hebrew revolt
against the Philistines under the leadership of Saul at Gibeah. The
story then relates one particularly heroic deed of Saul's son
Jonathan, who led a daring raid through the Geba Pass against the
Philistine positions at nearby Michmas, expelling this enemy from
the area of central Benjamin.

The first גבע-root place-name appears in the notice (13.2) that Saul
stationed one thousand troops with Jonathan in 'Gibeah of Benjamin'
(גבעת בנימין). The very next verse (13.3) then reports that Jonathan
struck down the Philistine governor[50] in 'Geba' (גבע). It is noteworthy
that an earlier notice in the story of Saul's mysterious mission (10.5)
had placed this same Philistine governor at another גבע-root site,
Gibeath Ha-Elohim. Adding further confusion to this narrative is the
notice one verse later (13.4) that indeed *Saul* struck down the
Philistine governor!

Following these conflicting reports about the puzzling attack on
the Philistine governor, the story pictures Saul and Jonathan
gathering the rebellious Hebrews to meet Philistine forces massing at
Michmas (13.5-14). 1 Sam. 13.15 places Saul's army at 'Gibeah of
Benjamin' (גבעת בנימן), yet in the very next verse (13.16) Saul is
placed with Jonathan at 'Geba of Benjamin' (גבע בנימן).

After an account explaining how the Philistines had previously
disarmed the Hebrews, the notice in 14.2 places Saul 'at the outskirts
of Gibeah (הגבעה) under the Pomegranate, which is in the Migron',
an enigmatic phrase which we will explain in Chapter 2. Meanwhile,
Jonathan reportedly led a daring raid on the Philistine outpost at
Michmas from his base at Geba. The account of this attack (14.4-6)
contains unusually detailed topographical information which will
eventually assist us in our search for Gibeah. The vignette pictures
Jonathan crossing between two columns of rock ('Bozez' and
'Seneh') that marked the pass in the valley between Michmas, on the
north, and Geba (גבע) on the south. In the midst of this raid, Saul's
men on the watch in 'Gibeah of Benjamin' (גבעת בנימן) reportedly
saw the confusion in Michmas (14.16) and joined Jonathan in driving
the Philistines away from the area.

This narrative is widely regarded as an important source for
historical information concerning the Hebrew revolt against the
Philistines and the subsequent establishment of the Israelite monarchy.[51]
Two related problems impede a confident historical reconstruction of

these events, however. The first difficulty pertains to the apparent presence of two conflicting literary traditions in the piece which credit both Saul and Jonathan with the expulsion of the Philistines from Benjamin.[52] The second problem relates to the presence in the narrative of the two גבע-root toponyms 'Gibeah' and 'Geba' in such a confusing entanglement that no less an historian than Noth despaired of ever separating and locating these toponyms in order to reconstruct properly the course of events.[53]

Scholarly solutions to the complicated intertwining of 'Gibeah' and 'Geba' in this narrative tend to follow basically one of the three following approaches: (1) the Hebrews operated from two separate base-camps, Geba and Gibeah, with Saul shifting back and forth between them;[54] (2) two accounts of separate and unrelated Israelite attacks, one by Saul at Gibeah, and one by Jonathan at Geba, lie behind the present tradition;[55] (3) 'Gibeah' and 'Geba' were variant names for the same city, and either scribes have interchanged the names in the transmission of the text, or each place-name derives from a distinct source.[56] We shall find a solution to this puzzle in Chapter 2. At this point we merely note that this is the second time 'Gibeah' and 'Geba' have appeared interchangeably within the same story.

Ultimately, we cannot reach topographical conclusions about Gibeah and Geba until we identify and analyze the literature in which each toponym appears. Several sources are discernible in 1 Sam. 13.2–14.23. Clearly, 13.2 was not a part of the original narrative at all, but is a fragmentary notice which bears signs of Dtr inclusion into the story; moreover, since its report actually fits the military scenario *after* the battle of Michmas, Miller suggested that the verse introduces the subsequent battle narrative by foreshadowing its outcome—a technique employed elsewhere in biblical literature.[57]

1 Sam. 13.3-4, which first ascribes the attack on the Philistine governor to Jonathan and then mentions that Saul accomplished the same feat, contains the kind of contradictory information that usually signals a duplication of sources. The latter account, which we take to be a part of a tenth-century cycle celebrating its hero Saul, prevails throughout most of ch. 13, though it now includes secondary additions such as the motif of Samuel's rejection of Saul.[58] The sources evidently shift at 13.23ff., which begins a long narrative describing Jonathan's raid on Michmas and the subsequent sacrilege caused by the rash oath of his father, Saul (13.23–14.46).[59] In this story, Jonathan is clearly the hero, and Saul a virtual antagonist—

very much the role he will play in the 'rise of David' narratives which follow. There is good reason to suspect that the narrative emerged from tenth or ninth century court circles in Jerusalem as part of a grand literary effort to delegitimize Saul's kingship in support of the Davidic dynasty.[60]

Regarding the infamous confusion of 'Gibeah' and 'Geba' in these stories, one pattern stands out: Gibeah is normally associated with Saul, and Geba with Jonathan.

1 and 2 Samuel: The David Stories

In the 'rise of David' stories (1 Sam. 15–2 Sam. 5), an extensive body of literature in the books of Samuel describes the struggle between Gibeah-based king Saul and his surreptitiously anointed successor, David. These stories characterize Saul as a tyrant driven nearly insane by God's rejection of him as king, while they portray David favorably as a pious, skillful, and divinely chosen new king. This presentation literarily foreshadows and explains Saul's eventual death at the hands of the Philistines, and David's subsequent succession to the throne of Israel.

The MT of 1 Sam. 15.34 reports Saul's return to his home at 'Gibeah of Saul' (גבעת שאול). The next three גבע-root passages all present the same motif: Saul at Gibeah when messengers bring him news about his rival David. In 1 Sam. 22.6, news that David had been seen after his escape from Saul reached the king at Gibeah (גבעה) as he sat under a tamarisk tree. 1 Sam. 23.19 and 26.1 are literary doublets—in each case Ziphites divulge to Saul at Gibeah (הגבעתה) the location of David's hiding place. In these last three passages, LXX regards the name of Saul's residence as an appellative.

Critics largely agree that these stories, composed in the Davidic court in Jerusalem, literarily legitimize David's dynasty at the expense of Saulide claims. They almost certainly date to the tenth or ninth centuries.[61]

In a separate Davidic cycle, the conclusion to a description of David's Philistine wars (2 Sam. 5.25) contains an example of Gibeon-Geba textual confusion. The MT states that David 'drove the Philistines in flight from Geba (גבע) to Gezer', but LXX has 'from Gibeon' (Γαβαών), a reading found again in the Hebrew and Greek of 1 Chron. 14.16. It is difficult to judge which was the original reading; if 'Geba', the notice may represent an early Judean editor's attempt to credit David with Israelite victories won under Saul's leadership (1 Sam. 13–14).

2 Samuel 21.1-9 describes David's extermination at Gibeah of Saul's surviving progeny (except Mephibosheth, who was kept under a kind of house arrest in Jerusalem). The account of this mass execution, ostensibly an act of revenge on behalf of the Gibeonites, opens a series of historically reliable stories (2 Sam. 21–24) which seem to originate in Davidic court circles of the tenth century.[62] Since no other tradition records Saul's alleged attack on the Gibeonites (21.1), it is probable that this story represents the attempt of Davidic court scribes to conceal the real reason for the murder of the remaining Saulide claimants to Israel's throne: elimination of potential threats to the hegemony of the Davidic dynasty.[63] The execution of the Saulides reportedly occurred at 'Gibeah of Saul' (גבעת שאול).[64]

Both 2 Samuel and 1 Chronicles cite men from Gibeah in their long lists of David's heroes and allies. There is no reason to doubt that these lists derive from Judean court records of the Davidic-Solomonic administration. 2 Sam. 23.29 mentions Ittai son of Ribai from 'Gibeah of Benjamin' (גבעת בני בנימן), a name repeated in 1 Chron. 11.31. 1 Chron. 12.3 lists Ahiezer and Joash, sons of Shemaah 'the Gibeathite' (הגבעתי).

Notices in 1 and 2 Kings and 2 Chronicles
The historical books of 1–2 Kings and 2 Chronicles, which treat the period of the Israelite-Judean monarchy (1000–586), contain far fewer references to Benjaminite גבע-root place-name cities than are found in books describing the pre-monarchical era. Yet the two that refer to Geba provide valuable information about the role of that city in Judean history.

1 Kings 15.16-22 records that King Baasha of Israel invaded Judah during the reign of King Asa (c. 900), fortified nearby Ramah, and thus threatened Judean access to Jerusalem. Reportedly forced by this invasion into an alliance with Ben-Hadad of Damascus, Asa eventually repulsed the Israelites from their southern fortification as Ben-Hadad applied military pressure to Israel's northern region. Asa then dismantled the former Israelite fortress at Ramah and constructed with its stones and timbers two new sites: Mizpah and 'Geba of Benjamin' (גבע גנימן).[65]

There is no reason to doubt the essential historicity of this report, which evidently originated in early Judean court records. After Asa's action, the Geba and Mizpah fortresses evidently guarded the northern border of the Kingdom of Judah until its demise in the sixth century.[66]

Almost three centuries after the fortification of Geba, the city is mentioned again in late seventh-century Judean Dtr accounts describing the so-called 'Josian Reform' (2 Kgs 23.1-25). This purge of the Judean cult included the elimination of priests and the desecration of their 'high-places' in all the cities outside of Jerusalem from 'Geba' (גבע) to Beersheba (2 Kgs 23.8).[67] The expression 'from Geba to Beersheba' probably designated the northern and southern limits of Judean territory by naming the border fortress complexes which guarded the borders of Judah.

Ezra and Nehemiah

The books of Ezra and Nehemiah are a valuable source of historical information regarding the Jewish community in Palestine as it reconstructed itself in the century or so after the Babylonian Exile.[68] The documents in these books frequently include town-lists, census data, and other information which relate to two גבע-root toponyms in Benjamin: Geba and Gibeon. Since the latter site lies outside the scope of our survey, we shall discuss information pertinent to Geba.

Ezra 2, and Nehemiah 7 which is nearly identical with it,[69] contain what purport to be lists of Jewish exiles who returned to Palestine after the Babylonian captivity. Scholars differ regarding the original purpose of these lists, but generally agree on their setting in Persian colonial times.[70] Both Ezra 2.26 and Neh. 7.30 number the combined populations of Ramah and 'Geba' (גבע) at 621.

Neh. 11.31-36 is a short list of Benjaminite towns, purportedly dating to the period after the return from exile, which appears in the so-called 'Memoirs of Nehemiah'. Determination of the precise original purpose and dating of this list has proved difficult; it likely descends from a document written in Persian colonial times.[71] Included in the list is mention of 'Geba' (גבע).

Neh. 12.27-43 describes the Levitical celebration marking the dedication of Jerusalem's new wall. Among the singers listed in Neh. 12.29 are those from the region of 'Geba' (גבע). This material is usually regarded as the sort of cultic archival information which the Chronicler inserted into the book of Nehemiah.[72]

This survey of texts stemming from official Judean monarchical records and Persian-era postexilic documents shows a clear and simple pattern regarding two גבע-root toponyms. 'Gibeah' does not appear in official Judean documents after the Davidic-Solomonic era; 'Geba', on the other hand, does not appear in these texts _until_ this era, and is mentioned regularly in various literary contexts from the monarchical through the postexilic period.

Hosea

The prophetic books of Israel and Judah represent a body of literature with language, style, and purposes distinct from those provided in the official documents edited by DH or the Chronicler. Several passages from prophetic works contribute valuable historical and topographical information about Gibeah and Geba.

References to a mysterious sin at 'Gibeah' play an important role in the preaching of the eighth-century Israelite prophet Hosea. Two distinct passages (9.9; 10.9) imply that an ancient crime at Gibeah symbolizes the sinfulness of Israel's entire national life; the latter reference even suggests darkly that an imminent disaster at Gibeah will fittingly bring about the destruction of Israel. A third passage (5.8) warns Benjamin of an impending attack on three of its cities, including Gibeah.

Hos. 5.8 exhorts the citizens of three Benjaminite towns to sound war-alarms as an unnamed army descends upon them.

> Blow the horn in Gibeah,
> the trumpet in Ramah;
> Sound the alarm in Beth-Aven:
> Behind you, Benjamin!

This mention of 'Gibeah' (גבעה)[73] opens a unit which, according to Alt's old theory, warns Israelite-occupied Benjamin of an expected Judean counter-attack after the Syro-Ephraimite invasion of Jerusalem in the late eighth century.[74] Though the theory is widely accepted by several generations of scholars,[75] the fact that no other evidence of such a counter-attack exists, and that the passage lacks specific details concerning the identity of the aggressors or the direction of the attack, means that the passage is susceptible to a more satisfying interpretation; we shall offer such a fresh explanation in Chapter 5.

Hosea next refers to Gibeah in 9.9, where he compares his contemporaries to ancient scoundrels: 'they make their corruption deep, as in the days of Gibeah' (הגבעה). Though the poor textual quality of the preceding verse makes an interpretation of this passage an especially difficult procedure,[76] interpreters are in general agreement that the phrase 'days of Gibeah' is a Hosean allusion to a great evil committed by Israel in its ancient past. Opinions differ as to whether the prophet referred to Saul's institution of kingship (1 Sam. 10–13),[77] to a sexual crime committed at Gibeah (Judg. 19),[78] or to a pan-tribal attack on the Benjaminites in Gibeah (Judg. 20).[79]

'Gibeah' appears twice in Hos. 10.9. Hosea again indicts Israel for her history of sin 'since the days of Gibeah' (הגבעה), but also alludes to punishment for this sin through an imminent battle at Gibeah (גבעה). This indictment opens a unit (10.9-15) which accuses Israel of the injustice of false trust in her weaponry, a sin for which war will punish the nation. Otherwise, Hosea's threat here lacks any detailed information which would give the passage an explicit historical context, and critics are therefore vague in their interpretations. In Chapter 5 we shall link all of these Hosean references to 'Gibeah' and find for them an illuminating historical/theological context.

Isaiah

The oracles of Hosea's Judean contemporary Isaiah mention both 'Gibeah of Saul' and the 'Geba Pass' in the same passage: Isa. 10.29. The context (10.27c-32) is an Isaian description of the steady progress through Benjamin of an unnamed invader *en route* to Jerusalem.

> He passed over the Migron, and left his gear at Michmas.
> He crossed the Geba Pass, and spent the night.
> Ramah trembled! Gibeah of Saul fled!

The MT of v. 29a, 'he crossed the Geba Pass' (מעברה גבע), refers to an important road in Benjamin also mentioned in Judges 20.33 and 1 Samuel 13.23 (where it is called the Michmas Pass). LXX reads 'he shall arrive at Aggai' (Ἀγγαί); this word surely transliterates the Hebrew הגי ('the valley'), referring to the impressive Wadi es-Suwenit, which was traversed by the pass between Geba and Michmas. The next line (v. 29b) mentions 'Gibeah of Saul' (גבעת שאול)[80] in close association with Ramah.

Critics are thoroughly divided in their attempts to find a plausible setting for this unit. In view of a reference to the Assyrians in 10.24, some scholars understandably connect the passage with an Assyrian invasion of Judah;[81] others hold that the oracle describes the invasion of the Syro-Ephraimite armies into Judah around 733;[82] and a third group of critics believes that the piece only represents the vision of some future invasion of Jerusalem.[83] In Chapter 5 we shall show how the passage relates to Hosea's 'Gibeah' oracles and the Syro-Ephraimite invasion.

Zechariah

The last chapter of the book of Zechariah offers an apocalyptic vision of the salvation of Judah and Jerusalem from foreign oppression. Zech. 14.10 promises that the whole land will be levelled 'from Geba (גבע) to Rimmon southwards', an ambiguous statement which could suggest either that Geba and Rimmon were considered the northern limits of Judah at the time of the oracle, or, more likely, that the two cities were considered as the northernmost and southernmost cities of Judah (cf. 1 Kgs 15.22; 2 Kgs 23.8).

Zechariah was a Judean prophet active in attempts to rebuild the Jerusalem Temple after the Babylonian Exile (c. 520).[84] Zechariah 9–14 in which the 'Geba' reference appears, however, is widely regarded as a collection of postexilic apocalyptic oracles, possibly dating to the third or second centuries.[85]

Summary Observations

These final prophetic references to Gibeah and Geba allow a few brief observations. In the prophets, 'Gibeah' appears in the late eighth century oracles of Hosea and Isaiah in contexts having to do with an imminent battle or invasion. Both prophets, however, use the term in 'archaizing' contexts, that is, in a rhetorical fashion relating Gibeah to an ancient crime in Hosea's case, or to its connection with Saul in Isaiah's usage. The latter appearance of 'Gibeah' again closely associates or identifies the toponym with 'Geba', a phenomenon we saw earlier in DH literature. 'Geba' is once again mentioned in a late postexilic context in Zechariah's oracle.

As we relate the historical and prophetic books, the following observations can be made regarding the Benjaminite גבע-root toponyms (see also Appendix 1).

1. 'Gibeon' appears in stories ranging from the pre-monarchical to the postexilic era. Except for occasional textual/spelling confusion with 'Gibeah' or 'Geba', it is clearly a distinct city in the literature, and can be located with confidence at the modern site of el-Jib.

2. The feminine toponym 'Gibeah' appears exclusively in stories set in the period of the Judges and the early monarchy (Judg. 19–20; 1 and 2 Sam.), or in prophetic passages which refer to that same period (Hos. 9.9; 10.9; Isa.

10.29). It is known variously and interchangeably in these texts as 'Gibeah', 'Gibeah of Benjamin', and 'Gibeah of Saul', the latter appellation prevailing in Davidic literature. There are no references to 'Gibeah' in official Judean documents after the tenth century.

3.   The masculine place-name 'Geba' appears in Judean stories and lists *composed* in monarchical and postexilic times though occasionally literarily *set* in earlier periods (i.e. the Benjaminite and Levitical town-lists of Joshua and the account of Jonathan's raid on Michmas in 1 Sam. 13–14). The toponym appears to have emerged after the tenth century and continued in use through the rest of the Old Testament period.

4.   The names 'Gibeath Kiriath-Jearim' and 'Gibeath Ha-Elohim' occur only once each in the Bible. Literary criticism, combined with topographical analysis, can determine with some degree of probability whether each name refers to an independent city or whether thee names are only variant designations for other sites.

Chapter 2

SEARCHING FOR GIBEAH

Our survey of the גבע-root place-names in Benjamin and the analysis
of their literary settings allows us to begin our geographical search
for Gibeah. Aside from the clearly distinct site of Gibeon (el-Jib), we
have identified four such toponyms: Gibeath Kiriath-Jearim, Gibeath
Ha-Elohim, Geba, and of course, Gibeah. We may now locate these
sites on the basis of information given in the biblical text or other
ancient documents, similarities with modern names, and archaeological
data.

Gibeath Kiriath-Jearim

Two biblical passages relate to the identification and placement of
Gibeath Kiriath-Jearim. The emended text of Josh. 18.28 refers to an
important 'hill' near Kiriath-Jearim, a city mentioned in the town
lists of Judah in Josh. 15.9 and identified again as a 'city of Judah'
(18.14-15) at a point on the southwe st boundary of Benjamin. While
this city lay just inside Judean territory, its 'hill' rose to the northeast
across the Benjaminite boundary. It was to Kiriath-Jearim that the
Philistines returned the captured Ark of the Covenant (1 Sam. 6.21-
7.1), which the men of Kiriath-Jearim then took to the house of
Abinadab on 'the hill' (גבעה).
    In view of its association with the Ark, it appears that the 'hill' of
Kiriath-Jearim was more than a generic mountain. The word here is
virtually a technical term for 'hill-shrine', and it is likely that the
'house' of Abinadab actually amounted to a typical ancient sanctuary.
The texts thus seem to indicate an important cultic site in Benjamin
immediatly adjacent to Judah.
    Since Robinson first identified Kiriath-Jearim with Kuryet el-
Enab (Abu Ghosh), the location of the biblical city has not been

seriously disputed; a mound 300 m. to the northeast of modern Abu Ghosh, Deir el-Azhar, is now widely regarded as the site of ancient Kiriath-Jearim.[1] The location of its 'hill' is much less clear. One theory gaining currency holds that the Hill of Kiriath-Jearim was none other than modern Nebi Samwil, an impressive mount northeast of Deir el-Azhar. In this view, the hill-shrine at Nebi Samwil later became identified with Gibeon (el-Jib), 1 km. to the north, where no trace of its famous high-place was found in archaeological excavations.[2] Whether the sanctuary of Kiriath-Jearim is to be sought at Nebi Samwil, or at some anonymous mount nearer Deir el-Azhar, in no case is this 'hill' to be confused with biblical Gibeah.

Gibeath Ha-Elohim

The identity and location of Gibeath Ha-Elohim is widely disputed, as often happens when a toponym is cited only once (1 Sam. 10.5). Since the theophoric element in the place-name (lit.: 'Hill of God') bears cultic significance, it is natural to assume that Gibeath Ha-Elohim housed an important Elohistic hill-shrine. Moreover, the fact that the toponym occurs only once in the Bible suggests that the sanctuary there may be known by another, more common name. A number of scholars argue that the name Gibeath Ha-Elohim denotes the 'high-place' of Gibeon on the assumption that Gibeon was the only city in the area which could both house a major sanctuary and serve as a Philistine military base as suggested by 1 Sam. 10.5.[3]

A number of problems beset such an identification, however. In the first place, the argument assumes the existence of only one major cultic site in Benjamin in Saul's time. Yet, as Wellhausen long ago noted, cult centers proliferated in ancient Israel;[4] one might note especially the numerous sites in Benjamin that at one time or another possessed sanctuaries: Mizpah (Judg. 20.1; 1 Sam. 10.17), Ramah (1 Sam. 8.4; 15.34; 19.18), Bethel (Judg. 20.26; 1 Sam. 10.3), Nob (1 Sam. 21.1), and Geba (2 Kgs 23.8). Surely Gibeon possessed no monopoly on worship in pre-monarchical Benjamin. Moreover, the strong probability that Gibeon's Hivite community worshipped a deity alien to Israel in this era cannot be dismissed. There is no textual evidence of an Israelite sanctuary at Gibeon until the time of David and Solomon (1 Chron. 16.39; 21.29; 1 Kgs 3.14-15; 9.2), suggesting that, if indeed a shrine at Gibeon existed prior to this period, the Israelites subsequently converted it to Yahweh worship.

Second, there is no basis for the suggestion that Gibeon's presumed importance determined its role as the base of the Philistine governor (1 Sam. 13.3-4). There exists neither textual nor archaeological evidence for the assumption that the Philistines occupied Gibeon at any point.[5]

The biblical text itself provides several clues that favor a different solution to the problem. 1 Sam. 10.5 states that Gibeath Ha-Elohim housed a Philistine governor; later, two conflicting notices record both that Saul killed this governor (13.4), and that Jonathan struck him down in Geba (13.3). It is evident that two separate literary traditions here attempt to credit the assassination to two different heroes. The Jonathan tradition remembers that the deed took place in Geba, but no independent account of Jonathan's murder of the governor at Geba exists.

The Saul tradition rather obviously identifies Gibeath Ha-Elohim with Gibeah. Saul reportedly arrived at Gibeah (10.10) after the 'man of God' sent him to Gibeath Ha-Elohim, 'where the Philistine governor is' (10.5). Though no direct account of Saul's assassination of the governor is extant, it is quite likely that it once appeared immediately after the scene in which Saul flies into a prophetic ecstasy (10.10-12); for some reason, later editors evidently suppressed the account.[6] Our attempt to identify Gibeath Ha-Elohim thus reaches a temporary impasse: one source rather clearly identifies the site with Gibeah, while another implies an association with Geba. A solution to the Gibeath Ha-Elohim problem must therefore await a resolution of the Gibeah and Geba identifications: were these cities separate sites so that the two assassination accounts give actually conflicting information, or are 'Gibeah' and 'Geba' merely variant names from different literary sources for the same city?

Geba

Geba is a distinct place-name in literature which derives from Judean monarchical or postexilic settings: the Benjaminite town lists (Josh. 18.24), the Levitical cities list (Josh. 21.17), Judean annals (1 Kgs 15.22; 2 Kgs 23.8), Jewish postexilic records (Neh. 7.30; 11.31; 12.29) and late apocalyptic material (Zech. 14.10). In two literary complexes, however, 'Geba' is confused with 'Gibeah': the Outrage of Gibeah story (Judg. 20.10; 20.33) and the 'Rise of Saul' stories (1 Sam. 13-14), where 'Geba' is so intertwined with 'Gibeah' that some scholars despair of determining whether two different sites are meant, or only one.

The location of Geba has not been seriously at issue since E. Robinson, noticing that the close association of Michmas to Geba in biblical writings was reflected in the geographical proximity of modern Mukhmas to Jeba, proposed that the Arabic names of these two villages faithfully retain their ancient Hebrew toponyms.[7] Robinson's identification of Geba with Jeba is almost universally accepted and has gained further support from Kallai's 1967 archaeological survey which found Iron II and Persian remains on the surface of the modern village.[8] Jeba has never been archaeologically excavated.

The Search for Gibeah

The toponym 'Gibeah' prevails in northern (Ephraimite or Benjaminite) literature and in pre-Solomonic southern (Judean) literature. The main occurrences of the place-name are (1) Judges 19-20, originally a Benjaminite war story which first passed into written form in northern circles before the fall of Israel; (2) the 'Rise of Saul' hero narratives (1 Sam. 9-15) from early tenth century Benjamin; (3) the Judean 'Rise of David' stories (1 Sam. 15-16) which employ the term 'Gibeah of Saul'; (4) various court records of the Davidic monarchy (2 Sam. 21-23); (5) the oracles of the eighth-century Israelite prophet Hosea; and (6) a speech of the eighth-century Judean prophet Isaiah. Each of these 'Gibeah' texts in some way points to events in that city before the division of the kingdoms in the late tenth century—even the eighth-century prophetic references, which poetically relate contemporaneous events to Gibeah's ancient reputation. When Judean writers employ the toponym, they usually link the city with Saul. All of these observations suggest that the importance of 'Gibeah' lay in Israel's distant past, in relation to historical events as elusive as its geographical location.

The modern quest for the site of ancient Gibeah began a century and a half ago with the American biblical scholar Edward Robinson's pioneering trip to Palestine. On Friday, May 4, 1838 Robinson led a small party on foot from Jerusalem toward the northeast. Three hours after departure, after passing through the Palestinian villages of Anata, Taiyibeh, and Hizmeh, the group arrived in the vicinity of Jeba. Robinson realized that this area related to the stories of the Outrage of Gibeah and the Battle of Michmas, but could not decide whether the Arabic name of the village of Jeba corresponded to biblical Gibeah or Geba. Robinson naturally looked for any ruins in this area which might solve his dilemma: several biblical texts seemed to indicate that *two* ancient towns—Gibeah and Geba—once lay across the large valley from Michmas, surely modern Mukhmas, a mile or so distant across the Wadi es-Swenit. Yet only one village—Jeba—was anywhere to be seen. After another search of the area on May 15, Robinson concluded that the Arabic toponym Jeba preserved the name of ancient Gibeah; as for Geba, Robinson surmised that its ruins might lie as yet undiscovered somewhere in the immediate vicinity of Jeba.[9] It is clear that Robinson's intuition was basically correct in one respect: several biblical texts do require that both 'Gibeah' and 'Geba' lie across the wadi from Michmas.

Yet a few years later, Robinson changed his opinion as a result of objections from a young German theologian who insisted that Gibeah must be located between Ramah (er-Ram) and Jerusalem.[10] According to his argument, the Levite couple travelling north from Jerusalem (Judg. 19.10-14) faced the choice of continuing the journey in order to stay the night in either Gibeah or Ramah, meaning that these cities were successive points north of Jerusalem on the watershed highway leading to Ephraim. Gibeah, according to this reasoning, must have therefore existed between Ramah and Jerusalem. Robinson subsequently changed his site identifications, and later editions of his *Biblical Researches* identified Geba with Jeba while placing Gibeah at Tell el-Ful, an impressive hill midway between er-Ram and Jerusalem astride the watershed highway. Robinson buttressed this site location with evidence from Josephus (Ant. 5.2.8) which placed ancient Gibeah 20 stadia north of Jerusalem (close to Tell el- Ful's actual distance of 22 stadia), and a report from the fourth century A.D. pilgrim Paula who paused at 'Gibeah' on her ascent from Emmaus to Jerusalem; Tell el-Ful would have lain directly on this route.[11]

Despite Robinson's site identification change, important scholars remained unconvinced by the Tell el-Ful—Gibeah equation. Foremost among them was the famous cartographer C.R. Conder, who in 1877 set forth several impressive reasons for placing Gibeah at Jeba.[12] Conder, noticing that two major narratives (Judg. 20 and 1 Sam. 13-14) seem to use the toponyms 'Geba' and 'Gibeah' interchangeably, explained that the feminine form 'Gibeah' probably referred to the countryside surrounding the city of 'Geba'. Conder also adduced other evidence from Josephus that supported a Jeba location for Gibeah. In his account of Titus' invasion of Jerusalem in 70 AD, Josephus stated that the Roman army bivouacked in the 'Valley of the Thorns, close to a village named Gabath Saul, which means "Saul's Hill", at a distance of about 30 stadia from Jerusalem' (Bell. 5.2.1). Conder pointed out that Jeba sits above the Wadi es-Swenit ('Valley of the Little Thorns') at a distance from Jerusalem of less than 40 stadia, close to Josephus' figure.

Conder's article concluded with an argument favoring Gibeah's location at Jeba which has never successfully been refuted. Noting that Saul's watchmen 'in Gibeah' reportedly observed the confusion of the Philistines in Michmas as Jonathan and his armor-bearer began their raid (1 Sam. 14.6), Conder claimed that the biblical author necessarily assumed the watchmen's location at Jeba, which enjoys a clear view of Mukhmas, 2 km. north across the Wadi es-Swenit; from Robinson's putative Gibeah, Tell el-Ful, it is difficult even to see the village of Mukhmas, much less observe events in it.

Nevertheless, the debate over Gibeah's location continued in scholarly journals over the next fifty years. W.F. Birch, finding both the Jeba and Tell el-Ful theories unconvincing, championed Khirbet Addaseh near the watershed highway, but E. Masterman quickly demonstrated that this site contained only Roman pottery.[13] Eventually, the discovery of Iron Age sherds at Tell el-Ful led the famous American archaeologist William F. Albright to undertake in 1922 the first full-scale modern archaeological excavations at the site.

Albright confidently claimed that preliminary results from three seasons of excavations (1922-23 and 1933) had clinched the placement of Gibeah at Tell el-Ful.[14] Albright's findings reportedly included the ruins of the village destroyed in the pan-Israelite attack after the Outrage at Gibeah, and the Iron Age 'fortress' where Saul based his kingdom. Albright's identification of 'Gibeah of Saul' became well established in archaeological circles in the next few decades, and still predominates in most scholarly studies and biblical atlases. However, when Lawrence Sinclair, a graduate student of Albright's at Johns Hopkins University, finally published detailed results of the 1933 expedition in 1960, fresh doubts about Tell el-Ful began to arise.[15] Sinclair's study contained chronological and interpretive revisions of Albright's previous findings serious enough to re-open the whole debate over Gibeah's location.

H.J. Franken suggested in 1963 that the archaeological evidence unearthed at Tell el-Ful was insufficient to make a positive identification with Gibeah.[16] So as bulldozers prepared to destroy the site in preparation for a new palace of King Hussein of Jordan,

Paul Lapp conducted a final archaeological probe of Tell el-Ful in 1964. Lapp's preliminary report, while revising Albright's Tell el-Ful chronology in important ways, claimed that the identification of an Iron Age tower as Saul's Gibeah Fortress 'rests on evidence about as strong as archaeology is ever able to provide'.[17] Yet just a decade later, J.M. Miller criticized the entire literary, topographical, and archaeological case for Gibeah at Tell el-Ful, and proposed that Gibeah and Geba might represent variant Hebrew toponyms for the same biblical city located at modern Jeba.[18] The debate over Gibeah's location had come full circle since Robinson's original identification nearly 140 years earlier.

In the final report of the Lapp expedition published in 1981, J.A. Graham, in support of Albright's Tell el-Ful identification, claimed that Miller's critique tended 'to misunderstand or misuse the archaeological evidence to support his conclusions, rather than to let the evidence speak for itself'.[19] It is appropriate at this point to determine if the literary, topographical and archaeological evidence in support of the Gibeah–Tell el-Ful equation does, indeed, 'speak for itself', or whether a more compelling site location for Gibeah can be found.

Problems with the Case for Gibeah at Tell el-Ful

The rationale for placing Gibeah at Tell el-Ful involves a complicated series of assumptions based on literary evidence, topographical information in biblical and extra-biblical texts, and the results of archaeological excavations. Each of these assumptions is extremely problematical.

Textual Evidence

A key textual question for scholars searching for Gibeah is the rather basic issue of whether one can actually distinguish Gibeah from Geba on the basis of the biblical text. Albright, for example, adduced four texts as proof for this distinction.[20] First, the reading 'Gibeath-Kiriath' (emended to 'Gibeath and Kiriath') in Josh. 18.28 purportedly proved a 'sharp' distinction of Gibeah from Geba, which is also mentioned in the list (18.24). Yet we have shown that the original term probably read 'Gibeath Kiriath-Jearim', a site known from 1 Sam. 7.1, and that 'Gibeah' itself never appeared in the town-list. Second, Albright supposed that mention of both Gibeah and Geba in Judges 19–20 proved that the battle, which began at Gibeah, later shifted to Geba. However, his reconstruction involved the emendation (without manuscript or versional support) of several toponyms in order to arrive at this conclusion. Third, Albright imagined that the 'Gibeah' and 'Geba' mixture in the account of the Battle of Michmas (1 Sam. 13–14) demonstrated that the Hebrews fought the Philistines with two armies, one led by Jonathan at Geba, and the other commanded by Saul at Gibeah. No such 'army' is associated with Jonathan, however; the story mentions only a single armor-bearer. More importantly, this explanation still fails to explain how Saul's watchmen could observe the turmoil in Philistine-controlled Michmas from Gibeah if this city were located at distant Tell el-Ful. Finally, Albright claimed that the description of the invasion of Judah in Isa. 10.27b-32 proved the Gibeah-Geba distinction, translating the passage so that the invader leaves Michmas and spends the night at Geba (10.29a), causing 'Gibeah of Saul' to flee (10.29b). Albright even rearranged the order of the Isaian verses, placing Gibeah nearer to the site of Tell el-Ful in order to create the impression that Gibeah and Geba were indeed separate sites. The Isaian passage, however, is more accurately translated, 'he crossed the Geba Pass, and spent the night. Ramah trembled, Gibeah of Saul fled!' In short, none of these textual distinctions clearly separates 'Gibeah' from 'Geba', and only serve to sharpen the suspicion that the names might merely represent variant toponyms.

Literary-Topographical Evidence

Proponents of Gibeah's location at Tell el-Ful cite three ancient passages which purportedly provide topographical support of their identification. The main geographical argument follows from Judg. 19.13, which pictures a Levite couple travelling north from Jerusalem trying to decide where to spend the night: in 'Gibeah or Ramah'? This expression is taken by some interpreters to mean that Gibeah must lie between Jerusalem and Ramah (er-Ram, 8 kms north of Jerusalem). Following this logic, Tell el-Ful, a prominent hill on the highway midway between Jerusalem and Ramah, is a natural candidate for Gibeah.

This biblical verse, of course, is susceptible to more than one interpretation. The phrase 'let us spend the night in Gibeah or Ramah' is evidence in favor of Tell el-Ful only if one assumes that the watershed route was the only road leading north to Ephraim from Jerusalem. In fact, no biblical text even explicitly suggests that the watershed route existed in ancient times, though such a road can well be hypothesized on the basis of passages like 19.13. The existence of another route, however, is clearly indicated by Isa. 10.27-32 and the writings of Josephus, which provide evidence of a northern route from Jerusalem to Ephraim which passed through Gibeah: the eastern highway.[21] Though Albright contended that this route was too difficult to use in ancient times, this opinion evidently was shared neither by the unnamed army in Isaiah nor the forces of the Roman general Titus.[22] The passage in Judg. 19.13 can be read as evidence that *two* routes to the Ephraim hill country extended north from the Jerusalem area: the eastern highway through Gibeah and the Geba Pass, and the watershed route through Ramah. The Levite's dilemma in the Judges story is thus explainable as a choice between routes to two towns which were roughly equidistant from Jerusalem. Geographically speaking, Judg. 19.13 can be used definitively only in associating Gibeah somewhat closely with Ramah, and then not necessarily to its south.

If Judg. 19.13 amounts to questionable support for Gibeah at Tell el-Ful, several other biblical texts make such an identification all but untenable. Most notable is the previously mentioned text which has Saul's watchmen 'in Gibeah' observing the Philistine disarray in Michmas after Jonathan's attack (1 Sam. 14.16). Albright's explanation that Gibeah's (Tell el-Ful's) 'fine watchtower' permitted such observations strains credibility since the enormous 7 km. viewing distance between Tell el-Ful and Mukhmas is in no way lessened by the height of a building.[23]

Another difficult passage for Tell el-Ful partisans is 1 Sam. 14.2, which locates Saul 'on the outskirts of Gibeah under the Pomegranate which is in the Migron'. The Pomegranate הרמון here is surely not a pomegranate tree (under which Saul and 600 men could hardly camp!), but the Rock of Pomegranate (סלע הרמון) located directly to the east of Gibeah in the desert (see Judg. 20.45-47).[24] No such feature exists anywhere near Tell el-Ful. Moreover, the Migron is specifically associated with the Michmas/Geba Pass region in Isa. 10.28-29, which implies that Gibeah existed immediately adjacent to this area, not at Tell el-Ful some 7 kms away.[25]

The account of the ambush of Gibeah in Judges 20 also poses insurmountable difficulties for a Tell el-Ful identification. The authors of the final edited version envisioned three successive attacks on Gibeah by the pan-Israelite armies based in Bethel. If Gibeah were located at Tell el-Ful, it is no wonder the Israelites were reported to have lost horrendous numbers of troops in the first two days: the round trip from Bethel (Beitin) to Tell el-Ful is approximately 30 kms! Though the final literary version of this battle is probably fictional, it is still unlikely that its creator would have understood Gibeah to exist at modern Tell el-Ful and thus expect his audience to believe that the armies of Israel would camp so far from the enemy. Moreover, the description of the ambush of Gibeah itself (Judg. 20.30-43), which may well preserve an historical memory, can not have had Tell el-Ful in mind as the target. This site enjoys a panoramic view of the entire Benjaminite countryside for many kilometers surrounding it; the concept of an 'ambush' springing out of its hiding place simply does not match the topography of the area around Tell el-Ful. Instead, Judg. 20.33 probably locates the ambush in the 'Geba Pass' (מעבר גבע) a cave-pitted canyon, ideal for a surprise attack, which is fully 7 kms. from Tell el-Ful. It would surely have been no surprise to Gibeah if this contingent attacked after taking an hour to spring from its hiding place and make its way across the open fields towards Tell el-Ful.

A final biblical geographical problem with Tell el-Ful as Gibeah admittedly amounts to 'negative' evidence. It seems strange that 'Gibeah', if at Tell el-Ful, is rarely associated in biblical texts with the important city of Jerusalem only 4 kms. away. On the contrary, OT texts associate Gibeah closely with sites appreciably to the north of Jerusalem, e.g. Bethel (Judg. 20.18, 23, 26; 1 Sam. 13.2), Rimmon (Judg. 20.45; Isa. 10.29), Mizpah (Judg. 20.3), Ramah (Judg. 19.13; 1 Sam. 15.34; Hos. 5.8; Isa. 10.29), Michmas (1 Sam. 13-14; Isa. 10.28), the Migron (1 Sam. 14.2; Isa. 10.29), and Gibeon (2 Sam. 21.6), leaving an overall impression that Gibeah sat in the heart of Benjamin, rather than virtually in the suburbs of Jerusalem.

Post-biblical Information
The ancient literary-topographical information most supportive of a Gibeah-Tell el-Ful identification derives from the post-biblical period. In the first century AD the Jewish historian Josephus located the 'Gibeah' mentioned in Judges 19-20 about twenty stadia north of Jerusalem, nearly the same distance from the city (4 kms) as Tell el-Ful.[26] One could well imagine that Josephus had precisely this ruin in mind. Similarly, Jerome's fourth century AD description of Paula's pilgrimage to Jerusalem also seems to assume that Tell el-Ful, or a site near it, was regarded as Gibeah in Christian times. The pious woman, after having ascended the Judean hills through Beth Horon, reportedly saw Aijalon and Gibeon on her right and stopped at the

ruins of 'Gibeah' to remember the crime of Judges 19 before continuing on to Jerusalem.[27]

Several factors make caution advisable when using these texts in the search for Gibeah, however. While Josephus's location of Gibeah in his paraphrase of Judges 19 matches closely a Tell el-Ful identification, one book later he identifies 'Gibeah' with the 'Geba' of 1 Samuel 13.3 and locates the site near Gilgal.[28] These two citations taken in tandem cause one to wonder whether Josephus knew two 'Gibeahs'. A third citation from Josephus supports this possibility. The account of Titus' invasion of Jerusalem places the invading army's camp in the 'Valley of the Thorns' near Gibeah of Saul, located thirty stadia from Jerusalem.[29] The 'Valley of the Thorns', probably the Wadi es-Swenit ('Valley of the Little Thorn-Tree'), lies 7 kms. from Tell el-Ful, which is only twenty stadia from Jerusalem.[30] These passages suggest that Josephus distinguished between the 'Gibeah' of Judges 19-20 (located at Tell el-Ful) and 'Gibeah of Saul' (located at Jeba).[31] Yet Josephus's data should not be accepted too readily in any case. We must remember that he wrote about these biblical events a full millennium after they occurred. His placement of the 'Gibeah' of Judges 19-20, for example, might be based on the same topographical assumption about Judg. 19.13 that guided Gross, rather than on any special information available to him in the first century AD.

No less ambiguous than Josephus's data is Jerome's description three centuries later. While his account of Paula's pilgrimage does indeed recommend Tell el-Ful as the site of her 'Gibeah', Miller has shown that two other references to 'Gibeah' in Jerome seem to place the city farther to the north, in close association with Ramah.[32] The information in Josephus and Jerome thus leads us to suppose that in Roman and Byzantine times the 'Gibeah' of Judges 19-20 was thought to have existed at or near Tell el-Ful, and 'Gibeah of Saul' at the site of modern Jeba. Yet two factors militate against proposing a 'two Gibeah' theory for earlier, biblical times: (1) its support relies solely on the ambiguous Judges 19.13 passage; and (2) the extra-biblical sources are up to 1,400 years distant from the biblical events which they describe and may employ false suppositions and use information which is in some ways inferior to modern data. Moreover, this hypothesis would neither explain the name duplications nor illuminate the texts which use the two names interchangeably.

Archaeological Problems at Tell el-Ful

Scholars seemed to discount the shaky textual and literary-topographical case for locating Gibeah at Tell el-Ful after Albright published the initial reports of his archaeological excavations of 1922-23. The excitement of discovering Gibeah of Saul, in conjunction with the assured bravado with which these results were proclaimed, seem to have foreclosed serious logical and scientific scrutiny of Albright's findings for nearly four decades. Sinclair's revisions of Albright's early conclusions, and especially the recent publication of Lapp's 1964 excavation report, allow a more cool-headed appraisal of the archaeological case for Gibeah at Tell el-Ful.

Period I: The Pre-Fortress Remains

The extensive narrative of the Outrage of Gibeah and its aftermath (Judg. 19–20) in the so-called Period of the Judges suggests that a site which claims to represent biblical Gibeah ought to exhibit the remains of an Iron I town or village. Publications from Albright's first excavations (1922-23) reported the find of a fortress datable to the thirteenth or twelfth centuries which exhibited the requisite characteristics of Gibeah of Judges, including an ash layer matching the reported destruction of the town in Judg. 20.48.[33] After Albright's return excavation of Tell el-Ful (1933), however, the fortress was removed from this time period, and all that remained of pre-monarchical Gibeah was a small stone installation, some sherds of collar-rim jars, and an 'appearance of a burned layer'.[34] By the time the Lapp expedition published the results of its excavations, Iron I Tell el-Ful possessed only a few fragmentary remains of housewalls with associated pottery and a possible grave, scattered over an area approximately 15 m. square (see Figure 1).[35]

A dispassionate interpretation of these remains might suggest the presence on Tell el-Ful in Iron Ia of a large house or even a small compound, but certainly not a significant village or town. Even granting that Judges 19–20 editorially exaggerates the size of Gibeah by claiming that 26,000 Benjaminite defenders crowded into the city, it is logical to assume that Gibeah in this period would display the remains of at least an average-sized Palestinian hill-country village of several hundred inhabitants. To claim, as Albright and his followers have, that the remains of this town were obliterated by the construction of the later Iron I fortress is to beg the question.

An even more fundamental problem in this regard relates to the severely restricted occupational surface available atop Tell el-Ful. In view of its steep hillsides, elevated location (high above water sources), and small summit, it is questionable whether Tell el-Ful ever supported a full-scale village, as indeed it has not in modern times. We might logically expect that biblical Gibeah, one of the foremost towns of Benjamin, would exhibit continual ancient and modern inhabitation as is apparently the case with neighboring Ramah, Michmas, Geba, or Gibeon. In fact, the site's commanding view of the surrounding countryside, in conjunction with its strategic position along the watershed highway, make it an ideal location for the construction of state defense fortifications such as watchtowers or fortresses, which is precisely its apparent role in antiquity as suggested by the archaeological record. It is noteworthy that, prior to the Six-Day War of 1967, Tell el-Ful was chosen as the site of a small palace of King Hussein of Jordan, a classic example of an artificially imposed state construction project, rather than the spontaneous natural development of a village.

Period II: The 'Fortress of Saul'

The strongest evidence supposedly linking Tell el-Ful to Gibeah is Albright's so-called 'Citadel of Saul', the foundations of an Iron I tower whose excavated remains supposedly form only the southwest corner of a major fortress.[36] Albright dated this structure to the period of Saul, claimed that its casemate walls represent the earliest example of this architectural feature in Palestine, and published a sketch of the imaginary citadel (see Figure 2). Soon secondary literature began to speak confidently of Tell el-Ful as Gibeah of Saul, and even referred to the 'fortress' virtually as the capitol building of Saul's nascent kingdom.

Lapp's 1964 excavations, however, found little evidence of Albright's projected fortress beyond the foundations of an Iron Ic tower. This expedition concluded that the walls were not of the casemate type, and that 'without any evidence of other towers at Tell el-Ful, suggesting a complete fortress is quite conjectural'.[37] Oddly, this same report concluded that 'archaeological evidence indicates that there was a fortress at Tell el-Ful, the date of which suggests identification with King Saul', and it published a new suggested reconstruction of the period II fortress (see Figure 3) which indicates a structure 'larger, at least from north to south (if there was more than a southwest tower) than Albright proposed'.[38]

Despite the lack of evidence for a major fortress, and its self-professed doubts about the existence of other towers, the final excavation report frankly seems more interested in perpetuating the notion of 'Saul's Citadel' than letting the archaeological evidence speak for itself. As was the case for the Judges-era 'Gibeah', the lack of evidence for an entire fortress is attributed to clearing operations for a later structure; the existence of other corner towers is 'suggested by a number of Israelite fortresses from late Iron I and Iron II which had corner towers', and so on.[39] A more sober analysis of the published data might suggest simply that late Iron I Tell el-Ful possessed a typical Palestinian watchtower with a few outlying buildings.

The dating of these structures to the Saulide era is also highly questionable. Refining Albright's early dating, Lapp placed the Tell el-Ful remains in the 1025-950 horizon.[40] By the estimation of most biblical historians, this seventy-five year period overlaps the reigns not only of Saul, but of David and Solomon as well. The final excavation report, nevertheless, continually assigns the Tell el-Ful ruins to Saulide construction when Davidic or Solomonic sponsorship is equally plausible.

The Iron Ic *migdal* watchtower and surrounding buildings atop Tell el-Ful might conceivably have been built by Saulide forces as a southern Benjaminite outpost late in the eleventh century. It is highly unlikely, however, that so tiny a complex could represent Gibeah of Saul, the most important city in Benjamin and center of the first Israelite kingdom. Moreover, if Gibeath Ha-Elohim is identical with Gibeah, then the city must have possessed a hill-shrine complete with a company of prophets, as well as a temporary Philistine garrison (see 1 Sam. 10.5; 13.3-4); neither cultic nor Philistine remains of any kind have ever been discovered at Tell el-Ful. The tower's construction there during this same period by Jebusite forces—defending Jerusalem against the rise of powerful Saulide Israelite forces to the north of Jerusalem—cannot be ruled out. Yet since the dating of the tower's construction falls wholly within the reign of David, it is more likely that David's administration erected the Tell el-Ful *migdal* as part of Jerusalem's northern 'early-warning' defense arrangement; certainly the Davidids had reasonable cause early on to fear northern attacks from the failing Saulide regime under Abner (2 Sam. 3.1) and later, to guard against northern insurrections (2 Sam. 20.1-2). Finally, one must also consider the possibility that the Solomonic government, which reportedly constructed military sites throughout the land (1 Kgs 9.15-23), built the Tell el-Ful tower sometime in the mid-tenth century.

Period III: 'Gibeah of Saul fled'

Even more serious problems with the Tell el-Ful–Gibeah equation relate to the period after the division of the kingdoms. In the first place, Albright himself had to retract his early association of Fortress III with Asa's ninth century stronghold of Geba (which Albright emended to 'Gibeah'—1 Kgs 15.22) when he reassigned the Period III structure to the eighth or seventh centuries.[41] Lapp's final excavation report redated this fortification even later, to the 650-587 horizon.[42] On the basis of this data, one could plausibly speculate that Tell el-Ful was reconstructed during the great Josian Restoration in the last quarter of the seventh century.

The great problem here is that Tell el-Ful apparently lay unoccupied throughout the eighth century (Period III); only some 'mid-field silo deposits' (c. 700) bear witness to any trace of inhabitation.[43] Yet several biblical texts imply that Gibeah was an inhabited town at least during the last half of this century, for during this period Hosea warned Gibeah of an impending attack (5.8) and predicted a war there (10.9); simultaneously, Isaiah reported the progress through this area of the unnamed army, which caused 'Gibeah of Saul' to flee (10.29). Unless we assume that the fleeing Gibeahites at Tell el-Ful took their streets and houses along with them, we are forced to find another site for Gibeah—one which exhibits occupation during this crucial era.

Concluding Observations

Two other problems with Tell el-Ful are also worthy of consideration. First, its name, ('hill of beans' in Arabic) clearly retains no linguistic links either with the ancient Hebrew name 'Gibeah' nor any discernible literary or historical tradition connected with Gibeah. Other Benjaminite towns in the immediate vicinity, by contrast, have retained recognizable remnants of ancient Hebrew toponyms throughout the centuries.[44] It would seem strange that a city so famous as Gibeah would not have done so. Second, excavations at Tell el-Ful failed to produce the kind of inscriptional evidence that constitutes a truly strong case for site identity, as may be seen, for example, in the finding of 'Gibeon' jar-handles at nearby el-Jib. No written material from Tell el-Ful provided any such link to Gibeah.

In summary, the case for a location of Gibeah at Tell el-Ful is as problematical from a literary-topographical standpoint as it is from an archaeological perspective; the evidence for a Gibeah identification simply doesn't amount to a 'hill of beans'! But if Tell el-Ful wasn't Gibeah, what was it? Archaeological excavation demonstrates that the site definitely flourished in various periods during the biblical era. It is likely that the name 'el-Ful' originally had nothing to do with 'beans', but is an Arabic corruption of the Benjaminite toponym 'Eleph' (הָאֶלֶף). This village is mentioned in the Benjaminite town list (Josh. 18.28) after Zela (usually identified with Khirbet es-Salah, 3 kms. northwest of Jerusalem) and immediately before Jebus (= Jerusalem, 4 kms, south of Tell el-Ful), a listing which closely matches Tell el-Ful's close proximity to the Jerusalem area. The name 'Eleph' sometimes connotes a military unit (see 1 Sam. 10.19) and may relate to Tell el-Ful's function as a Judean military outpost. Our dating of the Benjaminite town list to the monarchical era, moreover, corresponds to times when Tell el-Ful/Eleph possessed military watchtowers: the Davidic-Solomonic and the Josian eras.

The Gibeah=Geba Hypothesis

The only serious alternative ever proposed to Tell el-Ful as the site of Gibeah is Jeba, an identification first suggested by Robinson in 1838, defended by Conder in 1877, and resurrected by Miller in 1975. Each of these scholars grappled with literary and topographical data which seemed to locate *both* Gibeah and Geba in the Jeba vicinity; each proposed a solution which attempted to explain the dual toponyms. Robinson originally thought that the ruins of a distinct 'Geba' must lie very near his 'Gibeah' at Jeba; Conder suggested that 'Gibeah' referred to the countryside around Geba (Jeba), and Miller proposed that the two toponyms were linguistic variants for the same ancient biblical city located at modern Jeba.

The last solution best begins to unravel the tangled literary, topographical, and archaeological web impeding the search for Gibeah. We will advance this theory on the basis of three logical steps. First, biblical Geba must be sought at Jeba; as we have already shown, scholars have expressed no serious doubts about this identification. Second, we must demonstrate that Jeba is also the most satisfactory site location for the Old Testament city known as 'Gibeah'; we will review numerous texts which seem to lead to this conclusion. Third, we must explain how and why the biblical writers referred to the site of ancient Jeba by variant toponyms.

Literary-Topographical Evidence for Gibeah at Jeba
The sure literary case for placing Geba at Jeba is more than matched
by parallel arguments for locating Gibeah at the same site. The first
topographical hints appear in the Outrage of Gibeah story in Judges
19–20. Here we immediately encounter the most problematical
biblical text for our Jeba identification. We have already shown that
the Levite's comment 'we will spend the night in Gibeah or Ramah'
(19.13) is geographically ambiguous: it may not be interpreted solely
as an indication that Gibeah and Ramah were successive sites on the
watershed highway north of Jerusalem. We must also entertain the
notion that the sentence implies a choice of two routes from
Jerusalem into Ephraim: the watershed highway through Ramah (er-
Ram), and the eastern highway through Gibeah (Jeba). Each city is
roughly equidistant from Jerusalem.

Judges 20
The ensuing battle scenes in Judges 20 are much less ambiguous
from a topographical viewpoint. In the first place, the two theologically
fictionalized versions of the attack which place the gathering points
for the pan-Israelite armies at Mizpah and Bethel, while suspect
from an historical viewpoint, would have been geographically
plausible to their postexilic audiences. The Mizpah source (20.1)
would place the Israelite camp at Tell en-Nasbeh, 5 kms. (one hour's
march) from Jeba; the Bethel source (20.18) implies an 8 km. march
to Jeba from Beitin.
      The battle account even hints at the confusion of toponyms which
may derive from a conflation of sources: in 20.10 the MT expression
'all those who have taken the field against Geba of Benjamin'
suggests at least an editorial comfort with this appellation for the site
known elsewhere in the narrative as Gibeah; in other words, the
editors seemingly retained the textual variety of toponyms for what
they may have considered to be the same city.
      Several topographical comments in the ambush account point to
an identification of Gibeah with Jeba. Judg. 20.33 notes that the
ambush 'sprang from its place in the מערה־גבע, a mysterious term
often translated 'from the clearing of Geba' or 'from the west of
Geba'.[45] However, the phrase most likely originally read מעבר־גבע
('the Geba Pass'), a reference to the crossing over the Wadi es-Swenit
between Mukhmas and Jeba also known from Isa. 10.29a (מעברה גבע)
and 1 Sam. 13.23, where the same ford is called the 'Michmas Pass'
(מעבר מכמש).[46] The notice indicates that, while one band of Israelites

drew Gibeah's defenders away from the city several kilometers to the west near the crossroads of the watershed highway (leading to Bethel) and the road between Gibeah and Gibeon (20.31), another contingent in ambush burst out from its hiding place in the Geba Pass (1 km. to the northeast of Jeba) and came in 'from the east of Gibeah' (20.34). The Geba Pass region, located hundreds of meters below Jeba, is pitted with numerous caves and recommends itself as an excellent point from which to launch such a dastardly attack. Observers in Jeba could scarcely have seen the attackers as they scrambled up the steep wadi ravine over which the city sits.

As the tide of battle shifted in favor of the Israelites, the Benjaminite warriors reportedly turned and fled toward the 'desert road' (20.42), the easterly route which followed the wadis Swenit and Qelt through the desert toward Jericho and the Jordan Valley. The Israelites cut down most of the Benjaminites at a point 'east of Gibeah' (20.43), probably near the area of the Geba Pass itself, while 600 survivors then fled 'toward the desert to the Rock of Pomegranate' (20.45). This passage indicates that the Benjaminites followed the 'desert road' in the Wadi es-Swenit, which leads from the Geba Pass in a southeasterly direction. Nearly 2 kms. southeast of the Pass there exists a remarkable geological feature. Indented deep into the sheer rock face of the south wadi wall is the enormous cave 'el-Jaia', which local legend correctly describes as large enough to hold 600 men—a tantalizing saying in view of the Judges' story.[47] It is likely that this cave, pock-marked with thousands of small pits and suggesting a split-open pomegranate with its seeds removed, is the סלע הרמון or 'Pomegranate Rock' where the 600 Benjaminite survivors reportedly took refuge for four months (20.47).

1 Samuel 13–14

Topographical information given in the stories of the Battle of Michmas also strongly supports the location of Gibeah at Jeba. Saul's assassination of the Philistine governor at Gibeath Ha-Elohim (1 Sam. 10.5; 13.4) seemingly caused the Philistines to encamp at Michmas (Mukhmas) in order to attack Israel; this move suggests a threat to the nearest Hebrew city: ancient Jeba. If Saul originally triggered the Hebrew uprising with the assassination of the Philistine governor at Gibeath Ha-Elohim, it is logical to conclude on the basis of the Philistine response at Michmas that this site existed at or near the site of modern Jeba. It is likely that Gibeah Ha-Elohim is the cultic name for the sanctuary at Gibeah (Jeba), which Saul seized after the assassination. Supporting this identification is another version of the uprising (13.3) which reports that *Jonathan* killed the governor at Geba; both accounts recommend Jeba as the site of the fateful events at Gibeath Ha-Elohim.

Saul is reported to have countered the Philistine threat by mustering his troops at Gibeah of Benjamin (13.15), the site of modern Jeba across the wadi from Michmas. Many of his Hebrew warriors reportedly hid out in the caves which pockmark this valley (cf. 13.6; 14.11), while 1 Sam. 14.2 explicitly locates Saul and 600 men 'on the outskirts of Gibeah under the Pomegranate which is in the Migron'. This notice surely refers to the great cave el-Jaia, the impregnable Pomegranate Rock where the 600 Benjaminites had earlier sought refuge (Judg. 20.47). The Migron (מגרון, from the root נגר: 'to gush forth, flow') is probably the ancient Hebrew name of the Wadi es-Swenit itself; the parʿʾlelism in Isa. 10.28b/29a seems to equate crossing the Migron wiᴛh crossing the Geba Pass.[48] This key passage thus unmistakably associates Gibeah closely with two geographical features in the Geba Pass region. This topographical connection is confirmed by the notice which has Saul's men on the watch in Gibeah itself observe the confusion in Philistine-controlled Michmas when Jonathan raided the camp (14.16); modern Jeba correspondingly enjoys a clear view of Mukhmas, some 2 kms. directly across the Wadi es-Swenit.

Isaiah 10.27c-32
Isaiah's description of the invasion of Jerusalem from the north seems also to place Gibeah in close proximity to the Geba Pass. In 10.28a-29, the prophet describes the crossing of the Wadi es-Swenit, the probable border between Israel and Judah, in a passage constructed in classic Hebrew poetical parallelism:

> He crossed over the Migron—at Michmas he left his gear;
> he crossed the Geba Pass—and spent the night.
> Ramah trembled! 'Gibeah of Saul' fled!

This passage implies that crossing the Migron amounted to crossing the Geba Pass;[49] the force of the dramatic parallelism is captured when one realizes that such a 'crossing' (עבר) constituted an invasion of Judean territory and the outbreak of war. This breach of the border caused the population of Ramah (er-Ram, 3 kms from the Pass) to panic and 'Gibeah of Saul' (Jeba, 1 km. from the border) to flee. Isaiah apparently here used the ancient Judean epithet 'Gibeah of Saul' as a poetic archaism for Gibeah/Geba, a frequent rhetorical technique of the prophet, who often employed alternate names for the same city.[50]

Hosea 5.8
The prophet Hosea's warning to the Benjaminite cities of Gibeah, Ramah, and Beth-Aven also supports the identification of Gibeah with Jeba. The association of Gibeah with Ramah (3 kms. to the west of Jeba) is very frequent (e.g. Judg. 19.13; 1 Sam. 15.34; Isa. 10.29), yet Gibeah's obvious proximity here to Beth-Aven is also illuminating. Two passages indicate that Beth-Aven lay immediately to the west of Michmas (1 Sam. 13.5; 14.23), which would suggest the site of Tell Maryam, less than 2 kms. southwest of Mukhmas.[51] Jeba's location 2 kms. to the south of Tell Maryam suggests that the cities of Gibeah, Ramah, and Beth-Aven warned by Hosea existed in close proximity to each other along the Judean-Israelite border.

These topographical references show a clear trend—a number of biblical texts closely associate Gibeah with the Wadi es-Swenit (the Migron), and sites in and near it: Michmas, Ramah, Beth-Aven, the Geba Pass, and the Pomegranate Rock. Jeba, correspondingly, sits in the midst of this thicket of sites. Moreover, the Arabic name 'Jeba' clearly retains the ancient Hebrew toponym 'Gibeah'. But if Jeba seems to represent *both* ancient Gibeah and Geba, how does one explain the presence of two Hebrew variant toponyms for the same city?

The Variant Names 'Gibeah' and 'Geba'
Our survey of the Benjaminite גבע-root place-names and their literary settings reveals an unmistakable pattern (see Appendix 1). 'Gibeah' occurs in stories deriving from early Ephraimite or Benjaminite geographical settings (e.g. the 'Outrage of Gibeah' and 'Rise of Saul' narratives), Davidic literature (e.g. the 'Rise of David' narrative), and in prophetic literature in some way referring to Israel's antiquity (e.g. Hosea and Isaiah). 'Geba', by contrast, appears in Judean literature originating in monarchical and postexilic times (e.g. 1 and 2 Kings, Ezra) though occasionally literarily *set* in the premonarchical era (e.g. the Benjaminite town-list and the Jonathan 'Battle of Michmas' source).

Both geographical and chronological aspects emerge from this pattern. Geographically, the preference for the feminine 'Gibeah' in literature deriving from the north, and for the masculine 'Geba' in

Judean literature, may reflect dialectical or orthographical differences between the two language groups.[52] Yet even more compelling is the rather dramatic chronological cut-off point for usage of the 'Gibeah' toponym: the Davidic era. With the exception of archaizing references in Hosea and Isaiah, 'Gibeah' disappears from common usage in stories and official records during the Davidic era. It is precisely in this period, however, that 'Geba' begins to appear. This phenomenon may have a simple linguistic explanation. It is common for a longer word to become shorter over a period of time by a process known as apocope. In the case of 'Gibeah' (הגבעה), the older toponym not only lost its final sound, but also its definite prefix, so that the surviving place-name was simplified 'at both ends': גבע.

A more sinister explanation for the name-change in the Davidic era is also possible. Gibeah was the dynastic home of David's hated rivals, the Saulides. In fact, one of the last Judean prose references to Gibeah (2 Sam. 21.6), records that David's forces exterminated most of the remaining Saulide claimants to the throne of Israel at the city. Can it be that the whole city of Gibeah was abandoned—or massacred—on this occasion? Such a drastic 'final solution' to the Saulide problem may have included the official expunction of the toponym 'Gibeah' from subsequent official Judean usage. Less than a generation later, King Asa built a fortress on the site called 'Geba' (1 Kgs 15.22), a name which adhered to the city throughout the rest of the biblical period.

The Archaeology of Jeba

An archaeological judgment on the suitability of a Gibeah/Geba location at Jeba must remain tentative. Kallai's surface survey in 1967 revealed Iron II and Persian sherds at the site.[53] On the basis of this information, a Gibeah/Geba location at Jeba could be considered compatible with the Bible in every period except Iron I (the so-called era of the Judges, c. 1200–1000). Two factors mitigate the use of this data to prove or disprove the Gibeah/Geba theory, however. First, surface surveys are not always reliable in inhabited villages; modern occupational sites can cover parts of an ancient tell and 'seal off' percolation of potsherd fragments to the surface. In the case of Jeba, much of the hill on which it sits is covered by houses. Second, the differences between Iron I and Iron II diagnostic sherds is subtle, and too fine a line cannot be drawn between them on the basis of a surface survey. Indeed, recent rumors have circulated to the effect that an as yet unpublished re-survey of Jeba revealed Iron I sherds;

such a finding would hardly be surprising. In any case, until a thorough excavation of Jeba is accomplished, the presence of Iron I remains at the site cannot be excluded in view of the possibility that these remains might not have come to the surface.

One hopes that a limited excavation of open portions of Jeba might take place in the future, though political turmoil in the area might inhibit this possibility for some time to come.

Summary Observations

Our analysis of topographical and archaeological data relating to the גבע-root toponyms in Benjamin allows us to arrive at a number of conclusions relevant to the location of Gibeah.

1. Gibeath Kiriath-Jearim was a distinct Benjaminite site which referred to a hill-shrine in the vicinity of Kiriath-Jearim. Modern Deir el-Azhar, less than 1 km. northeast of Abu Ghosh, is the most likely location of this site.

2. Gibeath Ha-Elohim is probably the name of an Elohistic sanctuary in or near Gibeah/Geba. Analysis of two accounts of the Hebrew revolt against the Philistines suggests literary links of this cultic toponym both with 'Gibeah' and 'Geba'—a potential site-identification problem averted by our theory that these two toponyms referred to the same place.

3. Both literary-topographical and archaeological analysis undermine severely the identification of Gibeah with Tell el-Ful. Rather, this site probably served as a Judean military watchtower-settlement known as Eleph.

4. Topographical information in the Bible strongly supports the location of Gibeah at Jeba, 9 kms. northeast of Jerusalem. This city flourished during the period of the Judges and served as Saul's headquarters while he reigned as Israel's first king. David struggled against the Gibeah-based Saulides throughout most of his rule, and eventually exterminated most of them in a mass-murder at Gibeah. Whether for purely linguistic or patently political reasons, the city ceased to be called 'Gibeah' by contemporary Judeans after the Davidic period. After the construction there by Asa of a fortress at the beginning of the ninth century, the city was called 'Geba', its official name in stories and records emanating from the Judean capital of Jerusalem throughout the rest of the monarchical and postexilic period.

Chapter 3

THE OUTRAGE AT GIBEAH

The most ancient Gibeah traditions are embedded within the editorially complicated strata of tales which now comprise Judges 19–21. The product of a long and fascinating literary history, this narrative in our Bible now tells the story of a tragic mistake which triggered hair-raising violence and, ultimately, civil war.

The story relates how a Levite sets off from Ephraim in order to retrieve his runaway concubine from her father's house in distant Bethlehem. Regaled for five days with his father-in-law's extravagant hospitality, the Levite finally leaves Bethlehem late in the day with his wife and servant in tow, only to face a difficult decision: where to spend the night in a foreign land. He tragically chooses Gibeah of Benjamin, where a fellow Ephraimite innocently offers a gracious welcome at his home. At night, men of Gibeah surround the house and sexually threaten the visiting Levite. Horrified at this danger to his guest, the host offers his own daughter instead. Suddenly and inexplicably, the Levite grabs his prized concubine and throws her to the assembled miscreants, who rape her all night and leave her for dead at the door the next morning. On returning to Ephraim, the Levite carves up her body into twelve pieces, which he sends to the Israelite tribes as a call for revenge on Gibeah. Outraged, the whole nation dispatches 400,000 soldiers to punish Gibeah and the tribe of Benjamin which speeds to its defense. After two horrendously unsuccessful sorties on Gibeah, the Israelites win divine help and set a clever ambush near the city. While one contingent of troops draws off the Benjaminite warriors from the city, thus leaving Gibeah undefended, another springs from its hiding place in the Geba Pass region and slaughters the civilian inhabitants of the city. When the Benjaminite soldiers see smoke in the city, they panic and flee into the desert with the Israelite troops in hot pursuit. Only 600 Benjaminites survive, taking refuge for four months in the Pomegranate Rock, a redoubt near Gibeah. Grieving that a whole tribe of Israel verges on extinction and seeking reconciliation with Benjamin, the assembled tribes of Israel seek wives for the 600 soldiers. Accordingly, they massacre the people of Jabesh-Gilead, sparing 400 virgins as peace-offerings to the Benjaminite warriors. Moreover, the Benjaminites, encouraged by the whole community of Israel, raid a feast at Shiloh and carry off more girls, with whom they begin to repopulate their tribe. The tragedy ends with the lesson that such civil tragedies ensue when no king rules Israel.

The events related in this long narrative purportedly took place in the chaotic years before the establishment of kingship in Israel (Judg. 19.1; 21.25). Most scholars agree that, although some elements in the narrative do indeed hark back to this era, much of the material in the story clearly derives from various literary circles many centuries removed from the events it claims to describe. The composite nature of the stories, and the obvious presence of later editorial re-working of the tradition, means that we can discover the historical roots of the passage only after identifying and understanding several layers of literary accretions to the original Gibeah tradition. Our search for the earliest historical memories of Gibeah will thus take us through an absorbing tour of a centuries-long literary and theological process which repeatedly shaped and re-shaped the oldest Gibeah stories.

First, we will identify additions made to the Outrage of Gibeah tradition during the postexilic period. The most obvious place to begin this investigation is with the Deuteronomistic redaction which evidently joined the Gibeah narrative to the main body of the book of Judges in the process of completing the great Deuteronomistic History (DH). Yet even when classical Dtr terminology and concerns are identified, it is clear that other late literary and theological influences pervade the Gibeah stories. These concerns bear a striking resemblance to the Priestly (P) corpus of biblical literature, and it is probable that the Outrage of Gibeah tradition passed through priestly hands before its final incorporation into DH.

Next, we shall examine in detail what is left of the Gibeah story after we have 'peeled off' obviously late DH and P accretions. We find a coherent narrative betraying strong tendencies and biases which help us identify the Israelite setting in which the first written version of the story (the 'core narrative') arose.

Finally, we shall identify, with the help of the prophet Hosea's oracles, which elements in this written core narrative might represent oral traditions tracing their origins back to the murky era of the 'judges'. Only then can we venture an historical guess as to what outrage actually occurred at Gibeah.

The Deuteronomistic Redaction

For many years, scholars offered two main reasons for their claim that Judges 19–21 had been appended as an independent narrative to the already-formed Deuteronomistic History many years after its initial publication.[1] First, the moral of the story—lack of kingship creates chaos—seemed to clash with the supposed 'anti-monarchical' bias of DH; and second, the style and structure of Judges 19–21 hardly related to that of the 'main body' of the book (Judg. 2.6–16.31); indeed, the only point of unity between the narrative and the rest of the book seemed to be its setting in the pre-monarchical period. Critics frequently regarded the Outrage of Gibeah story as little more than an appendix—an editorial afterthought—to the Book of Judges.

Several scholars have seriously challenged this assumption in recent years on two main grounds.[2] First, it is becoming clear that Judges 19–21 contains phraseology that implies a Dtr revision; and second, the way in which the entire Gibeah outrage episode is 'framed' with introductory and concluding comments, and thereby placed into the context of the overall DH, suggests that the Dtr editors found a way to incorporate an already existing piece into the corpus of DH.

Deuteronomistic Terminology

At least eight separate instances of phraseology in Judges 19–21 link the narrative to similar word-use elsewhere in DH, or to evident Dtr concerns. Since these glosses are comparatively minor in relation to the rest of the narrative, it is evident that the editor made the changes mainly to incorporate smoothly an already existing written Gibeah tradition into the larger DH. These additions are as follows:

a. A gloss in 19.10 identifies Jebus as Jerusalem, a very questionable topographical statement, indeed.[3] The only other instances of such an identification of Jerusalem in the Bible (Josh. 15.8; 18.28) also occur where a Dtr editor or copyist incorporated late material (the

Judean boundary list and the Benjaminite town list) into DH. All three passages are thus linked by an editorial quirk deriving from the same Dtr hand.

b. In two places (19.22; 20.12) the wicked Gibeahites are described as 'men of the sons of Belial'. This odd term, suggesting utter worthlessness, is a favorite Dtr expression and describes negatively select figures throughout DH.[4]

c. The repeated use of נבלה ('outrage') as a term describing the gang-rape (19.23; 20.6, 10) suggests Dtr influence since the word is found elsewhere primarily in Deuteronomistic contexts, and frequently with regard to sexual crimes.[5]

d. The Levite's exclamation after the rape-murder that 'nothing like this has happened or been seen since the days the Israelites went up from the land of Egypt till this day' (19.30b) is an obvious Dtr addition. This phrase strongly echoes several other Dtr passages.[6]

e. Concern for the perfectly complete number of twelve Israelite tribes marks much of the material in Judges 20–21. The word for 'tribe' (שבט) used here is frequent in Dtr material but almost never used for example, in P.[7]

f. The report of the attack on Gibeah repeatedly notes that it was not merely Israelite soldiers, but the 'whole people' (כל־העם) which acted (20.2, 8, 26; 21.2). This term has a strong Dtr flavor,[8] especially when it occurs in conjunction with קהל ('assembly'), another classic Dtr term.[9]

g. The final narrative awkwardly shifts the base-camp of the combined Israelite forces back and forth between the sanctuaries at Mizpah and Bethel, a sure sign of editorial interference. It is likely that references to Bethel (20.18, 26-28; 21.2) represent Dtr intrusions for the purpose of explaining or exemplifying why Bethel was holy in ancient days, in stark contrast to its subsequent profanation as a shrine of Jeroboam, a key villain in DH.[10]

h. The edited battle account is marked by highly exaggerated military statistics and fantastic casualty reports (20.16, 21, 25, 35, 44-46) of the kind that seem to be indicative of Dtr battle reportage (see Joshua 8; Judges 7).

The Deuteronomistic 'Frame'
Additional evidence of Dtr activity in Judges 19–21 is the formula which serves both as an introduction and conclusion to the piece, framing it for inclusion into the overall Dtr message concerning the era of the Judges. The opening phrase 'in those days there was no

king in Israel' (19.1) suggests to the reader that the horrible story which follows is explicable only in terms of the absence of a strong central authority in Israel. The concluding sentence develops this message further: 'in those days there was no king in Israel, and a man did what was right in his own eyes' (21.25), an almost apologetic explanation for the story of chaos which precedes.

This obviously pro-kingship formula might at first glance seem out of place in the supposedly anti-monarchical DH.[11] A more sophisticated view of DH, however, would suggest that the work isn't simply anti-kingship, but merely offers strong warnings against an apparently necessary and inevitable institution—or, to paraphrase Churchill's comment about democracy, 'monarchy is a very bad form of government, but all the others are so much worse'. DH carries this ambivalent attitude editorially into the Gibeah outrage story, where the chaotic civil war it relates helps explain the people's demand for kingship which will follow in 1 Sam. 8.5.[12]

The Deuteronomistic Meaning

It is not possible to determine with much precision the place and dating of the Dtr redaction of Judges 19–21, except to propose that a postexilic Dtr editor may have attached the narrative to an earlier edition of the DH, both providing it a suitable literary frame as well as making certain glosses consonant with Dtr theology. The final canonical meaning of the Outrage of Gibeah narrative as provided by Dtr is thus that disobedience to Yahweh creates the kind of anarchy for which the establishment of a legitimate monarchy is a necessary, if flawed, solution. The problematical institution of kingship which followed the chaotic events of Judges would itself prove, in Israel's theological experience, to be a solution which fell far short of the complete obedience which Yahweh demanded.

The final Dtr additions to the Gibeah Outrage narrative were as follows: 19.1a, (10b-11a), (22), 23b, 24b, (29), 30; 20.2, 6b, 8-10, 12-13, 17, (26); 21.2-4a, 5b-6, 9, 15, 17, 19b, 25.

The Priestly Redaction

After the apparent Dtr additions are 'peeled' from the Outrage narrative, the piece still exhibits classic literary signs of editorial interference such as doublets, redundancies, and exaggerations. Taking our cue from Eissfeldt, who long ago proposed that Judges 17–21 underwent a P redaction,[13] we will examine in detail those signs which suggest that Priestly or Levitical circles substantially edited an original Gibeah Outrage story, shifting the emphasis in the narrative to cultic concerns. This Priestly edition made major changes in each of the three chapters of the narrative.

The Levite and his Concubine (Judges 19)
The phrase איש לוי ('Levite man') which introduces the protagonist in 19.1 (and the call to revenge in 20.4) is redundant, and especially odd in view of the fact that the man's Levitical status seems to have no direct bearing on the rest of the narrative; these clues suggest that his identification as a Levite is a late and gratuitous insertion into the story.[14] If the character's Levitical status has no visible literary significance, we can assume that the addition served other purposes.

Since Levites were often equated with those in the Israelite culture who required special legal protection, we can assume that members of this community felt relatively vulnerable or marginalized.[15] Seen in this light, the story's graphic depiction of Israel's immediate response to the Levite's cry for revenge takes on a political hue. Now the story describes the kind of reaction that once could have been expected in Israel's 'Golden Age' if a Levite were harmed. This self-serving alteration of the story would have suited well the Levitical priestly order in its various postexilic controversies and conflicts since it ostensibly shows the power the brotherhood once had to unite the nation in the days of Israel's pristine youth.[16]

A similarly awkward and even contradictory situation exists with regard to the woman in the story, who is repeatedly called a concubine (פילגש), though her father is called the Levite's 'father-in-law' (חתן), a term implying full marriage. We can assume that the wife's transformation into a mere concubine is a Priestly alteration in order to save the story from two moral dilemmas. In the original story, the wife committed adultery (זנה) against the husband (19.2).[17] The Levitical Holiness Code, however, prescribed death for such an adulteress.[18] In order to retain symmetry with this law, the Levitical redactors may have changed the 'wife' into a mere 'concubine', which, in turn, might have improved her legal position. Moreover, the admittedly bizarre scene of a Levite pushing his wife out to the surrounding Gibeahites (19.25) may have shocked the Priestly editors into substituting the word 'concubine' in order to soften the scurrilousness of his action.

This wife-to-concubine alteration also required one final series of changes. While the text already identified the Bethlehemite father of the wife as a 'father-in-law' the Priestly redaction merely refers to him as the 'father of the girl,' an odd and awkward redundancy which again implies a legal relationship somewhat short of formal marriage.

The Community Responds (Judges 20)

The Priestly editors made even more sweeping changes to the original account of Israel's attack on Gibeah in Judges 20. These alterations almost certainly account for the long-held but probably mistaken scholarly impression that two separate and independent sources comprise the chapter.[19] The resulting edited version of the attack on Gibeah presents four classically Priestly features:

a. The forces which gather against Gibeah are identified as one 'community' (עדה), a late theological term characteristic of Priestly writing.[20]

b. The editors now identify the combatants as the 'sons of Israel', and the 'sons of Benjamin'. The expression 'sons of Israel' (בני ישראל) is a term much used in P material, and its usage here is strongly suggestive of late P authorship.[21]

c. The Levitical redaction places the staging area for the Gibeah attack at the sanctuary of Mizpah, most likely modern Tell en-Nasbeh,[22] some 5 kms. northwest of Jeba. This attempt to underscore the cultic legitimacy of Mizpah as a valid sanctuary is especially understandable in exilic times, when the city became the capital of Judah after the destruction of Jerusalem (2 Kgs 25.22-26) and site of a 'house of the Lord' (Jer. 41.4-8). This latter reference might also illuminate the notice in Judg. 20.27-28 that 'the Ark of the Covenant of God was there in those days, and Phinehas son of Eleazar son of Aaron stood before him'. Inasmuch as the appearance of 'Bethel' here is a later Dtr addition,[23] the notice probably originated in the Priestly gloss referring to Mizpah. Similarly, an earlier reference to the 'house of the Lord' (Judg. 19.18) in Jerusalem is an anachronistic gloss, probably from the hand of P editors.

d. Most, if not all, of the overtly cultic material in the narrative derives from Priestly editors. In addition to usage of the term עדה, which implies an explicitly religious gathering,[24] several other passages betray Priestly cultic supplementation. The Israelite army now inquires of Yahweh both before the first two battles (20.18-25), and after the final victory (21.4-8), at shrines under sacerdotal control. After two horrific losses, the whole Israelite people ritually laments and fasts, sacrificing שלמים ('shared offerings')—a P term.[25]

These prayers are answered as Yahweh enters the battle, scattering Benjamin (20.35).

The Priestly redaction also pictures the gathering of the entire community of Israel in Mizpah to hear the Levite's story (20.4-6), which subtly changes the events reported in Judges 19.[26] The gathering of the 'sons of Benjamin' (20.14-16) is also added to the account, foreshadowing the monumental and tragic battle that is about to take place. The insertion of the notice that Judah led the community's attack (20.18), which commentators usually regard as a late interpolation,[27] reinforces the point of the whole P redaction: this war has united all parts of Israel on behalf of one aggrieved Levite. Two failed attacks by the community on Gibeah (20.21, 25) heighten the sense of tragedy, but also highlight the successful results that accrue to those who will finally fast and offer the proper sacrifices (20.26).

The Community Provides (Judges 21)

The bulk of the narrative in Judges 21 appears to have been attached to the original Gibeah narratives by P editors who created a narrative out of two disparate and originally independent folktales which related virgin abductions.[28] Whereas the original narrative ended on a note of triumph as Israel left 600 warriors from Gibeah trapped in a cave and the cities of Benjamin burning (20.48), the P redactors refashioned two raid tales in order to demonstrate the ability of the Israelite religious community to forgive Benjamin and provide for its surviving soldiers lest Israel lose an entire tribe.

According to the P introduction (21.2-9), each Israelite had sworn not to marry his daughter to a Benjaminite (21.1),[29] which demanded that the replenishment of the tribe could take place only with women whose husbands swore no oath. After offering sacrifice (21.4b), the community sought wives for the Benjaminite survivors from among the girls of Jabesh-Gilead, which did not take part in the attack.[30] The notice that the 400 captured young women were not sufficient (21.11) is surely a pretext for the incorporation of yet another ancient folktale, the raid on Shilo for virgins (21.19-23). Together, these tales allow the story to end on a solemn religious note: though the community punishes its wayward sons, it also reconciles them on behalf of Israel's unity.

The Setting of the Levitical Redaction

The affinities which the P redaction of the Gibeah Outrage story shares in terminology and theology with other P materials suggest that the P editors reworked an old narrative in exilic or post-exilic times. If the editorial references to Mizpah relate to its cultic importance in this period as reported in Jeremiah 40–41, then we might suppose that the redaction arose in priestly circles which conducted worship in Mizpah in the period between the destruction of the temple in Jerusalem in 586 and its reconstruction less than a century later.

The P edition considerably altered the original Gibeah Outrage narrative in order to demonstrate the power and magnanimity of the priestly community in ancient Israel. As that religious community once acted decisively to avenge an outrageous evil inflicted upon one of its priests—and forgave the punished villains as readily—so would the newly restored priestly community of Judah create law and order so that the people might live in peace and reconciliation in a period of renewed chaos.

Besides the minor additions already noted in Judges 19, the P edition supplemented the following verses: 19.12b; 20.1, 3-6a, 7, 14-16, 18b-19, 21-28 (minus references to Bethel), 30-31a, 32, (34), 35-36a, 39b, 44-46; 21.1, 4b-5a, 7-8, 10-14, 16, 18-19a, 20-24.

The Official Israelite Version

When we remove both the late Dtr and Priestly editorial accretions to the Gibeah Outrage story, we are left with the original core narrative, a stark story of intertribal savagery in early Israel (for the reconstructed text, see Appendix 2).

In its originally simplified form, the story relates how an Ephraimite man found unexpected and extravagant hospitality as he retrieved his run-away wife from her father's house at Bethlehem. Yet the couple's late departure for home caused them to make a tragic mistake: spending the night in Gibeah with a fellow Ephraimite. When men of the city gathered to humiliate the guest sexually, the host offered his daughter instead. Suddenly, the Ephraimite thrust out his own wife to the thugs, who raped her all night and left her dead at the doorpost. Returning to Ephraim, the husband divided her body in pieces and sent them to the tribes of Israel, who responded with a war party which set an ambush against Gibeah. As one contingent drew out the Benjaminites from the city, losing about thirty men to them, another sprang from its hiding place in the wadi below Gibeah, and put the civilians to the sword. When the Benjaminites saw the smoke signal, they turned and fled into the desert before the pursuing Israelites. Finally, 600 found refuge in the Rock of Rimmon, while the Israelites burned the surrounding Benjaminite cities, vowing never to marry their daughters to the survivors.

Composition of the core narrative
Perhaps the most striking feature of this narrative is its composition: most of the scenes in it are amazingly similar to episodes found elsewhere in the Old Testament! The appearance of such literary 'doublets' has long intrigued biblical literary critics. Most scholars have tended to think of doublets in the Bible as evidence of literary imitation or direct copying, and indeed, some of the material in Judges 19–20 is widely regarded by the critics as the product of deliberate postexilic plagiarism.

Intensive cross-cultural research into the dynamics of oral tradition, however, has yielded fresh theories which offer more satisfying and creative explanations for the kinds of doublets we see in the Gibeah story. Scholars such as R. Alter and R. Culley seek the explanation for doublets not at a late stage of literary imitation, but in the earliest oral phases out of which most of the biblical stories developed.[31] These critics theorize that ancient oral story tellers possessed in their memories a whole inventory of 'stock scenes' out of which they could spontaneously draw motifs and apply them artfully in appropriate narratives as circumstances dictated. In fact, W. Ong has shown that the use of such stereotypical or cliché elements in stories is a primary feature of oral culture.[32]

We will follow these modern critics' lead as we identify the component motifs of the oldest Gibeah narrative, compare them to similar biblical episodes, and analyze them with reference to their use in the entire story.

The Crime at Gibeah (Judges 19)
The first part of the narrative relates the tragic story of hospitality gone wrong, and how the wicked citizens of Gibeah brought upon themselves deserved punishment for their crime. After a brief introduction of the two protagonists, the author stitched together three stock 'type-scenes' in order to fashion a larger narrative.

The story opens with the introduction of the two nameless

principal characters: a man who lives on the flanks of Mt Ephraim,[33] and his new wife from Bethlehem of Judah. After she commits adultery[34] against him and flees back to her father's house, her husband undertakes his fateful journey from Ephraim to Bethlehem in order to 'speak to her heart' and win her back. There the husband receives an unexpectedly lavish welcome from his wife's father, who regales him with days of generous conviviality.

The Hospitality at Bethlehem (Judges 19.3-9)
Our story's account of the hospitality accorded the Ephraimite man in his father-in-law's house in Bethlehem is very similar in form and language to other hospitality type-scenes in the Old Testament, especially Abraham's welcome of angels (Gen. 18.1-16), Lot's hospitality to the angels in Sodom (Gen. 19.1-4) and these same Ephraimites' experience a few days later (Judg. 19.15-22).[35] The comparability of the key words and phrases in Judg. 19.3-9 to other hospitality type-scenes is apparent in the following list.

Judg. 19.3-9		Other scenes
3	Host *sees* visitors	Gen. 18.2; 19.1. Judg. 19.17
3	Host *meets* visitors	Gen. 18.2; 19.1
4,6,7	Host/guest *sits*	Gen. 18.1; 19.1. Judg. 19.15
4,6,8	They *eat*	Gen. 18.8; 19.3. Judg. 19.21
4,6	They *drink*	Gen. 19.3. Judg. 19.21
4,6,7,9,10	They *lodge*	Gen. 19.2. Judg. 19.20
5,7,9,10	*Getting up to go*	Gen. 18.16. Judg. 19.27,28
5,8	*Strengthening the heart*	Gen. 18.5
5	*Morsel of bread*	Gen. 18.5
6,9	Making the *heart glad*	Judg. 19.22
7	*Pressing* the guest	Gen. 19.13
9	*Get up, go your way*	Gen. 19.2

Two points are especially noteworthy about this list. First, it is clear that the basic elements in the Bethlehem scene are not copied mechanically in any one other version; on the contrary, the shared linguistic elements are scattered among all three. Similarly, the other three hospitality scenes sometimes share words among them *not* found in the Bethlehem scene. In short, none of the scenes is a literary copy of another. Instead, the basic elements of the hospitality accounts appear to have been drawn from a remembered oral fund of stereotypical expressions and scenery which was available to story-tellers in ancient Israel and employed in a given story according to the requirements of oral convention.[36]

The other obvious feature in the 'hospitality at Bethlehem' episode is the frequent repetition of stereotypical language within the same scene. Earlier scholars thought that this repetitiveness suggested the presence of two independent sources.[37] In fact, we have seen that some supplementation to the narrative did take place in the Priestly redaction. Yet modern critics have learned to appreciate that such repetitions evince oral and literary story-telling techniques rather than separate written sources.[38] Indeed, the Bethlehem scene's repeated mention of eating, lodging, and attempts to 'get up and go' serves two functions. First, it vividly contrasts the lavish hospitality which the Ephraimite receives in Bethlehem with the hostility he will soon suffer in Gibeah.[39] Second, the very repetitiveness subtly builds a certain dramatic tension within the story, climaxed by the final episode of extravagant hospitality which delays the couple's departure from Bethlehem, forcing them to find shelter in Benjamin at nightfall.[40]

The author of this narrative evidently elaborated upon a conventional hospitality 'type scene' in order to explain why an Ephraimite couple leaving Bethlehem could travel only so far as Gibeah after a late afternoon journey, and how, ironically, they were ultimately endangered by the extravagant kindness they received.

En route home, the Jebus interlude scene (Judg. 19.10-13) continues the dramatic build-up in the story by giving attention to the passage of time. This technique cleverly emphasizes the inevitable onset of a tragic night as the couple faces three lodging alternatives: Jebus, which the Ephraimite hastily ignores, and a choice between Ramah or Gibeah.[41] For the very first time in the story, the Ephraimite speaks: he chooses the homeward route through Gibeah.

The Outrage at Gibeah (Judges 19.14-24)
The account of the atrocity committed against the Ephraimite couple in Gibeah has elicited a wide variety of scholarly opinion over the years. One important school of thought believed in the essential historicity of the story,[42] but most biblical scholars since Wellhausen have regarded the story as what might now be termed 'historicized prose fiction'.[43]

The real debate over the origin and nature of this story centers around the reasons for its striking similarity to Gen. 19.1-11, the famous account of the threat experienced by innocent angelic visitors to Sodom. Most scholars theorize that the authors of the Gibeah outrage account basically copied or imitated the similar story in Genesis.[44] Before considering this possibility, the direct verbal similarities (underlined below) between the two stories should be demonstrated graphically.

Judges 19	Genesis 19
16 *In the evening*	1 *In the evening*
15 the man *sat*	1 Lot was *sitting*
17 the old man *saw* (guests)	1 Lot *saw* (guests)
15 *they turned aside to spend the night*	2 *turn aside, spend the night*
21 *they washed their feet*	2 *wash your feet*
20 *do not spend the night in the square*	2 *No. We can spend the night in the square*
21 *he brought him to his house*	3 *they went to his house*
21 *they ate and drank*	3 *they ate. . . a feast*
22 *men of the city, men of. . .*	4 *men of the city, men of. . .*
22 *surrounded the house*	4 *surrounded the house*
22 *bring out* the man!	5 *bring them out!*
22 *and let us know* him	5 *and let us know* them
23 *he went out to them*	6 *he went out to them*
23 *he said, no, my brothers don't do this evil.*	7 *he said, please don't do this evil, my brothers.*
24 *Look, my daughters. . . I will bring them out*	8 *Look, my daughters. . . I will bring them out*
24 *do to them what is good in your eyes*	8 *do to them what is good in your eyes*
24 *don't do a thing to this man*	8 *don't do a thing to these men*
23 *he came* (to my house)	8 *they came* (under. . . my roof)

While one can never totally exclude the possibility that one of these stories copies the other, such a solution to the similarity problem is unlikely for several reasons. First, the widespread assumption that the literary version of the 'early' Genesis 19 episode pre-dates the 'late' Judges 19 is highly questionable. In none of the many Old Testament references to Sodom, for example, is there the slightest mention of the outrage story which presently prefaces the report of its destruction, suggesting strongly that the story of Lot and the angels was subsequently prefixed to the ancient tradition of the city's wantonness and destruction by God.[45] Still less can one say that the Gibeah version cannot be properly understood without assuming knowledge of Genesis 19.[46] Surely an ancient audience would have grasped the full meaning of the outrage and its punishment without reference to the Genesis account. As for the suggestion that both versions derive from the same Yahwist document,[47] one must also consider the strong *dissimilarities* between the two stories. Whereas the entire Genesis 19 episode is thoroughly mystical, almost 'comic', and clearly set in the southern Judean realm, the original Judges 19 version is completely secular, unrelentingly 'tragic', and oriented to northern Ephraimite circles.

Most importantly, the similarity in language between the two stories (as indicated in our graph) is not strong enough to demonstrate deliberate *verbatim* copying, or 'wooden re-use of language'.[48] On the contrary, the shared use of common verbal roots and stereotypical language is indicative of *oral* mnemonic technique.[49] In brief, this style is characterized by the use of memorized *Leitwörter* (key words or phrases) in patterns which story-tellers employ according to their designs. Additional material is supplemented to the key-word pattern as the storyteller wishes.

The language-use comparison in our graph suggests a shared key-word pattern between the stories, yet great diversity in verb number, mood and tense, number of characters, and so forth. For this reason, a solution to the Genesis 19–Judges 19 puzzle along the lines of Alter's type-scene theory appears the most promising. Each story is the literary offspring of a common oral ancestor.

Yet technically speaking, the two versions share not just *one* type scene, but rather a *series* of four type-scenes: (1) a welcoming invitation by a countryman in a foreign and unfriendly city; (2) a description of an evening's conviviality, (3) a scene of sudden threat to guest and host, and (4) a quick action by the guest which saves himself. A perusal of the shared elements of the two passages, in fact, reveals the rudimentary outline of a 'type-story'[50] which dramatized a wicked city's brutal threat to a stranger and his clever move to save himself. Von Rad once proposed a solution precisely along these lines when he observed that the account of the crime at Sodom and the narrative which reported its subsequent punishment originated as two distinct stories.[51]

> Perhaps an ancient narrative, well-known in Israel, about a frightful violation of the law of hospitality was connected only secondarily with Sodom as the seat of all sin.

A process similar to the one which attached the outrage story to the Sodom tradition also appears to have been at work in the Gibeah narrative. In each case, the 'evil-city' outrage type-story provided a graphic depiction of a city so wicked as to merit total destruction.

The Original Outrage Type-Story

We might inquire at this point into the nature of our hypothesized original type-story, bearing in mind that, as an oral phenomenon, the narrative never existed as a precise entity 'on paper', but rather as a series of key-words forming a dramatic pattern which existed only in the memories of story-tellers and their audiences. This type-story had a life of its own, subtly distinct in meaning from its later re-use in two biblical written settings.

The opening scene pictures the welcome of an innocent stranger into a foreign city by one of his fellow countrymen living there as a resident alien. The tone of conviviality later in the night highlights the dramatic scene of danger which follows. At night, men of the evil foreign city surround the house, demanding in euphemistic but entirely obvious threatening language that the host deliver his guest to them for gang-rape.[52] The host attempts to save his position by offering his own virgin daughters to the crowd. The thugs' refusal forces the guest to take immediate and clever action to save himself.

The original themes, characters, and dramatic tensions of the type-story arose out of the Hebrew experience of intolerable oppression in ancient Canaan. This victimization is biblically expressed in the Book of Judges, where a swarm of pagan peoples surround and harrass Israel in one persecution after another, for which dangers Yahweh graciously sends a deliverer in each crisis. Yet modern researchers are less inclined to view Israel's endangerment as a purely religious or ethnic one, preferring to emphasize the vulnerable social status of the Hebrews as lower-class, marginalized 'outsiders'. It is likely that the scattered tribes of the people who were to become Israel lived in pre-monarchical times in isolated rural villages in the hill country, outside the dominant city-state social structure of Canaan.

The hero of our story appears as an innocent stranger in an ominous foreign city, recreating a common motif in early Israelite folklore which pictured the city as an evil and threatening place.[54] The host's character serves as a foil to our hero: as a countryman to the stranger he is the only city-dweller kind enough to offer hospitality, but his utter inability to handle the later threat to his guest probably offers a graphic symbol of the extent to which he has become urbanized. The villains are city people, utterly cruel and vicious thugs without the least trace of humanity. The theme of the story is obvious: the city is a dangerous place for country people, but one clever Hebrew can outwit a whole city full of gangsters when he has to!

The outrage story probably served several social functions. In addition to entertainment, it exemplified the all-important Middle Eastern cultural value of hospitality by picturing its use and abuse.[55] In this sense, it even shows how far a host must go to defend his guest —even to the sacrifice of his own daughter. Yet at a deeper level it dramatized a crucial social and psychological issue confronting the early Hebrews. It is important to realize that the threat to the stranger in our story is not a homosexual encounter *per se*. Aside from one twice-repeated legal proscription in the esoteric Levitical Holiness Code, there is no evidence in the entire Old Testament that the Israelite people historically considered homosexual relationships as especially noteworthy, much less immoral.[56] The real threat foisted on our hero by the city's hoodlums is an utterly degrading and humiliating gang-rape. Recent sociological studies regard rape, not so much as an act of lust, but as a particularly effective tool by which psychologically insecure oppressors create a sense of their own social superiority by degrading defenseless individuals and reminding them of their inferior status and vulnerability.[57] The type-story's threat of gang-rape thus almost painfully symbolized the Hebrews' sense of their own social vulnerability and marginality. Originally, the episode probably functioned as a kind of 'horror story', evoking powerful fears and animosity in its audience while at the same time bringing these emotions to a successful catharsis as the hero, by virtue of his wit and resourcefulness, somehow saved the day as he struck down his attackers.

It is not entirely clear in the original type-story precisely what actions the hero took to save himself. Bearing in mind that oral story-tellers freely elaborate upon the familiar story-patterns which they recount, it may be that the type-story provided the raconteur with an open-ended opportunity to include a climax of his/her own choosing. Since the supernatural version of the story in Genesis already utilized the well-known ancient motif of gods disguised as visitors, the story quite naturally ends with God's assistance to the guests, who blind their antagonists.[58] This supernatural version of the type-story provides a theological moral: God takes the place of the vulnerable, and punishes their oppressors immediately.

Use of the Outrage Tradition in Judges 19

The author of the Judges version, however, used the outrage type-story in an entirely different way, thereby altering its ending significantly. As the story's threat of homosexual rape recedes in importance, the emphasis shifts to the actual heterosexual rape and murder of the Ephraimite's wife.[59] The Ephraimite husband is now no hero—the selfish sacrifice of his wife represents an act of true desperation and cowardice.[60] This contradictory picture of Judges 19's protagonist (undertaking a dangerous journey to retrieve his wife, only to throw her to the wolves at the first hint of trouble) is explicable only when we realize that the author is hardly interested in the fellow—much less his wife! In fact, this is a nameless couple, with little character development and even less dialogue.

If the author of Judges 19 is embarrassingly uninterested in the feelings and experiences of the story's characters, one naturally seeks some point to the narrative other than artistic character development.[61] It seems apparent that the author is really only interested in the rape/murder itself—the outrage—and not in the characters who either inflicted it or suffered it. The primary intent of this story is to create a literary pretext, a virtual *casus belli*, in order to justify the ensuing account of the ambush and massacre of Gibeah (Judges 20). Whereas the Yahwist author employed the outrage type-story as a theodicy in order to justify the tradition of total divine destruction of the evil Sodom, another literary circle obviously utilized the same stock story to justify and explain a narrative which described the Israelite slaughter of the inhabitants of Benjaminite Gibeah.

The Call to Tribal War (Judges 19.29)

The account of the horrible rape and murder at Gibeah is followed immediately by another shocking episode which describes how the Ephraimite divided his wife's body and sent its pieces throughout Israel. Scholars have long noticed this pericope's striking similarities to a passage—interestingly enough, also associated with Gibeah—which pictures Saul calling the Israelite tribes to war in the Transjordan (1 Sam. 11.7).[62] The recurrent use of key linguistic terms in both passages clearly suggests that we have encountered yet another type-scene.

Judges 19	1 Samuel 11
29 *He took* a knife	7 *He took* a team of oxen
29 ind *cut* (her) *in pieces*	7 *and cut* (it) *in pieces*

29 *and he sent* her	7 *and he sent* it
29 *in every part of Israel*	7 *in every part of Israel*

These parallel texts suggest once again that their respective authors appropriated oral stereotypical language in fashioning their scenes. This particular type-scene, involving the dismemberment of a body and the parcelling out of its pieces as a prelude to war, may remember a practice, also known in the Mari texts, which once ritually called tribes to war.[63] The final version of the Judges 19 story containing the notice that the concubine was divided in *twelve* pieces is likely to be a Dtr gloss reflecting a later, idealistic twelve-tribe conception. The original version merely stated that her divided parts were distributed in every territory of Israel, that is, Ephraim.[64]

The Purpose of Judges 19

Our literary-critical reading of Judges 19 suggests that the narrative lacks dramatic profundity because of the superficial development of its characters. While one surely feels a hot justice-seeking anger at the hoodlums of Gibeah, this sentiment derives more from the story's provocative, even titillating violence, than from any spiritual identification with the victims. The narrative finally leaves the reader with a certain cool distance from its characters, not unlike that experienced in reading yet another account of murder in a tabloid newspaper. For just as sensational journalism is interested, not in the humanity of crime victims, but in selling newspapers to addicts of pornographic violence, so the author of this literary account basically is trying to 'sell' something: namely, a sense of righteousness for the story of Gibeah's punishment which follows. Ultimately, Judges 19 is a manipulative pretext written from oral stereotypical scenes in order to create a sense of just satisfaction for a tradition which related the total slaughter of Gibeah, a small village in Benjamin.

The Punishment of Gibeah (Judges 20)

The account of the ambush in Judges 20 is the center of the entire Gibeah Outrage tradition in Judges; chapter 19 introduces and morally justifies it, and chapter 21 heals its effects. Such a flurry of literary activity normally indicates that a narrative relates something truly astonishing: in this case, Israel's fratricidal massacre of Benjamin's village.

The original ambush report begins at Judg. 20.11 and extends (with Dtr and P intrusions) through 20.48. This narrative is clearly distinguished by the strange idiom איש ישראל (lit.: 'a man of Israel') as a designation for the Israelite troops.[65] This ancient term appears in biblical battle reports set in the period from the time of the Conquest to the Philistine wars, usually referring to soldiers from the northern tribes.[66] Interestingly, איש ישראל also designates those northerners who supported Absalom in his revolt against David (2 Sam. 15.13; 16.15, 18; 17.14, 24), and in 2 Sam. 19.42-44 and 20.1-2 the term specifically contrasts with איש יהודה (lit.: 'a man of Judah'), southern warriors who remained loyal to David after Sheba's revolt. The appearance of איש ישראל in the Gibeah ambush account strongly suggests two important facts about the narrative. First, the term designates only northern (i.e. Ephraimite-area) soldiers, and not all tribes in the imaginary so-called 'twelve-tribe confederacy' created by postexilic theologians. And second, this is a chronologically early term which originated in a period when 'Israel' still meant only Ephraim and perhaps a few associated northern tribes.[67]

The gruesome body-slicing scene of 19.29 dramatically anticipates the appearance of the 'men of Israel' as they quickly respond to the Ephraimite's call for revenge (20.11). This transition emphasizes the solidarity of the whole tribe with one of its members; whereas the Gibeahite thugs victimized one man (איש), now all the men of Israel (איש ישראל) respond 'as one man united' (כאיש אחד חברים). The ensuing ambush and attack on Gibeah is correspondingly decisive, swift and efficient, and justly inverts the outrage committed against the Ephraimites. Whereas the men of Gibeah had surrounded the house, lying in wait for the man of Ephraim (19.22), now the men of Israel surround Gibeah, waiting to deliver intertribal justice (20.29).

The Ambush of Gibeah (Judges 20.29-48)
The ambush scene of Judg. 20.29-48 closely resembles Josh. 8.10-29, which relates how the invading Israelite army under Joshua attacked the Canaanite city of Ai after entering the Promised Land. While the careful planning for the Ai ambush (Josh. 8.2-9) is not paralleled in Judges 20, the report of its execution bears obvious similarities in typical language and scenes to the Gibeah account.

Judges 20	Joshua 8
29 Israel *set up ambushers*	12 Joshua *set up an ambush*
31 *They were drawn out from the city*	16 *They were drawn out from the city*

33 Israel's *ambush* broke *from its place*	19 *The ambush* rose quickly *from its place*
34 (Gibeah) *didn't know* (the evil approaching)	14 (King of Ai) *didn't know* (there was an ambush)
40 Benjamin *turned behind and beheld the whole city going to the sky*	20 The men of Ai *turned behind and beheld the city's smoke going to the sky*
41 (Men of Israel) turned and pursued men of Benjamin	21 (Israelites) turned and struck the men of Ai
43 *They pursued* them	24 *they pursued* them
47 *to the desert*	24 *in the desert*
48 (Men of) *Israel returned and put them to the sword*	24 (all) *Israel returned and put* Ai *to the sword*

The presence in each of these versions of similar but not identical scenery, and stereotypical but not *verbatim* linguistic forms, indicates once again a common origin for the accounts in oral tradition rather than in direct literary imitation.[68] This fact leads to a fascinating literary and historical question: where did this particular ambush tradition originate?

It is quite possible, of course, that the account derives from stock type-scenery portraying the well known 'ambush-feint-attack' motif known elsewhere in the ancient world.[69] In this case, both the Ai and Gibeah episodes derive from a purely fictional oral war story with which ancient Hebrew raconteurs regaled tribal celebrations. In view of the historical paucity of our sources, this explanation remains a live option. Yet the possibility that the ambush scene remembers an actual event in Israel's early days cannot be dismissed, either. We shall explore the historical implications of this prospect shortly as we discuss the historicity of the Gibeah Outrage.

The core narrative ended on a just and triumphant note: the men of Israel chased the Benjaminite warriors into their desert redoubt at the nearby Pomegranate Rock, and returned to burn the cities of Benjamin as punishment for their outrage.

The Origin and Purpose of the Core Narrative
Our search for the purpose, setting, time and place which generated this core narrative first requires a clear summary of some of the story's distinctive characteristics. Perhaps the most obvious is the strongly pro-Israelite and anti-Benjaminite tendentiousness of the piece. The main protagonists are Ephraimite or Israelite: the man and woman, the host, and the 'men of Israel'. The villains are

Benjaminite: the Gibeahite thugs and the 'men of Benjamin' who flock to their side. Indeed, the piece basically functions as a tale relating why Benjaminite Gibeah richly deserved extermination.

The narrative betrays its Israelite origins in other respects, as well. The symbolic geographical orientation of the story implies that Ephraim is a safe home, point of origin and return, and land of righteous order. The Benjaminite territory, on the other hand, is threatening foreign territory where lawlessness reigns. Moreover, the strong use of the term איש ישראל, indicating an army comprised of northern tribal elements, suggests composition in an Israelite environment.

It is somewhat more difficult to ascertain the time period in which this Israelite story appeared as a written document. Since the Kingdom of Israel disappeared around 722, we may adopt this date as a *terminus ad quem*; theoretically, the story may have emerged at any time within three or four centuries before this date. Yet we may argue that such documents originate only in literate, leisured, and organized settings, and reason that the work therefore reflects a monarchical milieu.

In ancient times writing was an expensive, arduous, and rare undertaking. We must ask, then, what author or group took the great trouble to write down this story—and why? What function did this narrative serve in the Kingdom of Israel? Ordinarily, we can answer such a literary and historical question only in general sociological, political and theological terms; in the case of the Gibeah Outrage narrative, however, two related biblical texts suggest a more specific answer to these questions.

Hosea and the Sin of Gibeah

We can find the key to unlocking the direct purpose of the core narrative in Hos. 9.9 and 10.9. In both passages, the eighth-century prophet Hosea alludes mysteriously to some evil in Israel's past which happened at Gibeah. While we can never be entirely sure that the Bible anywhere actually records the Gibeah sin in question, it is quite probable that Hosea refers to an event remembered in Judges 19–20. We can establish this relationship on the basis of the contexts in which each Hosean passage occurs. Hos. 9.9a seems to compare the prophet's own contemporary endangerment by his Israelite countrymen with a similar sinister entrapment by ancient Ephraim:

Ephraim lies in wait at the prophet's tent,
    he sets a trap on his every path—hostility even in the temple
    of his God!
They make their corruption deep
    as in the days of Gibeah.

Further elucidation of the Gibeah allusion occurs in 10.9-15, where Hosea indicts his own nation for its history of militarism:

Since the days of Gibeah you have sinned, Israel.
There they took their stand in rebellion. . . .
Because you have trusted in your chariots,
    in the number of your warriors,
The tumult of war shall rise against your tribes.

                                            (Hos. 10.9a, 13b-14a)

We shall discuss scholarly interpretations of this passage in detail in Chapter 5. At this point we need say only that the contexts of Hosea's oracles surely do not permit an interpretation linking the 'sin at Gibeah' to the establishment of the Israelite monarchy under Saul. Most commentators correctly link Hosea's allusion to the Gibeah outrage tradition. Yet a more careful analysis of the passages reveals that Hosea did not allude to the sex-crime and murder episode of Judges 19 as most of these critics assume. For the object of both Hosean indictments is not Gibeah or Benjamin, but Ephraim/ Israel—Hosea's own nation! Hosea's accusation, understood within its anti-military context in 10.9-15, is an indictment of *Israel* for her bellicosity as evidenced in antiquity by the treacherous trap (Hos. 9.8-9) in which she massacred the populace of Gibeah, the city of a fellow Hebrew tribe.

We conclude, therefore, that Hosea knew an Israelite oral tradition which remembered a shameful ambush and massacre of Benjaminite Gibeah by men of Israel in its earliest days. The 'sin of Gibeah' connoted in Hosea's prophetic circles a shameful deed which Israel committed in the distant past. Moreover, there is no evidence that Hosea knew the rape and murder story in Judges 19; for him, the 'outrage' of Gibeah consisted in what Judges 20 reports as Gibeah's 'punishment'!

The Sin of Gibeah and Israelite Nationalism
If we assume that an oral tradition circulated in eighth-century Israelite prophetic circles which remembered the Ephraimite war-crime at Gibeah centuries earlier, we might then ask what circles

would wish to oppose this memory with an entirely different version of the event. One thinks naturally that the royal court, that bastion of nationalism and tradition, would possess the literary resources and the will necessary to sanitize Israel's history of all traces of national shame. If this is indeed the case, the core narrative is much more than a simple, popular, anti-Benjaminite story. It serves more seriously as an official Israelite narrative of national exculpation. Its authors justified the ancient attack on Gibeah by creating out of stereotypical stock scenes an account of a tragic journey to Gibeah, which they then prefixed to a pre-existing account of the ambush and massacre. Now, the incident was all Gibeah's fault, it got what it deserved, and the soldiers of Israel acted justly after all, as of course they always do.

Whether this official Israelite core narrative arose in direct opposition to Hosea's unpatriotic preaching, or only in response to the irritating oral tradition which he employed, must remain a mystery. Less mysterious now is the fact that this militaristic, heroic and self-righteous narrative belongs to a literary genre all too familiar to moderns: nationalistic propaganda.

Historicity of the Events at Gibeah

As we search for the history of Gibeah, we must 'peer behind' the veils of literary and oral traditions to see if an actual event is visible. Thus far, we have attributed much of Judges 19–21 to late editorial intrusions and propagandistic re-use of fictional oral type-scenes. Yet one tradition remains for our historical investigation: the account of the ambush and massacre of Gibeah in Judges 20. The main problem with this narration from an historical viewpoint is that it suspiciously resembles passages in Joshua 8; both accounts cannot be historical. Assuming that the original oral story of the ambush is not in itself completely fictional, we are left with the real possibility that such an ambush actually happened. The problem lies in determining whether historically it occurred at Ai or Gibeah.

Unquestionably, the Ai narrative is the least historically certain of the two. Not only is the historicity of the entire Joshua conquest tradition itself highly doubtful, but the specific account of the Ai ambush probably amounts to little more than a simple Israelite folk aetiology which explained how the city got its name: 'Ai' means 'ruins'.[70] Yet the strong possibility exists that the ambush type-scene which comprises the fictional aetiology for Ai (modern et-Tell) originated in the historical memory of a genuine battle at nearby Gibeah (Jeba).[71] The aetiological Ai Benjaminite war-story may then have been incorporated into the Joshua cycle as one episode in the saga of the Israelite conquest of Canaan.[72] If the Ai version does not stand on its own as a plausible historical report, we must test the historical credibility of the Gibeah ambush account.

In general terms, the battle report itself provides no inherently implausible literary qualities such as fantastic numbers of troops and casualties, supernatural intervention, or overreaching individual heroism, which would suggest a purely fictional folkloric genre. The only casualty figure, a twice-repeated report of 30 Israelites killed (20.31, 39),[73] is a credible ancient figure. Moreover, the ambush's tactic of drawing the defenders away from a fortified city with one contingent, while another falls on the city from its hiding place, represents rather standard ancient military strategy.

It is also quite plausible that such an inter-tribal skirmish involving Benjamin could erupt in the first place. Several other biblical passages, e.g. Gen. 49.27, where Benjamin is called a 'ravenous wolf', and Gen. 35.18-19, which names it 'the son of affliction', bespeak a certain approbrium attached to the tribe. Some scholars suggest that the historical hostility between the tribe of Ephraim and Benjamin originated when the latter tribe, whose name means 'son of the south', separated itself violently from its larger and more powerful northern neighbor; others propose that the tribes feuded over land, or clashed because of Benjamin's 'brigandage and murder' against its neighbor.[74]

While we cannot trace precisely the origins of this ancient Ephraimite-Benjaminite enmity, we can determine with some confidence that it issued in a tragic slaughter at Gibeah. The existence of an independent tradition of a warlike sin 'in the days of Gibeah' in Hos. 9.9 and 10.9, in conjunction with evidence of patent efforts of Israelite nationalists to justify the actual account of this massacre in Judges 20, suggests that a real Ephraimite war-crime inflicted a painful wound that ached in Israel's national psyche for generations.

Reconstruction of the Gibeah Ambush

It is notoriously difficult to determine who started an inter-tribal feud. We may assume that a succession of incidents and insults fueled growing tensions between Ephraim and Benjamin some time in the twelfth or eleventh centuries. Perhaps the tribes argued over wells, clashed over disputed land, or even raided each others' villages. But at some point, matters escalated to the point that Ephraim hatched plans for a deadly attack on its closest Benjaminite target, the city of Gibeah.

Gibeah sits on a hill high above the Wadi es-Swenit, which marked the boundary between southern Ephraim and northern Benjamin. Gibeah's exposed position on the Ephraimite frontier marked it as an obvious target for a sneak attack. A war-party of Israelite fighting men probably left Michmas in the darkness and crossed the Geba Pass area. One contingent broke off and scattered its warriors in the numerous caves that pockmark the wadi on the northern side of the hill on which Gibeah sits. Later, the other band climbed the highway to Gibeah, where they staged a feint attack designed to draw off Gibeah's defenders. The ruse worked.

The written account (20.31) states that the Benjaminites chased the Israelite warriors away from their position near Baal Tamar (an unknown site) and towards two highways, one leading to Bethel, and the other to 'Gibeah' (which is probably a textual mistake for an original 'Gibeon'). It suggests that the two forces clashed approximately 2 kms. west of Gibeah near the crossroads where the watershed highway leads toward Bethel on the north, and the road from Gibeah continues west toward Gibeon. This encounter cost Israel around 30 men, as the story mentions twice (20.31,39). While the Gibeahites chased Israel away to the west, the ambushcade burst from its hiding place in the wadi, clambered up the thorny hillside, and fell on the unprotected women and children of Gibeah. They spared no one (20.37). Then, as the surviving Benjaminite soldiers saw the black smoke rise from Gibeah, they realized the cost of their tragic mistake. Traumatized, they abandoned the battle and ran along the highway back toward the desert, with the Israelites in hot pursuit. They fled past Gibeah and down into the Pass, whence they made their way along the desert highway for a further kilometer or so to their refuge in the Pomegranate Rock, a giant cave in the sheer wall of the wadi. Meanwhile, the Israelites reportedly burnt Gibeah, and perhaps other small villages in the vicinity.

Summary Observations

We have traced the development of the Outrage of Gibeah tradition from its distant roots as an oral memory of an historical war-crime, through its passage into written literature as Israelite propaganda, to its final canonical redactions into the narrative we now recognize in the Judeo-Christian scriptures. The shock of the original Gibeah atrocity echoed so sharply in Israelite tradition throughout the centuries that the prophet Hosea could still allude to its shame half a millenium later when he indicted Israel for its history of militarism on the eve of the Syro-Ephraimite War. In an attempt to explain and justify this crime in Israel's earliest days, nationalistic circles in Samaria evidently prefixed a stock type-story depicting a wicked city's sexual crime to the old Gibeah massacre tradition, creating a new exculpatory written narrative.

After the destruction of Samaria in 722, the document passed into the hands of Priestly editors, probably in Jerusalem, whence it eventually emerged in exilic times as a tale describing how the whole theocratic community of Israel once responded to retaliate against Gibeah for its crime against a Levite couple passing through the city. These editors made various additions of a cultic nature to the old Israelite core narrative, including the incorporation of two formerly bawdy folk tales which were transformed into pious descriptions of the community's attempts to insure posterity for the shattered tribe of Benjamin.

The Priestly edition found its way in the postexilic period into the Deuteronomistic History, where secondary Dtr redactors made slight alterations to the account in accord with their entire theological scheme. The piece was finally appended to the already-formed Book of Judges, where as a pre-monarchical story it naturally belonged. This canonical placement has the ultimate effect of summing up the period of Judges as a time of anarchy, for which the popular demand for a king which will shortly follow in 1 Samuel appears to be an irresistible, though ultimately inadequate, solution.

Chapter 4

GIBEAH AND THE RISE OF THE ISRAELITE MONARCHY

Gibeah plays an important role in biblical narratives relating to the
establishment of monarchy in Israel. From a purely literary
viewpoint, events at the city symbolized mass anarchy for the Dtr
editors who employed their final redaction of the Outrage of Gibeah
tradition (Judges 19-21) as an illustration of the chaos in Israel
which would shortly occasion Israel's popular demand for a king 'like
the other nations' (1 Sam 8.5). Yet Gibeah's part in the rise of
Israelite kingship was far more than a merely literary one.

Several ancient traditions inextricably link Gibeah to historical
events which saw the rise of two competing tribal warlords—Saul of
Benjamin and David of Judah—to the office of King of Israel. The
'rise of Saul' stories imply that the crucial incident which triggered
the Hebrew uprising against the Philistines occurred at Gibeah, and
that the hero of this revolt secured the city as his base-camp in the
wars of Hebrew liberation, of eventually founding there the first
'capital' of the nascent kingdom. In pro-Davidic literature, however,
'Gibeah of Saul' symbolized the threatening and entrenched
establishment which Saul's Judean rival and successor David had to
overcome before he brutally rose to power and moved the Israelite
capital to his own city, Jerusalem. Yet whether the city signifies
revolutionary liberation in the Saul cycle, or royal oppression in the
David stories, there is no historical doubt that the key events relating
to the rise of kingship in Israel did, in fact, occur in and around
Gibeah, a site we might somewhat anachronistically term 'the first
capital of Israel'.

Before we attempt to reconstruct the likely course of historical
events at Gibeah in this momentous period, we must analyze very
carefully the various conflicting literary traditions about these events
which have come down to us in the Books of Samuel. For we are not
dealing here with a coherent, continuous or contemporary historical

record of experiences early in Israel's national life. On the contrary, the Bible's final account of the transition from the period of the Judges to the monarchical era of Saul and David is a rather late Dtr fabrication which weaved together disparate and even contradictory ancient folk tales and traditions, and supplemented them with editorial additions according to a profound theological plan.[1]

Our study will examine the earlier received traditions which DH so thoroughly interrupted, rearranged, and re-worked. These old folktales and narratives told Israel about the rise of Saul as king at Gibeah and about his struggles there with the upstart Judean commander David. These stories may be broadly classed as Saulide (pro-Saul) or Davidic (pro-David), and though both types tendentiously celebrate their own heroes, they provide enough unintentional information to allow the creation of a credible historical scenario of events in the late eleventh and early tenth centuries in Israel.

The 'Rise of Saul' Stories

After we remove from historical and literary consideration several blocks of obviously late Dtr-influenced material in the narrative cycle relating to Saul (i.e. 1 Sam. 7.2-8.22; 10.17-25; 12.1-25),[2] three 'rise of Saul' episodes remain: (1) 9.1-10.16 (Saul's anointment as prince before a mysterious mission to Gibeah); (2) 10.26-11.15 (Jabesh-Gilead's rescue appeal to Saul at Gibeah, which led to his acclamation as king at Gilgal); and (3) 13.2-14.46 (the victory of Saul/Jonathan from their base at Gibeah/Geba over the Philistines at Michmas). Each of these narratives connects Gibeah to the events which saw Saul lead the beleaguered Hebrews in an uprising against the Philistines and to a new experience in state government.

While these traditions possess great antiquity and potential for historical analysis, there are two strong reasons to suspect that their original historical and literary sequence has been disturbed. The final canonical arrangement first describes Saul's inspired mission to Gibeah, where he performs some mysterious feat (9.1-10.16). A short time later, messengers from Jabesh-Gilead call Saul from Gibeah to rescue their city across the Jordan Valley; his success there leads to his investiture as the new king of Israel (10.25-11.15). Later, he and his son Jonathan lead the Hebrews to a successful attack on the Philistine outpost at Michmas, across the wadi from Gibeah (13.2-14.23).

Many scholars find it implausible that Saul would have abandoned Gibeah in order to undertake a distant military battle in the Transjordan while his home-base still fell under Philistine domination, and they therefore propose that the rescue of Jabesh-Gilead historically occurred after the Hebrew defeat of the Philistines, when most of Benjaminite territory came under Saulide control.[3] Moreover, literary-critical evidence also suggests that later editors interfered with the original narrative sequence of events. Miller noticed that Saul's mission to Gibeath Ha-Elohim ends too abruptly and anti-climactically in 10.13, and proposed that some dramatic event once climaxed the long tale at this point.[4] Miller's theory suggests that Dtr editors interrupted the original narrative chain and intruded the Mizpah lottery scene while switching the later Jabesh-Gilead rescue account into the story *before* the story of Saul's capture of Gibeah and Michmas (1 Samuel 13–14).

It is not entirely clear whether the original radical rearrangement of these accounts occurred under Dtr auspices.[5] One might also strongly suspect that Davidic literary circles in Jerusalem inherited the piece and re-edited it according to their own designs centuries before the narratives ever passed into Dtr hands. The literary effect of these obviously anti-Saulide alterations is obvious: they rob Saul of credit for instigating the Hebrew uprising, and thoroughly diminish his role in the Battle of Michmas. Yet on historical and aesthetic-literary grounds, we can still reconstruct the narrative flow of this hypothesized Saul story.

Outline of the original 'rise of Saul' story
The old folk tale may have begun with a marvelous account of Saul's birth, remnants of which still exist in 1 Sam. 1.20, 27-28. Though apparently this aetiology was later borrowed and inserted into the Samuel narrative, where it now appears, it obviously originally explained the meaning of *Saul's* name through repeated plays on the verb שאל ('ask', 'lend').

The Saul saga probably next related the story of Saul's encounter with an unknown seer as he searched for his father's asses in the land of Zuph (9.1-13). There an anonymous 'man of God' sent Saul on a mission to Gibeath Ha-Elohim, where he was to fall into a prophetic ecstacy in the company of a band of prophets. When this sign was given, Saul was to 'do whatever your hand finds to do' (10.7). Everything happened just as the seer prophesied. Yet after Saul fell into the predicted prophetic rapture, the narrative ends abruptly and no clear account of Saul's actions remains (10.13). The original saga probably related here how Saul, in a state of prophetic ecstasy, struck down the Philistine governor in Gibeah (see the notice in 13.4 which suggests this action). This assassination encouraged the Hebrews to rally around Saul as he led an uprising against the Philistines at Gibeah.

Fragments of the tale's next scene exist in 13.3b-6 and possibly 16-22. Hebrews from the Canaanite hill-country flocked to Saul at the tribal sanctuary of Gilgal, where the seer had commanded Saul to go after the assassination (10.8). Meanwhile, the Philistines mustered their troops and fortified Michmas, across the wadi from Gibeah, threatening the Hebrews who had hidden themselves in the numerous caves which pockmark this region. Saul then gathered 600 troops and came to their rescue (13.16-22), leading the beleaguered Israelites to a victory over the Philistines in Michmas from his headquarters at Pomegranate Rock in the Migron Valley outside of Gibeah (14.2). Saul and his men then chased the Philistines away from Benjaminite territory (14.21-23).

The narrative next described how messengers from Jabesh-Gilead ran to Saul at Gibeah, where he had set up his home (10.26). Responding to their plea for help, Saul called together the tribes and rescued this Hebrew city in the Transjordan from an Ammonite attack, an heroic deed which finally won him, at Gilgal, the office of King of Israel (11.6-15). This scene may have climaxed the old 'rise of Saul' tale. (For the reconstructed text of this tale, see Appendix 3.)

Clearly, other interests have editorially interrupted this literary complex, which probably originated in Saulide circles in Gibeah late in the eleventh century. While Samuel may originally have appeared in the tale as the king-maker at Gilgal, there is no question that later circles, especially Dtr, greatly expanded his role in the story of Saul's rise. Moreover, the account of Saul's battle at Michmas has been largely replaced with a later and longer narrative (14.1-15.46) which credits *Jonathan* with the victory, and which subtly undermines Saul's royal legitimacy. We shall discuss the purpose of this account later in the section on the David stories.

Identification of this Davidic and Dtr literary interference, and reconstruction of the original 'rise of Saul' narrative, allows us to investigate the earliest traditions which relate how Saul maneuvered himself into kingship over the Israelite state at Gibeah. The mysterious mission from the man of God provides a fascinating starting point.

The Mission from the Man of God

Remnants of the first 'rise of Saul' folktale are still visible in 1 Sam. 9.1-10.16.[6] Birch points to several characteristics which place this story in the genre of fable: (1) the fanciful theme—how Saul, as a young man, went to search for asses and found a kingdom; (2) the ideal picture of a young man who excels above all others in stature and appearance; (3) the namelessness of the city to which Saul and his servant come, and the anonymity of the seer who dwells there; (4) the indefiniteness of time; and (5) the entire atmosphere of the story which moves in the realm of wonder rather than fact.[7]

Birch rejected the suggestion that every aspect of the fable was fictional, and concluded that the tale served two purposes: (1) to provide a story of Saul's unwitting encounter with Samuel as a youth (into which account a later editor inserted the tradition of Samuel's anointing him), and (2) to provide an aetiology of the popular proverb found in 10.10-13, 'is Saul also among the prophets?'[8] If the seer was identified later in the original folktale as Samuel, one might well imagine with Birch the 'delight' of an ancient audience as the anonymous 'man of God' reveals himself to the unsuspecting Saul as Samuel, the great prophet who would eventually make him king.

Yet considerable doubt exists as to whether the figure of Samuel was in any way native to the original folktale.[9] Mayes found it most unlikely that Samuel would have been described first as a paid seer from an anonymous village, and proposed that

> the original story was a folktale which described how Saul, as a
> young man in search of his father's asses, was honored by a seer, a
> story which would have been related in order to illustrate how from
> the beginning Saul, an outstanding young man, was destined for
> great things, and how his physical attributes commended him to
> the people to be their king.[10]

One evident purpose of the tale was to show how God destined young Saul to become king of Israel—a common folkloric device which introduced and theologically legitimated later stories reporting his actual royal deeds.

Perhaps more importantly, the tale explains who authorized Saul to perform his revolutionary feat in Gibeah. Everything in the piece suggests that the 'man of God' acted under the authorization of God (אלהים) in sending Saul on his fateful journey to Gibeah. The seer's predictions (10.2-6), uttered by Samuel in later editions, provide an uncanny element of fate to the story. The reported fulfillment of the signs (10.9) only confirms what the listeners have begun to suspect: something decreed by God is about to take place. The fulfillment of all these predictions also convinces Saul of his divine empowerment to perform his explosive deed: 'when these signs happen, do what your hand finds, for God is with you' (10.7).

The fact that Saul performed this action while in a state of prophetic ecstasy, causing the people around to inquire, 'is Saul among the prophets?' raises intriguing literary and historical issues. From a literary perspective, it is sometimes claimed that the function of the account of the prediction and accomplishment of Saul's prophetic frenzy was simply to explain the ancient independent saying connecting Saul to the prophets (also found in 19.24).[11] Yet it is difficult to believe that the only purpose of the story of the encounter with the seer and his sending of Saul to Gibeah was to explain an ancient proverb.

Edelman suggests with greater plausibility that the saying here historically recalls an actual ruse used by Saul as he took part in a prophetic ceremony in order to gain access to the Philistine governor.[12] Moreover, a number of scholars propose that the otherwise unmentioned 'uncle' (דּוֹד) of Saul (10.14) is a Dtr alteration of the honorific דּוֹד, a term which originally referred to this same official.[13] If these claims are true, then the fabulous elements earlier in the folktale simply anticipate and authorize the *historical* tradition which remembered Saul's assassination of the Philistine overlord.

While a description of the attack on the governor is missing at present, we might reconstruct the story as follows. Saul, a Benjaminite leader intent upon eliminating Philistine oppression over the Hebrew tribes, disguised himself as a cult prophet in a religious ceremony attended by the Philistine overlord at the high-place (בּמה) of Gibeath Ha-Elohim in or near Gibeah. Mimicking the classic prophetic frenzy, he approached the official in the ecstatic band and promptly struck him down. The assassination electrified the assembled Hebrew tribesmen, and Saul immediately escaped in the midst of the confusion to the safety of the Israelite shrine at Gilgal in the Jordan Valley, where fellow Hebrew warriors joined him in rebellion.

This decisive act signalled the outbreak of the Hebrew *intifadah* (Arab.: 'shaking off'). But why are so few literary fragments remembering it found in the final biblical text? The canonical version of the story suppresses the assassination account and ends in a most unsatisfactory literary fashion: at the height of his frenzy, Saul simply goes home (10.13). One can only conclude that anti-Saulide literary circles subtracted credit for the Hebrew rebellion from Saul's reputation; in fact, they even attributed the achievement to Jonathan (13.3)! These editorial culprits almost certainly represented the rival Davidic dynasty (see 'the David stories' below).

The original Saul folktale also explains how it was that Saul first came to Gibeah. The frequent assumption that Gibeah was Saul's birthplace is, in fact, entirely without textual support; still less likely is the claim that Saul hailed from nearby Gibeon.[14] Saul's ancestral home was most likely Zela, probably modern Khirbet es-Salah, some 3 kms. northwest of Jerusalem.[15] The mission to Gibeath Ha-Elohim, the high-place at Gibeah, portrays Saul's initial journey there as divinely commanded. One may assume, however, that Saul eventually established himself at Gibeah for less theological reasons; he, like the Philistines who had first seized it, appreciated Gibeah's strategic military location.

Saul and the Battle of Michmas

The Saul story next shifted its attention to Gilgal, the famous Israelite sanctuary where Saul fled immediately after the assassination as commanded by the 'man of God'. 'When Israel heard that Saul had killed a Philistine governor, and that the name of Israel stank among the Philistines, they answered the call to arms and joined Saul at Gilgal' (13.4). Word of the revolt also spread to the Philistines, who amassed huge numbers of troops at Michmas, directly opposite newly liberated Gibeah across the Geba Pass (13.5).[16] Apparently, some Hebrew rebels had also remained in the Gibeah area, for 13.6 pictures them hiding out from the Philistines in the caves, holes, rocks, and pits which mark the Geba Pass region. The battle lines were drawn, and Saul's military prowess faced its first test: could he lead his motley army to Michmas and successfully dislodge the Philistines?

The dramatic original narrative is severely interrupted at this point with an obviously secondary and irrelevant polemic pitting Samuel against Saul, who reportedly committed a minor cultic infraction which doomed his dynasty forever (13.8-15a).[17] The earliest story had Saul leave Gilgal and gather 600 men around him at Gibeah of Benjamin (13.5). This same army also appears again with Saul 'on the outskirts of Gibeah under the Pomegranate which is in the Migron' (14.2). This notice provides interesting geographical information. In the first place, it suggests that, while Saul called his troops together in Gibeah, he actually camped with them on the outskirts of the city, presumably in a safer location. The 'Pomegranate' is surely the Pomegranate Rock, the same site where another 600 Benjaminite soldiers—the survivors of the Gibeah ambush—also found safe refuge (Judg. 20.47).[18] The Migron is probably the ancient Hebrew name for the impressive Wadi es-Swenit (see also Isa. 10.28).[19] We can conclude that Saul set up his rebel headquarters before the Battle of Michmas inside the 'Pomegranate Rock', a massive cave in the sheer rock wadi wall of the Migron, almost 2 kms. east of Gibeah and 2 kms. south of Michmas.

Davidic editors apparently rewrote most of the original account of Saul's battle against the Philistines as a later Judean version of the event which credited Jonathan with the victory (see 'the David stories'). Among the surviving fragments are probably the comment that the Philistines deprived the Hebrews of iron for use in making weapons (13.19-22), and a description of Saul leading a charge into Michmas, which encouraged his Israelite warriors to chase the Philistines back toward their territory (14.20-23). We might surmise that the full account detailed some clever or stealthy strategy which allowed the Hebrews to overcome their deficits in men and weaponry and open the way for Saul's battlefield charge.

The notice that Saul stationed 2,000 men with him in the Michmas-Bethel region, and 1,000 with Jonathan in Gibeah (13.2-3), which now appears as an introduction to the canonical report of the battle, may originally have concluded the story of the Battle of Michmas.[20] This historically plausible passage indicates that Saul split his combined forces immediately after the Philistine defeat in order to control both the north and south flanks of the Migron around the Geba Pass region, a position the Philistines held before the Hebrew revolt. Such a military posture evidently allowed control not only of the key eastern highway which linked Ephraim and Benjamin through the Geba/Michmas Pass, but also of the desert road, which led down the Migron towards Jericho and Gilgal.

The History of the Hebrew Uprising under Saul
Literary analysis of the hypothesized 'rise of Saul' narrative, including determination of certain purely folkloristic elements within it, permits us to propose a general picture of the historical situation in which these events took place. At some point late in the eleventh century, Philistine forces rose from their homeland on the southeast coastal plain of Palestine and established control over key positions

in the central hill country, the Hebrew homeland. It is possible that the Philistines cemented their domination of Benjaminite territory with their victory at Ebenezer reported in 1 Sam 4.1-2. This site is located in 7.12 as lying between Mizpah (Tell en-Nasbeh) and Jeshanah ('the tooth' of 14.4-5?), which would place the battle in the general vicinity of the Geba/Michmas pass region and Gibeah. The Philistines evidently needed an outpost at Gibeah in order to control a strategic point on the eastern highway between Ephraim and Benjamin, and the desert highway to Jericho, providing an effective wedge between major Hebrew population centers and a valuable checkpoint for controlling traffic between the tribes.

In response to this threat, Saul, an up-and-coming military 'strong-man' (*condottiere*) from the tribe of Benjamin, disguised himself as a prophet during a prophetic trance ceremony attended by the Philistine governor at the shrine of Gibeath Ha-Elohim. In the middle of the frenzy, Saul struck down the enemy official and fled down the desert highway to Gilgal. The act electrified the Israelites and encouraged disparate Hebrew elements to unite under Saul's leadership.[21] Gathering his rag-tag and poorly armed troops together, Saul returned to the Gibeah region in order to expel the Philistines from their newly fortified position at Michmas. After driving the enemy from the Benjaminite heartland, Saul established a rudimentary 'chiefdom' based in Gibeah which won allegiance from the allied Israelite tribes of Ephraim and Judah.

The presence of a continual Philistine threat during Saul's rule had provoked a popular crisis among the Israelites which threatened to diminish their traditional values of tribal independence in favor of the growing economic and military demands of centralized authority. Partly in response to these tensions, the remnants of which may be seen in the references to discontentment with Saul among certain Israelite factions (e.g. 10.27; 13.8), the Saulide establishment commissioned a compilation of folk traditions about Saul for a written narrative which allegedly divinely sanctioned Saul's leadership and celebrated his military abilities. This account, of which major fragments survive in 1 Sam. 9.1–10.12 and 13–14, circulated among Saul's proud Benjaminite countrymen along with other stories celebrating his military exploits.[22]

Saul's Rescue of Jabesh-Gilead
One of Saul's most dashing victories is remembered in 1 Sam. 10.26–11.15, the account of a rescue raid at Jabesh-Gilead, a Hebrew city

across the Jordan River over 70 kms. northeast of Gibeah.[23] Historians largely accept this description of Saul's deliverance of Jabesh from Am..ionite seige since the deed corresponds well with other biblical notices of this period regarding the city: distant Jabesh's ethnic ties with the Israelites in Canaan (Judg. 21.1-8), the city's otherwise inexplicably valiant rescue of the bodies of Saul and Jonathan from the Philistines at Beth Shan (1 Sam. 31.10-13), and the explicit statement that Saul was lord over the city (2 Sam. 2.4b-7).[24]

There exists serious doubt as to whether the Jabesh rescue occurred at so early a stage in the historical 'rise of Saul' as the text suggests. Many scholars now place the Jabesh rescue chronologically after Saul's defeat of the Philistines at Michmas rather than before the battle as indicated in the canonical text.[25] It is improbable both that Saul would have abandoned the Gibeah region while it still lay under Philistine control in order to mount an attack in the distant Transjordan, and that he would have been militarily prepared to do so in view of the reported Philistine weapons-embargo against the Hebrews (1 Sam. 13.19-22).[26] It is even more unlikely that the simple 'farm boy' depicted in 10.21-25 could have mobilized Israelite warriors for such a dangerous venture in a distant land.[27]

The Jabesh-Gilead campaign surely occurred well after Saul's victories over the Philistines in the Benjaminite heartland, at a time when Sau! had secured his throne against all enemies, foreign and domestic. Edelman argues cogently that Jabesh-Gilead may already have sworn a vassal treaty with Saul (see 2 Sam. 2.4b-7) when he achieved dominance over the Hebrew tribes. The city's appeal to Saul during the Ammonite Nahash's seige, then, simply compelled Saul to honor his treaty alliance with Jabesh.[28]

The beginning of the Jabesh narrative pictures Saul and a small army returning to his house in Gibeah (10.26).[29] This verse may continue the narrative threads of the story which immediately before concluded the account of Saul's expulsion of the Philistines from Michmas and the Benjaminite hill-country (13.2), in which case it belonged to the original 'rise of Saul' saga; or it may belong to some other collection of stories such as the 'battle source' hypothesized by Edelman.[30] The arrival at Gibeah of messengers from Jabesh seeking help (11.4) opens a dramatic scene in which destiny wrenches Saul, seemingly the successful warrior returned to a peaceful occupation, from his pastoral chores for the good of the people. Saul's startling division of his farm oxen and his parcelling out of their pieces not only symbolizes graphically the tragic end of his bucolic career, but ritualistically enacts an apparent call to war (see Judg. 19.29).[31] The appearance of the slicing motif as a call-to-war ritual in both major literary complexes involving Gibeah may illustrate the tendency of an oral tradition connected with a geographical area to appear with great plasticity in stories connected with that region.

It is debatable whether the story of Saul's acclamation as king at Gilgal after the Jabesh rescue (11.12-15) originally belonged to that episode or is a later addition.[32] It is certainly plausible that Saul's victory at Jabesh catapulted him fully from the position of military chief over Israel to full royal status, yet one cannot exclude the possibility that Saul had already won acclamation as king when he fled to Gilgal after assassinating the Philistine governor at Gibeah. In either case, the original presence of Samuel in the piece as king-maker is highly questionable since he represents the whole theological case which favors the Davidic dynasty's divine right of kingship.

It is quite unclear what other war stories also existed in the early pro-Saul 'battle source'. The summary of Saul's reign (1 Sam. 14.47-52), remarkable for its positive assessment of Saul, may have concluded the whole Saul cycle. The summary mentions wars against the Moabites, Edomites, and the king of Zobah in addition to the well-known battles against the Philistines. The fact that no record of these battles exists may indicate that written versions of these battles were removed from the Saul cycle, leaving only war stories involving the Ammonites, Philistines, and Amelekites. It is even possible that editors have transferred the story of Saul's campaigns in southern Palestine to the Joshua cycle (Josh. 10.29-43).[33] Despite such editorial shenanigans, Gibeah's role in Saul's rise to power remains visible in this early cycle of tradition.

Gibeah and Saul

Recently, a theory was proposed that Saul actually established his home-base in Gibeon—though no biblical passage directly associates Saul with that city, and one text even reports the conflicting information that Saul massacred Gibeon's citizens (2 Sam. 21.2).[34] Mention of Saul at home at Gibeah in the Jabesh account, taken in conjunction with Saul's association with the city in the Battle of Michmas report (cf. 13.15 and 14.2) and the clinching connection of Saul with Gibeah in the 'rise of David' stories (15.34; 22.6; 23.19; 26.1), provide convincing evidence that Saul based himself at Gibeah during his rule over Israel. While it may be anachronistic to regard Gibeah as a full-scale capital of Israel, there can be no serious question that it served, at least, as Saul's military base and center of his chiefdom. The Jabesh account would imply that Gibeah was a sizable hill-country town where Saul and his warriors lodged.

Why did Saul base his kingdom at Gibeah? Once crucial to the Philistine domination of the central Palestinian hill country, the city sat at a strategic location which enabled Saul to station his small army in a secure position between the Hebrew tribes of Benjamin and Ephraim. This site not only placed Saul in the midst of the Hebrew population centers, but afforded him a secure base from which to conduct military operations as distant as the Transjordan. The city guarded the Geba/Michmas Pass area, where two important routes crossed: the eastern highway which connected Ephraim in the north with the major Hebrew tribal areas of Benjamin and Judah to the south, and the desert road in the Migron Valley (Wadi es-Swenit), which connected the Ephraim-Benjamin hill-country with Hebrew villages such as Jericho and Gilgal in the Jordan Valley.

Too little historical material remains from this period to allow a detailed reconstruction of Gibeah's role in Saul's rule. Even if the summary in 1 Sam. 14.47-52 contains reliable information, the sketchy quality of this material makes it impossible to understand exactly how Saul's headquarters in Gibeah related to these military campaigns. Though it is questionable whether Saul extended Israelite control directly over Edom, Moab, and Ammon, it is undoubtedly accurate to speak of Saul's royal domination over the Benjamin/Ephraim area immediately surrounding Gibeah.[35]

In view of the paucity of information, describing Gibeah as Saul's 'capital', a term which implies the presence of a sophisticated government bureaucracy, is somewhat questionable.[36] Equally problematical is the term 'kingdom' for his rule over the central Palestinian hill country and certain Hebrew ethnic areas in Judah and the Transjordan.[37] Gibeah could be viewed simply as a strategic village which Saul seized from the Philistines for use as a control-point and base-camp from which he militarily controlled his mountainous territory and conducted wide-ranging campaigns, the last of which resulted in his death at Gilboa (1 Sam. 31).

The David Stories

Gibeah is mentioned four times (1 Sam. 15.34; 22.6; 23.19; 26.1) in the literature which describes the rise of David to kingship in Israel (1 Sam. 15–2 Sam. 5). It is widely recognized that a major concern of the 'rise of David' literature is to legitimize David's dynasty. Scholars agree that such an obvious intentionality bespeaks an origin for this literary complex in a Davidic court in Jerusalem attempting to win legal and theological support for itself; the critics are only divided on the question of whether this work appeared as early as the tenth century or as late as the ninth century.[38]

It is a political fact that the promotion of one political group always occurs at the expense of another. The strongest concrete threat to the Davidic dynasty was the Saulide family, which could claim its own legitimate rights to dynastic kingship over Israel on the basis of Saul's royal acclamation at Gilgal. Against the Saulide house the Davidids long warred, so that 'David grew steadily stronger while the house of Saul became weaker and weaker' (2 Sam. 3.1). Eventually, David pounced on the survivors of his weakening foe and had them slaughtered (2 Sam. 21.1-10).

It is clear that the Davidic purge of the Saul dynasty later extended even into the literary sphere. We have already seen abundant evidence that a pro-Davidic literary tendentiousness worked its way into the original Saul-cycle in the form of editorial insertions portraying Samuel's renunciation of Saul, and the apparent robbery of stories which celebrated Saul's heroism and faith. The anti-Saul bias in these Judean-edited narratives makes it difficult to recover information about the historical Saul, and so we are forced to hypothesize on the shape and tone of the original literature.[39]

The Gibeah Complex

The literary vendetta against Saul is even more obvious in the 'rise of David' stories composed by the Davidids. One evident technique is to portray the first king as a raving madman, i.e. possessed by an evil spirit. Among the passages portraying Saul's tormented condition are scenes set at the royal court of Gibeah (1 Sam. 16.14-23; 18.6-29; 19.1-7) which Ward termed the 'Gibeah complex'.[40] In the first scene, David's wisdom, handsomeness, and musical gifts deliver Saul from his paranoid attacks, but later, David's military success precipitates a frenzy in Saul so severe that the king tries to murder his young troubadour (18.11). In the final Gibeah court scene, Saul announces his deliberate intention to kill David (19.1).

These fictional stories surely reflect the sophisticated social and governmental conditions of the tenth or ninth-century Jerusalem court back into the time of Saul at his primitive Gibeah redoubt.[41] In view of its tendential artificiality, this portrayal of the court of Gibeah should not support the otherwise unproven assumption that Saul possessed a royal palace or even an impressive fortress at Gibeah.[42] One text, in fact, speaks of nothing more grand at Gibeah than a house (1 Sam. 19.9), while another seems to place him simply at Gibeah's 'high place' (1 Sam. 22.6).[43]

Though the 'rise of David' narratives are of little use in recovering information regarding Saul's trappings at Gibeah, much less his psychological state or personality, their placement of David there in mortal tension with Saul confirms the impression that Saul did indeed base himself at Gibeah. The Gibeah court functions in the Davidic literature as something of a symbol of the cruel and entrenched régime against which David had to struggle on his climb to power.

The Slaughter of the Saulides
The long political and military struggle between the Saulide and Davidid houses came to an horrific end when David arranged to have Saul's descendants—the Davidic dynasty's potential competitors for the throne of Israel—exterminated (2 Sam. 21.1-9). As one might expect, Davidic scribes covered up the actual political motives for this massacre with a literary account attributing theological motives to the king. A three year famine had caused David to 'consult the Lord', who blamed the drought on Saul's murder of the Gibeonites. No other biblical texts corroborate Saul's alleged massacre, but it is quite plausible that the tradition remembers Saul's attempt to purge foreign ethnic groups like Gibeon's Hivites from the Benjaminite hill-country.[44] Supposedly as an act of expiation to the Gibeonites, and under the Lord's orders, David then arranged to have the Gibeonites eliminate Saul's progeny. Seven sons of Saul were reportedly hurled to their death 'before the Lord' in Gibeah of Saul (2 Sam. 21.6, 9).[45] One imagines that a morbid cultic ceremony of some kind took place at Gibeah's high-place before the men were thrown down the steep sides of the wadi wall above which Gibeah perches. Whatever the final theological justification for the murders, the actual historical event to which the passage refers surely had as its sole purpose the total elimination of any further Saulide

opposition to Davidic rule over Israel.[46] Though David evidently drew at least some support from individuals in Gibeah (2 Sam. 23.29/ 1 Chron. 11.31 mentions Ribai from Gibeah of Benjamin as one of his thirty military strongmen),[47] one can assume that Gibeah of Saul was regarded in Jerusalem as a hostile and threatening place.

'Gibeah' Becomes 'Geba'

As we have seen in our study of biblical literature relating to Gibeah, it is approximately in the tenth or ninth centuries that Judean texts show a change from use of the toponym 'Gibeah' to the related place-name 'Geba'. It is within the context of outright Davidic hostility to Gibeah that we can countenance a wholesale change in the nature of the city as well as its name during this period.

One theory which might explain this change is inherent in Albright's suggestion that the Levitical cities list of Joshua 21, which mentions Geba (21.17; see also 1 Chron. 6.45), derived from a Judean document dating to David's time.[48] According to Albright, this document represented David's attempt to reorganize his kingdom under central planning. Building on this proposal, Mazar hypothesized that the cities in the list, including Geba, not only provided lodging for Levites but also served as fortified settlements on previously hostile ground.[49] If this view is correct, then Geba, which is here the new Judean term for 'Gibeah', became a Levitical settlement in the Davidic era not only to provide close proximity to the Temple in Jerusalem for its priestly community, but also to serve as a royal control over the inhabitants of that town, who could have been considered hostile to a Davidic régime. It is therefore possible that the name-change of 'Gibeah' to 'Geba' is only one, albeit minor, function of the wholesale Davidid attempt not only to exterminate Saul's offspring and undermine his heroic role in the Hebrew revolt, but to extirpate even the name of his home-base, Gibeah. David's capture of Jerusalem and his establishment of a fully fledged capital there (2 Sam. 5.6ff) should also be regarded as part of this wide-ranging policy designed to break totally free from Saul and every last vestige of his rule at 'Gibeah of Saul'.

The Term 'Gibeah of Saul'

The toponym 'Gibeah of Saul' (נבעת שאול) merits special attention at this point. Though, as we have observed, 'Gibeah' is a place-name preferred by northern Israelite or Benjaminite literature, it also appears six times in specifically Judean contexts—but only in connection with the proper name 'Saul'. The special form 'Gibeah of Saul' appears twice in the 'rise of David' literature: 1 Sam. 15.34 and 2 Sam. 21.6.[50] The only other occurrence of the term is in Isaiah 10.29b, which is clearly written from a Judean perspective. This latter usage suggests that 'Gibeah of Saul' existed as a toponym for Geba over three centuries after Saul stationed his armies in the city; in this regard Isaiah's usage is poetically anachronistic.

Three nominative forms of נבעה also appear in the Judean 'rise of David' stories (1 Sam. 22.6 and the doublets 23.19 and 26.1), yet they exist only in immediate linguistic relation to the name 'Saul'. All six of these usages demonstrate that the feminine toponym 'Gibeah', whether used in construct with 'Saul' or in the same immediate phrase with his name, appears in Judean literature only when used in connection with 'Saul'. Except for the late Isaiah passage, the literary context for the term in each case is highly negative: 'Gibeah of Saul' is a dangerous and threatening place. Aside from Isaiah's archaizing reference, the toponym 'Gibeah' never again occurs in Judean literature after the Davidic-Solomonic era.

Jonathan's Raid

Among the many attempts of the Davidic dynasty to detract from Saul's rightful place as the instigator of the Hebrew uprising against the Philistines and the heroic first king of Israel is a case of major editorial interference in the original Benjaminite Saul narrative. Only bare fragments of the story crediting Saul with victory over the Philistines at Michmas now survive; much of the original story was apparently rewritten in a parallel account largely assigning credit to Jonathan for the victory (1 Sam. 13.3, 14.1–15.46).

The later Judean version of events at Michmas can be distinguished from the original Saul story in several ways. First, from 13.3 onwards, when Saul alone appears, he is associated with 'Gibeah', but whenever Jonathan alone appears, he is connected with 'Geba'. Second, the contradictory notices giving credit for the striking of the Philistine governor both to Saul (13.4) and to Jonathan (13.3) suggests the presence of different literary sources.[51] Third, and most striking, is the entirely different tone which marks the Jonathan account from the fragments of the Saul story. While we recognized some supernaturality in the folkloric 'call narrative' of Saul where אלהים ('God') is actively involved, the stories of his military enterprises are clearly secular in nature—Saul succeeds through cleverness or bravery. The narrative of Jonathan's raid and sacrilege, however, possesses a thoroughly religious or cultic quality in which יהוה ('Yahweh') is the divine actor.[52] After the notice concerning the presence of the sacred ephod (14.3), Jonathan plans to punish the 'uncircumcized' under the protection of Yahweh (14.3); in the ensuing battle, it is Yahweh who wins the victory (14.10, 12b, 23), sending the Philistines into a 'panic' (14.15), a word typical of holy war terminology.[53] The account of Jonathan's sacrilege (14.24-46) is even more obviously cultic in nature.

Most important, the Jonathan account displays a marked anti-Saul tendency. In addition to the fact that the later version pictures Saul as uninvolved in and ignorant of Jonathan's raid on Michmas, the sacrilege story which follows emphasizes Saul's foolishness in swearing a rash oath (14.24, 39, 44), a potentially deadly mistake from which he is rescued only by the intervention of the people (14.45). Jonathan is portrayed, on the other hand, as resourceful and brave in mounting his solo attack on the Philistines, and as an innocent victim in the sacrilege affair, his very life having been endangered by his father's foolishness.

Blenkinsopp has demonstrated the Jonathan narrative's Judean origins in noting its deep affinities with Yahwistic literature.[54] If the raid and sacrilege account is seen in conjunction with the other 'rise of David' narratives in which Jonathan is prominent (1 Sam. 18.1-5, 19-20), then cognizance of its Judean viewpoint provides an insight into the reasons for its composition. Since this particular story credits Jonathan with the responsibility for winning the initial battles in the Hebrew revolt while at the same time eclipsing Saul's role, the meaning of the later depiction of Jonathan's obsequiousness to David begins to emerge more sharply. As part of the overarching literary scheme designed to legitimize the Davidic dynasty, Judean writers depicted not only the transfer of Jonathan's royal claims (as symbolized by his cloak, sword, bow, and belt) to David (1 Sam. 18.4), but even the glory and honor accompanying the earliest events which attended the eventual establishment of the Israelite kingdom.[55] In other words, the 'rise of David' literature not only provided a theological basis for David's dynasty through the editorial intrusion which described Samuel's rejection of Saul and choice of David, but it reinforced its claims to the royal throne of Israel with the story that Saul's own son Jonathan handed over all legal rights to David in a passionate act of love. Lest Jonathan appear as a mere fop, Judean authors created an account of his virile heroism at Michmas in order to buttress the magnanimity of his deference to the even more worthy David.

In addition to the patently political tendentiousness of the piece, several other factors militate against the acceptance of the Jonathan story as an historical account. First, the tale's strong cultic tone betrays theological rather than reportorial concerns. Second, the literary form of 'single-combat' heroism, in which a lone figure virtually wipes out an army without the knowledge or permission of his commander, suggests that the story belongs to the realm of fiction rather than history.[56] And third, the sudden appearance from nowhere of Jonathan, and his absence from the other accounts of Saul's battles, suggests that his character has been subsequently intruded into the Philistine war stories in which he probably had only a subsidiary role.[57]

Though the narrative of Jonathan's raid on the Philistines is fictional, the story contains topographical remarks which suggest that its author possessed a detailed knowledge of the Geba-Michmas region, especially the pass through the wadi separating the two villages. Since the actual road-crossing over the Wadi es-Swenit is so deep in the valley that it is not visible from either Jeba or Mukhmas, it is noteworthy that the Philistines reportedly needed to post a force on a ridge above the 'Michmas Pass' (1 Sam. 13.23–14.1). The following account then explicitly identifies two rock prominences on either side of this pass: 'Bozez' (בוצץ) and 'Seneh' (סנה), one on the north near Michmas, and one on the south near Geba (14.4-5). Two rock formations corresponding to this description stand directly east of the wadi crossing.[58] The name Seneh ('thorny'?), moreover, might relate etymologically to Josephus's location of 'Gibeah of Saul' in the 'Valley of the Thorns', as well as to the present Arabic name Wadi es-Swenit, 'Valley of the Thorn-Tree'.[59] The description of Jonathan's climb up the precipitous slope toward the Philistines (14.13) also reflects the treacherously steep sides of the ravine immediately east of the wadi pass.[60]

The Gibeah-or-Geba Problem

Our suggestion that the account of Jonathan's raid on Michmas is a separate, Davidic-oriented story subsequently edited into the original Saul narrative provides an appealing solution to the 'Gibeah or Geba problem' which has for years vexed scholars analyzing The Battle of Michmas account (1 Samuel 13-14).[61] 'Gibeah' is the name of Saul's home-base in the original Benjaminite (northern) version dating to the late eleventh century, while 'Geba,' the later name of the city under the Kingdom of Judah, is employed in the Davidic (southern) Jonathan account a century or two later. The editors who melded the two versions retained the toponym proper to each text. As a result, the text of 1 Samuel 13-14, rather than exhibiting 'confusion' over the sites as many scholars have assumed, is on the contrary a remarkably faithful indicator of the duality of sources in these chapters.

Summary Observations

Our analysis of the 'rise of Saul' literature revealed a pro-Saul cycle which remembered Gibeah as the headquarters of the first Israelite king. Though later Davidic and Dtr editors severely disrupted and reorganized this account, literary reconstruction permits us to imagine a continuous narrative which once described how the young Saul encountered a mysterious seer who sent the youth on a mission to Gibeah in order to assassinate a Philistine governor. Fleeing to Gilgal, Saul rallied his Hebrew warriors and returned to Gibeah to eliminate the Philistine garrison at nearby Michmas. The pro-Saul cycle also included a story which related how Saul left his base at Gibeah in order to rescue distant Jabesh-Gilead when it fell victim to Ammonite attack. The narrative then reported the royal acclamation of Saul at Gilgal, though it is no longer clear whether this account appeared after the description of Saul's flight to Gilgal, or after the Jabesh rescue. All of these early pro-Saul stories, arising in Benjamin, remember 'Gibeah' as the city which Saul wrested from the Philistines and subsequently made his military headquarters.

The 'rise of David' cycle, arising in Davidic-Solomonic circles, described how its hero survived Saul's paranoia at the Gibeah court and eventually succeeded to the Israelite throne. These literary interests attempted to legitimate the Davidic dynasty not only with the portrayal of Saul as a divinely rejected and insane king and the claim that Yahweh graciously chose David through Samuel, but also through a subtle literary device involving Jonathan. The Davidic court commissioned a narrative which transferred credit for the Michmas victory to Saul's son Jonathan, adding heroic weight to accounts picturing the infatuated boy essentially abdicating to David in passi ate love. The author of this story, intimately familiar with the Geba-Michmas region, labelled Jonathan's base by its ninth-century Judean name 'Geba'. The editors who conflated both the fragments of the Saul version and the whole Jonathan piece did not alter the toponyms into a uniform place-name, so that the final version implies that Saul operated from Gibeah and Jonathan from Geba as if the villages were distinct sites.

After David ascended the throne of Israel, he made Jerusalem the capital of united Israel, slaughtered Saul's progeny at 'Gibeah of Saul', and resettled friendly Levites at the city, now renamed 'Geba', as part of a program to assert royal control over previously hostile areas. There... the city was known in royal records and Judean literature as ⲅ

Chapter 5

'BLOW THE TRUMPET IN GIBEAH'

After the Davidic-Solomonic era, old tensions between the northern
Israelite and the southern Judean tribes once again flared to the point
of explosion. When the hapless new king Rehoboam journeyed to
Shechem from Jerusalem to receive his royal acclamation from the
Israelite elders gathered in assembly, he faced a firestorm of protest
(1 Kings 12). A generation of high taxes and forced labor under
Solomon had built the resentment of the northern tribes to flash-
point. When Rehoboam foolishly listened to his hot-headed 'young
Turk' advisors and ruled out any concessions, the northerners
seceded from the United Kingdom and retrieved the rebel Jeroboam
from Egyptian exile in order to proclaim him the new king of
Israel.

It is quite likely that the new boundary between the Kingdoms of
Israel and Judah passed immediately below the old city of Gibeah
(now renamed Geba) in the Migron, the modern Wadi es-Swenit.
Since 1 Kgs 12.21 states that the tribe of Benjamin remained with
Judah under the Davidid dynasty, we may assume that the
traditional tribal border between northern Benjamin and southern
Ephraim (see Josh. 16.1; 18.11-13) in the Wadi es-Swenit now
became an international frontier. This hypothesis is indirectly
supported by 1 Kgs 12.29-33, which notes that Jeroboam erected
golden calves in Dan and Bethel, ostensibly to draw his northern
constituency away from its attraction to the Davidic temple in
Jerusalem. This explanation is surely a Dtr creation with literary
connections to Aaron's golden calf (see Exod. 32.1-6); Jeroboam
almost certainly built shrines at Dan and Bethel simply to serve as
border-sanctuaries at the northern and southern extremes of his
kingdom. Bethel, then, remained in Israel as the southern sanctuary

along the watershed highway leading into the kingdom. On the other side of the frontier lay Gibeah/Geba, awaiting its role in future affairs between the kingdoms.

The Fortress at Geba

A few decades after the division of the kingdoms, warfare erupted along the Israelite-Judean border (1 Kgs 15.16-22; 2 Chron. 16.1-6). Apparently, military tensions ran high throughout the reigns of Baasha of Israel (c. 906-883) and Asa of Judah (c. 908-868).[1] At some point, Baasha's army invaded Judah and seized northern Benjamin, effectively controlling access to Jerusalem from the north (15.17). The Israelites attempted to consolidate their gains by fortifying Ramah (er-Ram), which sat astride the watershed highway only 9 kms. north of Jerusalem.

Asa reportedly responded to this threat by sending gold and silver from the temple to King Ben-Hadad of Damascus, bribing him into an alliance which might save Judah (15.18-20). A willing Ben-Hadad then invaded Israel and seized territory in the north. Baasha was forced to abandon his fortifications at Ramah and fall back to a defensive position at his capital of Tirzah. Asa, in turn, reoccupied northern Benjamin and decreed that every man in Judah join in dismantling the stones and timbers of the former Israelite stronghold at Ramah in order to fortify Geba of Benjamin and Mizpah (1 Kgs 15.22). This was an essential strategic move if Judah was to protect its northern border from future invasions.

The fortress at Mizpah (Tell en-Nasbeh) evidently guarded the watershed highway which led into Judah at a point just a few kilometers south of the Israelite border.[2] Geba, meanwhile, controlled access to Judah from Israel across the strategic Geba Pass, through which passed the eastern highway (see Judg. 19.13; 20.33; 1 Sam. 13.23; Isa. 10.27-32; Josephus's *Wars of the Jews* V, 2.1).[3] The Judean-Israelite border itself probably extended from south of Jericho, an Israelite possession (1 Kgs 16.34), westward along the modern Wadi el-Qelt to the point where it meets the Wadi es-Swenit. From this point, the border followed the Wadi es-Swenit in a northwesterly direction, passing just north of Geba and crossing the Palestinian watershed near el-Bireh. This border apparently remained unchanged until the fall of the northern kingdom, becoming the boundary between the Assyrian province of Samaria and the kingdom of Judah until the period of Josiah's northern expansion.[4]

Mizpah and Geba each sat near a major Judean highway approximately 1 km. south of this border. These twin posts undoubtedly garrisoned troops who could engage an enemy along the highways in times of war, or control traffic and collect tolls in more peaceful times. Decades of military tension with Baasha obviously led Asa to believe that both routes leading from Israel into Judah must be protected.[5] Recent archaeological excavations, taken in conjunction with a notice in 2 Kgs 23.8, also suggest that these border fortresses played an additional role.

The Royal Border-Sanctuary
The appearance of Geba in connection with an event centuries after its foundation as a border fortress, the so-called Josian Reform of the late seventh century, provides information relevant to its role throughout Judean history. Around 622, King Josiah enacted a series of harsh measures in Judah that suggest in many respects a fundamentalist purge of the entire Judean cult. One feature of the crackdown entailed the round-up of priests and the desecration of their hill shrines 'from Geba to Beersheba' (2 Kgs 23.8). Aharoni's excavations of a ruined temple complex at Arad, apparently a Judean border-post deep in the Negev, suggested to him that such sanctuaries might have been an integral part of border fortresses:

> We may now assume that a temple was erected at Geba in the days of Asa or Jehoshaphat with the stabilization of the Israelite-Judean border... 'from Geba to Beer-Sheba' became a slogan for the borders of Judah, similar to 'from Dan to Beer-Sheba' in the days of the United Monarchy. These were the royal citadels which dominated the border areas; a vital part of each of them was evidently the royal and sanctified temple.[6]

According to Aharoni, these cultic sites in military fortifications on Judah's borders afforded travellers the opportunity either to request Yahweh's favor as they entered the land under his protection, or to thank him for his benefits as they left.[7] Aharoni's discovery in 1973 of a dismantled altar at Beer-Sheba (Tell Beer-Sheva) confirmed part of his 'border-sanctuary' theory,[8] and increased the possibility that archaeologists might one day unearth such a complex at Geba (Jeba), which also probably functioned both as a military post and cultic site. The presence at Geba of a Levitical community (Josh. 21.17) is consonant with this view; no doubt the Levites served at the Geba sanctuary until their recall to Jerusalem during the Josian Reform.

Moreover, if our analysis is correct, the tradition of a sanctuary at Gibeah/Geba traces back to the pre-monarchical period, when Saul was missioned to the high-place at Gibeath Ha-Elohim (1 Sam. 10.5, 13) and later sat at this same במה at Gibeah (1 Sam. 22.6).[9] The execution of Saul's sons at Gibeah 'before the Lord' (2 Sam. 21.6) probably took place at this same sanctuary. That Geba retained cultic significance even after the demise of its role as a royal border sanctuary can be inferred from Neh. 12.29, where it is reported that Levitical singers from the 'region of Geba' performed at the dedication of the new wall of Jerusalem. Geba thus seems to have served not only as an important fortress guarding the northern Judean border at the key Geba Pass, but as a royal border-sanctuary of Judah from the time of Asa at least until the rule of Josiah.[10] In this role Geba found itself in the swirl of events surrounding a terrible chapter in relations between Israel and Judah.

The Syro-Ephraimite War

No biblical text mentions Gibeah/Geba for well over a century after the city's fortification by Asa (i.e. 890–750). This era, for all its domestic strife within the kingdoms, was characterized mainly by peaceful relations between Israel and Judah, possibly because Judah served as a virtual vassal to its rich and powerful neighbor to the north.[11] In the last half of the eighth century, however, the city appears in the prophecies of Hosea and Isaiah in literary contexts mentioning invasion and war. This fact signals a new historical situation in which conflicts along the Judean-Israelite border once again arose. The events which occasioned these new tensions revolve around the so-called 'Syro-Ephraimite War'.

Although a number of problems exist pertaining to the identification of sources and the ascertainment of a chronology for this conflict, there seems to be little doubt as to the major historical factor behind Ephraim's attack on Judah (2 Kgs 15.37; 16.5): the political turmoil that boiled over in the Near East as Tiglath-Pileser III of Assyria (744–727) began to dominate the Eastern Mediterranean seaboard. Formerly, most scholars believed that the war resulted simply from an attempt by Rezin of Damascus and Pekah of Israel to force Judah under Ahaz into a coalition in order to block the Assyrian onslaught on the eve of Tiglath-Pileser's invasion of Philistia in 734.[12] This view, while basically sound, is not entirely satisfying. While it is undoubtedly necessary to view the invasion of Judah against the backdrop of this Assyrian advance, it is difficult to make sense of the biblical accounts of these events if the Assyrian threat is seen as the *sole* precipitating factor for the war, and at so late a date as 734, when Tiglath-Pileser's armies were already on the march in Palestine. Three other problems with the traditional scholarly view are: (1) a joint Syro-Ephraimite invasion of Judah in 734 would have significantly weakened, rather than enhanced, an anti-Assyrian coalition; (2) internal strife in the Levant itself is historically the cause of conflict in the region, and not external threats; and (3) according to 2 Kgs 15.37, the war against Judah began in Jotham's reign, undermining the view that Ahaz's obstinacy triggered the allied invasion.[13]

A more recent theory suggests that, in addition to the defensive purpose of the anti-Assyrian coalition, the Syro-Ephraimite alliance originated in the attempts of Rezin of Damascus to gain hegemony over Syria-Palestine by seeking to recreate a 'Greater Syria' along the lines of Hazael's achievement a century earlier.[14] Assyrian texts from the eighth century associate Rezin with Tyre and Philistia, which suggests that Rezin may have drawn these two states into his coalition at an early stage of his designs on the Palestinian region.[15] Later, the accession of Pekahiah to the throne of Israel after Menachem's death likely provided Rezin with an opportunity to gain control over Samaria. Early in this new king's reign, Pekah, probably an Israelite commander in the Transjordanian region adjacent to Rezin's kingdom of Damascus, overthrew Pekahiah with the help of fifty Gileadites (2 Kgs 15.25). One suspects that Rezin engineered Pekah's accession to the throne as a puppet; certainly, biblical texts consistently mention Pekah *after* Rezin, as if he ruled in a subordinate position.[16]

Judah was now outflanked and pressured on the north by Tyre, Syria, and Israel, on the west by the Philistines (2 Chron. 28.18), and on the south and east by Edom (2 Kgs 16.6 [reading 'Edom' for 'Aram'] and 2 Chron. 28.17) as Rezin attempted to bring Jerusalem under his control.[17] Isa. 7.6 records that Rezin and Pekah conspired to invade Judah in order to place 'the son of Tabeal' on the throne in Jerusalem.[18] Attempts to identify this figure had been unconvincing until recent publication of an annal of Tiglath-Pileser.[19] In a list of tributaries to Tiglath-Pileser dating to c. 738, the mention of Rezin of Damascus and Menachem of Samaria is immediately followed by the name 'Tubail of Tyre'. Rezin probably attempted to place the son of the Tyrian Tubail on the throne in Jerusalem in order to complete his hegemony over Syria-Palestine.[20] This effort took the form of a joint

Syrian-Israelite invasion of Judah (Isa. 7.6) and siege of Jerusalem (2 Kgs 16.5) in the reign of Ahaz around 735.[21] Tiglath-Pileser's invasion of Philistia in 734 was thus a response to, and not a direct cause of, the anti-Assyrian coalition in Syro-Palestine.[22]

It is within these historical circumstances that Gibeah/Geba once again appears in biblical literature, for the city guarded the northern border of Judah which the allied armies breached on the road to Jerusalem. The anxieties caused by this imminent invasion of Judah at Geba are permanently recorded in the oracles of the Israelite prophet Hosea and his Judean counterpart Isaiah.

Hosea and the Sin of Gibeah

'Blow the Trumpet in Gibeah' (Hosea 5.8)

The prophet Hosea mentioned Gibeah three separate times in his prophecies: Hos. 5.8; 9.9; 10.9. The first instance occurs within a passage rousing three cities in Benjamin:

> Blow the trumpet in Gibeah,
>   the horn in Ramah;
> Sound the alarm in Beth-Aven:
>   Behind you, Benjamin!
>   (Hos. 5.8)[23]

Though some critics interpret this passage as a ritual or liturgical pericope,[24] most scholars agree that these verses open an actual prophetic battle-alarm issued to Benjaminite cities during the Syro-Ephraimite War.[25] The international political comments that follow in Hos. 5.8-15, in conjunction with concrete references to warfare around Gibeah in a related passage (Hos. 10.9-15), surely disallow a purely liturgical background for this passage, and indicate that the text refers to an actual contemporaneous event.[26] Though specific historical details are lacking in this battle-warning, its address to Benjaminite cities, and its presence in a literary context mentioning tensions between Israel and Judah, suggests an origin in the only situation in the late eighth century when the border area of Benjamin is known to have been at issue: the Syro-Ephraimite War.[27] The pertinent historical issue involves the determination of the precise nature and purpose of Hosea's alarm in the context of this war.

Alt proposed that the passage constituted the opening lines of a unit that extended from 5.8–6.6 and consisted in Hosea's warning to Israel of a Judean counter-attack after the original Syro-Ephraimite siege of Jerusalem (2 Kgs 16.5).[28] Though no historical information concerning such a Judean counter-attack exists, Alt hypothesized such a reprisal on the basis of three assumptions about this passage. First, Alt took the statement of 5.10, 'the rulers of Judah act as men who displace landmarks', as an indication that the Judean invasion had already begun to expand Jerusalem's control over formerly Israelite territory.[29] Second, Alt assumed that the three cities of Gibeah, Ramah, and Beth-Aven all belonged to Israel at the time of this supposed counter-attack.[30] Finally, Alt claimed that the order of the cities mentioned in the verse indicated the northerly direction of the attack from Judah: Gibeah (Tell el-Ful), Ramah (er-Ram), and Beth-Aven (Beitin) were all believed to be successive points along the central Palestinian watershed route which led from Judah into Ephraim.[31] Alt's assumptions have been widely accepted in studies relating to the Syro-Ephraimite conflict.[32]

Alt's thesis depends heavily on his location of Gibeah, Ramah, and Beth-Aven as successive points along the watershed highway leading north from Jerusalem. Yet of these cities, only Ramah (er-Ram) can be confidently placed along this route. Gibeah probably ought to be sought at Jeba astride a completely different highway, and in any case, archaeological investigation at Alt's 'Gibeah', Tell el-Ful, reveals no trace of occupation in the eighth century when Hosea delivered his warning to the city.[33] Moreover, since no evidence exists to suggest any changes in the Israelite-Judean border from the early ninth through the late eighth century, then both Ramah (er-Ram) and Gibeah (either Tell el-Ful or Jeba) must be assumed to have rested within *Judean* territory during Hosea's time. What, then, of Beth-Aven?

Alt assumed that the toponym 'Beth-Aven' actually referred to the great Israelite sanctuary at Bethel, an identification frequent in Hosean studies since Beth-Aven can be translated pejoratively as 'house of wickedness', reflecting the prophet's hostility to the Bethel cult.[34] While Hosea does indeed seem to use אָוֶן in this sense to refer to Bethel in Hos. 4.15 and 10.5, in two other places he uses the word root אוֹן in an opposite sense, meaning 'strength' or 'wealth' (Hos. 12.4, 9). R. Coote's study of Hosea's intricate word play on אוֹן in reference to Bethel revealed the prophet's clever alternating usages of 'nothingness' and 'wealth'.[35] These biblical references suggest that Hosea's sobriquet for Bethel in 10.5 was a pun on the name of an actual city named 'Beth-Aven' ('House of Wealth') mentioned earlier in a non-rhetorical fashion in Hos. 5.8. Where was this village?

The Location of Beth-Aven

Josh. 7.2 (MT) places a site called 'Beth-Aven' (בית און) near Ai ('east of Bethel'). Josh. 18.12-13 locates a region called the 'wilderness of Beth-Aven' on the northern Benjaminite border; the area is clearly distinguished from Bethel.[36] 1 Sam. 13.5 situates Michmas 'to the east of Beth-Aven', while 1 Sam. 14.23 records that the Israelites drove the Philistines off from Michmas past Beth-Aven, presumably toward their home territory to the west. Albright suggested that the original Canaanite name of this site was 'Beth-On' ('House of Wealth'), a pronunciation preserved in the LXX of Josh. 18.12 (Βαιθων), and probably altered to 'Beth-Aven' by scribes who vocalized און so as to give the meaning 'nothingness' and 'wickedness'.[37] The location of this Beth-Aven/Beth-On is widely disputed. Albright, who once identified Beth-On with Ai (et-Tell), later favored Burqa, which is northwest of Mukhmas and near et-Tell.[38] Kallai-Kleinmann proposed Tell Maryam, 1 km. west of Mukhmas, which fits 1 Sam. 13.5 and 14.23 (west of Mukhmas), and possibly Josh. 7.2 (near Ai, if et-Tell was Ai).[39] Given biblical texts which associate Beth-Aven with both Ai and Michmas, one is forced to find a site in proper relation to each. Unfortunately, finding a location near Ai for Beth-Aven is an extremely problematical undertaking since, in the first place, the reference in Josh. 7.2 is textually uncertain, with LXX omitting any mention of Beth-Aven with Ai.[40] Second, the location of Ai has itself proved to be problematical. Since biblical notices place Ai 'east of Bethel' (Gen. 12.8; Josh 7.2; 8.9, 12; 12.9), most scholars locate Ai at et-Tell on the assumption that Bethel was located at modern Beitin.[41] It would seem prudent, therefore, on the basis of 1 Sam. 13.5 and 14.23, which place Beth-Aven west of Mukhmas, and Josh. 18.12-13, which places the 'wilderness of Beth-Aven' on the northern border of Benjamin between Jericho and Bethel, to accept Kallai's proposal to identify Beth-Aven with Tell Maryam.[42] A location west of Michmas for Beth-Aven means that in the eighth century, Beth-Aven lay in *Judean* territory immediately south of the Judean-Israelite border, which extended northwest from Michmas towards the Palestinian watershed. Our placement of Beth-Aven thus situates the city in close proximity to both Ramah and Gibeah/Geba, all of which were located within a few kilometers of each other south of the Judean-Israelite border.

The Imminent Attack on Judah

In the light of these topographical considerations, it appears that Hosea's oracle warns, not Israelite cities, but the most northern cities of Judah adjacent to the eastern highway leading southward from Israel to the Judean capital of Jerusalem. Rather than providing evidence of an alleged Judean 'counter-attack' which is not known from any other source, Hos. 5.8 almost certainly witnesses to Hosea's prophetic warning of the original Syro-Ephraimite invasion of Judah known from 2 Kgs 16.5; Isa. 7.5-7; 2 Chron. 28.5-7; and probably Isa. 10.27c-32.[43] Hos. 5.8 thus opened a speech condemning the impending Syro-Ephraimite invasion of Judah with a bugle cry of alarm to the cities most likely to be engulfed immediately in battle.

The Hosean speech which follows this alarm (5.8-15) presently alternates accusations against Ephraim and Judah, implying that Hosea regarded both sides in the conflict as responsible for the punishment in war which they were both about to receive. Yet the condemnation of Judah seems out of place in a speech which also warns its northern cities of an attack. Nor would one expect an exhortation to Judah in the context of a speech delivered in, and directed to, Israel. These considerations lead some scholars to propose that the word 'Judah' has been substituted for 'Israel' in the oracle by later redactors wishing to make the passage relevant to a much later period, when only Judah existed.[44] In this case, Hosea originally levelled the indictment of 'Judah' for 'moving a boundary' (5.10) at *Israel* as it breached the Judean frontier during the invasion of the Jerusalem. The present alternating indictments of Ephraim and Judah (5.12, 13, 14) thus originally read 'Ephraim and Israel', a case of typical Hosean parallelism (e.g. 5.3; 5.5; 5.9; 6.10; 7.1; 7.8-11; etc.). When read as an indictment of his native Israel, Hos. 5.8-15 plausibly appears as the prophet's denunciation of Israel's collusion with Syria in the fratricidal act which they were about to commit against Judah. Such a policy would enjoy no more success than Israel's previous flirtations with Assyria (5.13).[45]

'The Days of Gibeah' (Hosea 9.9)

Hosea's second reference to Gibeah is difficult to interpret chiefly because of the poor state of the text of the preceding verses, which are among the most difficult passages in Hosea.[46] Yet the underlying sense of 9.7-9 is clear enough: Hosea is attacking adversaries who had declared him 'mad' (9.7b)—the nearest thing we have to a report on Hosea's public ministry and the people's response to him.[47] Yet the enigmatic phrase צפה אפרים ('Ephraim lay in wait')[48] in 9.8 suggests that the danger to the prophet consisted in more than merely verbal threats, for this phrase is followed immediately by the parallel sentence, 'traps are set for him (פח יקוש) on all his paths'. This treachery motif suggests that active plots against the life of Hosea had been set in motion by official contemporaries who waited at the prophet's tent (emending אלהי נביא in 9.8 to אהל נביא) and even the 'house of God' in order to terrorize the prophet. Hosea seems to capsulize Ephraim's hostility in a reference which compares such evils to the 'days of Gibeah'.

> 'The prophet is a fool, the inspired man is mad'
>   But only because of your great sins and iniquity!
> Ephraim lies in wait at the prophet's tent.
>   Traps are set for him on all his paths.
> Enmity even in the house of his God.
>   They deepen their corruption, as in the days of Gibeah.
> He will remember their iniquity and punish their sins!
>
> (Hos. 9.7c-9)

Interpreters are divided in their understanding of the Gibeah allusion. One group sees 'the days of Gibeah' as a reference to Saul and the beginning of kingship in Israel.[49] This view is based on the assumption that Hosea belonged to an anti-monarchical tradition related to Deuteronomistic ideology. Aside from the fact that no traditions remember Saul becoming king at Gibeah, but rather at Mizpah or Gilgal, there is no evidence that Hosea was hostile to the institution of kingship itself, but only to a series of corrupt kings in Hosea's day, most recently the puppet king Pekah.[50] More importantly, nothing in this unit hints at such an anti-Saul or anti-monarchical interpretation.

A more prevalent tendency is to relate the Gibeah allusion to the events now recorded in Judges 19–20; namely, the sexual outrage committed against the Levite couple. While this interpretation at least matches the tone of treachery in Hosea's oracle, it is finally unsatisfactory since in Judges 19–20 Ephraim did not commit the *crime*, but rather, delivered its just *punishment*.[51]

Hosea's comment surely has to do with the tradition underlying Judges 19–20 in which *Israel* was considered a guilty party at Gibeah. This oral tradition remembered a devious massacre of the people of Gibeah by Israelite soldiers early in the days of the Judges, and occasioned the official Israelite core narrative which later justified this war-crime (see Chapter 3). In order to describe the sinister plots being hatched against him, Hosea hearkened back to the most shameful analogy in Ephraim's past available to him: the old tradition of Ephraim's ambush and massacre of the Benjaminites at Gibeah. As Ephraim once lay in wait for Gibeah, now it sets traps for the prophet of God.

'In Gibeah, a War' (Hosea 10.9)
Twin references to Gibeah mark the prophet's final use of the Gibeah tradition.

> Since the days of Gibeah you have sinned, Israel.
>> There they took their stand in rebellion.
> In Gibeah there will be war on these sons of injustice.
>> (Hos. 10.9)

This passage, also alluding to the oral tradition that remembered Ephraim's ambush and massacre of Benjaminite Gibeah, opens a unit (10.9-15) that concludes with a reference to yet another war-crime, the slaughter of women and children by Shalman at Beth-Arbel (10.14b).[52] The phrase, 'in Gibeah there will be war', suggests that Hosea chose this tradition as an examplar of divine poetic justice: as Israel began its national life with a sinful attack on a brother tribe, so will an imminent battle in the same region, namely, the attack on Jerusalem through the Judean border fortress at Gibeah (Geba), issue in Israel's just punishment.

This saying is closely associated with Hos. 5.8, the prophetic warning to the Judean cities of Gibeah, Ramah, and Beth-Aven of an impending invasion by Syro-Ephraimite forces; both passages foretell an imminent outbreak of hostilities around Gibeah. Perhaps rumors of Israel's intended incursion into Judah electrified the atmosphere in Samaria for weeks as preparations for the attack progressed. Hosea may have delivered 5.8-15 in an outspoken attack on the puppet Pekah's collusion with Rezin of Damascus. This speech, in turn, could have been viewed by the political establishment as an almost treasonous announcement of Ephraim's battle strategy, creating a tense situation which would help explain the environment of treachery and threat in which the prophet found himself (9.8-9). The delivery of 10.9-15 would then represent Hosea's final prophetic judgment on the impending attack: it would end in utter defeat for Israel.

Exactly how Hosea envisioned this result is not clear. Hos. 10.10 mentions eventual retribution by unnamed 'peoples', but nowhere in this pericope is a defeat by Judah explicitly mentioned; in fact, while Hosea's ominous words concerning Gibeah ambiguously hint at a disastrous battle at the northern boundary of Judah, this outcome evidently did not materialize.[53] Hosea prophesied a battle at Gibeah as the symbolic and fitting end to Israel's history: as in the earliest days of its origins Israel had resorted to treachery there against its brother tribe of Benjamin, so in the final days would it choose the same fratricidal policy at the identical place against Judah. These two outrages are undoubtedly the 'two deeds of shame' (שתי עינתם—10.10b) which frame Israel's history and which merit a final punishment.

Hosea contrasted these 'two deeds of shame' at Gibeah with God's original plan for Israel (10.11-12): a national life of domestic obedience on the land, and fundamental reliance on principles of justice.[54] But whereas Yahweh had harnessed the heifer Ephraim to the plough so that she would 'sow justice and reap faithful love', Israel sowed wickedness and reaped injustice (10.11-13b). For Hosea, the two war-crimes at Gibeah symbolize Israel's life-long national sin: reliance on warfare rather than righteousness—a crime known in modernity as militarism.

> Because you have trusted in your chariots,
>   in the number of your warriors,
> the tumult of war shall rise against your tribes.
>
> (Hos. 10.13b-14a)

The tradition of the outrage at Gibeah thus reached its moral zenith in Hosea's condemnation of Israel's approaching invasion of Judah: there it was used to symbolize the sinful reliance on the implements of war, rather than the precepts of justice, as an instrument of national policy.[55]

The Prophet 'Oded'

A passage in 2 Chron. 28.9 implies the existence of prophetic opposition to the Syro-Ephraimite invasion of the kind that we hypothesized from Hosea.

> A prophet of the Lord was there, Oded by name; he went out to meet the army as it returned to Samaria and said to them, 'it is because the Lord the God of our fathers is angry with Judah that

he has given them into your power; and you have massacred them
in a rage that has towered up to heaven'.

The Chronicles text continues with a description of Oded's
condemnation of Israelite plans to enslave captured Judean war
prisoners; these were later returned to Judah as a result of opposition
among the chief Ephraimite leaders (28.10-15).

It is possible that the prophet 'Oded' mentioned here is none other
than Hosea himself. The Hebrew root עוד, probably meaning 'to give
a message', appears to have been an ancient term for 'prophet' which
the late editor of Chronicles may have mistaken as a proper name.[56]
If this is the case, the Chronicles version may have recorded a
tradition in which the 'Oded' Hosea needed to explain why his
prediction of the invasion's failure (Hos. 10.9) itself failed: the Lord
was angry with Judah. In any case, the story in 2 Chronicles certainly
confirms that significant opposition, including that from the prophetic
groups and other Ephraimite leaders, developed in Israel against the
Syro-Ephraimite invasion.

'Gibeah of Saul Fled!' (Isaiah 10.27-32)

A speech of Hosea's eighth-century Judean counterpart Isaiah also
describes an invasion of Judah (Isa. 10.27c-32). On its march toward
Jerusalem, the anonymous army from the north crosses the Geba
Pass and causes Gibeah of Saul to flee. In view of the mysterious
quality of the passage, a wide range of opinions as to its historical
provenance has naturally developed.

One school of thought interprets this invasion scenario in terms of
the oracle's present literary setting, which explictly mentions the
threat from Assyria (Isa. 10.5; 12; 24). These historians hypothesize
that the passage describes the Assyrian invasion of Judah under
Sennacherib in 701.[57] The major problem with this opinion,
however, remains formidable: the Assyrian invasion in that year
appears to have approached Jerusalem from the Shephelah to the
southwest, and no evidence of a northern attack exists.[58] While it is
possible that the Isaian oracle witnesses to an otherwise unrecorded
Assyrian attack on Judah from the north shortly after the Fall of
Israel, the lack of evidence for such a shocking move by Sargon II
makes this explanation doubtful.[59]

The fact that no independent evidence of an Assyrian invasion of
Judah from the north exists gives rise to another opinion: that

Isaiah's dramatic and detailed description of the invasion was only visionary, and described the *imagined* route of a feared future Assyrian attack.[60] The detailed description of the invasion's route, however, and the unusual course which it took, undermines the likelihood of this view.[61] The use of past-tense verbs in 10.27c-29a, in contrast to the present/future tense of the verbs in the remaining verses, moreover, makes it apparent that Isaiah delivered the oracle in the midst of an actual military advance which had just progressed to the Geba Pass vicinity, throwing the surrounding countryside into panic in the expectation of an imminent push at Jerusalem within the day (10.32).

The realistic elements in Isaiah's speech lead yet a third group of scholars to relate the passage to the only known event which featured an attack on Judah from the north in the late eighth century: the Syro-Ephraimite invasion.[62] Though set by Isaian editors after a speech mentioning Assyria, its literary placement does not necessitate direct historical linkage with this empire, but suggests only a later redactional decision possibly uninformed by the actual historical origins of the passage.[63]

The case for placing Isa. 10.27-32 during the Syro-Ephraimite invasion is enhanced by relating Hos. 5.8 to the same event. Hosea's explicit warning to the three Benjaminite towns of Gibeah, Ramah, and Beth-Aven near the Judean frontier is matched closely by Isaiah's description of the actual course of the attack, which crossed the international boundary and caused Ramah to 'tremble' and 'Gibeah of Saul' to flee (10.29b).

Isaiah's Description of the Invasion

The mystery surrounding the invasion's point of origin can also be solved within such an historical setting. The opening sentence of the passage (10.29c) reads 'he came up from Shamen' (שמן: 'oil, fatness'), a site otherwise unknown from biblical or extra-biblical records. A number of scholars emend the text to read רמון, a place-name preserved in the modern Arabic Rammun, a village nearly 7 kms. northeast of Mukhmas.[64] This reading is implausible since Rammun sits in the desert 'in the middle of nowhere' and is an unlikely point of origin for an invasion of Judah. Emendations to ישימון ('desert') or צפון ('north') are equally vague and no more helpful. Emending the text to read שמרן ('Samaria'), however, supports the theory that the invasion originated at the Israelite capital of Samaria.[65]

The next geographical point listed, 'Aiath' (10.28a), surely refers to the famous ruins of Ai (cf. Joshua 7–8), now usually identified with et-Tell. This notice indicates that the army left the main watershed highway near Bethel (Beitin) and headed in a southeasterly direction along the eastern highway. The following lines contain topographical information that needs to be read in its Hebrew literary context, namely, *parallelismus membrorum*. The first half of the parallelism states: 'he crossed the Migron, at Michmas he left his gear' (10.28b). This notice imparts the factual data that the army continued from Ai approximately 6 kms to the south, where it left its support equipment at the last Israelite city, Michmas, before breaching the international frontier with Judah in the Migron (Wadi es-Swenit). Yet the line also forms the first half of a unit which poetically emphasizes the crucially important crossing of the border: עבר במגרון. The second half of the parallelism (10.29a) also begins with the verb עבר, only this time in the plural: עברו מעברה גבע ('they crossed the Geba Pass'), which also means that they crossed the fateful border.[66] Whereas the second half of 10.28b notes that the army left support equipment at Michmas, the second half of 10.29a states that the army set up camp, presumably near the Pass. This dramatic military move caused the reactions recorded in the final past-tense section of the pericope: 'Ramah trembled, and Gibeah of Saul fled' (10.29b).

The news of the incursion must have reached Jerusalem quickly; Isaiah may well have delivered his speech the morning after the Syro-Ephraimite army bivouacked, for the verses which follow switch to the imperative for warnings to the Benjaminite towns of Gallim, Laishah, Anathoth and Madmenah and the future-tense prediction that the invader will shake his fist from Nob at Jerusalem 'this very day' (10.32).

> He came up from Samaria,
>> he arrived at Aiath.
> He crossed the Migron, and left his gear at Michmas.
> They crossed the Geba Pass, and spent the night.
>> Ramah trembled! Gibeah of Saul fled!
> Raise your voice, O daughter of Gallim!
> Watch out, O Laishah! Sound a warning, O Anathoth!
>> Madmenah is in flight! Gebimites flee for safety!
> Standing at Nob this very day, he will shake his fist
>> at the mountain of the daughter of Zion,
>> the hill of Jerusalem.
>
> (Isa. 10.29c-32)

Isaiah's speech (and Hos. 5.8) indicate that the Syro-Ephraimite army avoided the comparatively easier watershed route in favor of the eastern highway, almost certainly to achieve surprise and to avoid the watershed highway and the major fortress of Mizpah, which possessed massive walls which now show no signs of historical destruction.[67] This tactic implies that the coalition's strategy may have excluded a heavy assault on the south to devastate the Judean forces (which might have been needed against Assyria later) in favor of a lightning attack designed to capture Jerusalem quickly in order to force Ahaz's abdication and enlist Judah in the alliance (cf. Isa. 7.6). In leaving some military equipment in a secure position in Israelite Michmas, the Syro-Ephraimite army seems to have planned to establish supply lines through Benjamin in support of Jerusalem's hopefully brief siege. Its choice of the Geba Pass area (some 12 kms. and two or three hours' march from Jerusalem) as a base-camp suggests that the army intended a quick strike at Jerusalem early the next day, a strategy basically repeated eight centuries later by the Roman general Titus, who camped in the same area before attacking Jerusalem.[68] The success of this *Blitzkrieg* may, in part, explain the lack of any reported Judean military response to the attack (2 Kgs 16.5; Isa. 7.1).[69]

It appears that the Geba fortress failed to protect Judah from the surprise attack. It is possible that Isaiah deliberately used the anachronistic and ancient term for the stronghold as a pejorative allusion to the city when he succinctly remarked, 'Gibeah of Saul fled' (10.29b). For partisans of the Davidic Royal Zion tradition, everything connected with Saul fails!

Geba in the Postexilic Period

After the Syro-Ephraimite War and the subsequent demise of the Kingdom of Israel, the toponym 'Gibeah' does not appear again in biblical literature. 'Geba', the surviving Judean dialect's name for the city, however, does continue to appear in the Old Testament through late postexilic times.

Geba does not appear in biblical documents from the time of the Syro-Ephraimite invasion until the reign of Josiah (c. 640–609) when the sanctuary there was closed and its priests brought into Jerusalem as part of the so-called Reform (2 Kgs 23.8). The ancient cult at Geba, Beersheba, and other Judean high-places evidently offended the sensibilities of fundamentalist Yahwists who demanded strictly orthodox worship in Jerusalem alone. The sanctuary at Geba probably suffered the same fate as its counterpart at Beersheba, which was apparently dismantled during this period, the stones of its altar serving as the foundation for a storehouse under construction at the same time.

It appears that Josiah re-extended Judean rule during this period over certain areas which formerly lay within Israelite territory, including Bethel (see 2 Kgs 23.4, 15). If Josiah achieved control at least over southern sections of the old kingdom—including all of tribal Benjamin—then the Benjaminite town-list (Josh. 18.21-28) may derive from an administrative document citing the main villages in the district, including Geba (18.24), during this period.[70]

Shortly after Josiah's reign, the Babylonian invasion (c. 597) devastated the Benjaminite and Judean regions. One can assume that so major a military post as Geba would not have escaped destruction, though no biblical text or archaeological excavation confirms this. After the return of the exiles from Babylon a half-century later, however, Geba reappears in Jewish literature, though in a modest role. Ezra 2.26 and Neh. 7.30 each number the returning Jewish exiles who settled in Ramah and Geba at 621,[71] and Neh. 11.31 also indicates that Geba was one of the main Benjaminite cities from this period. Unfortunately, we can glean little information from these texts which would indicate the identity, purpose, or quality of life of the Jews who resettled the ancient city. Yet one other text suggests that Geba retained some cultic significance in the postexilic period. Neh. 12.29 relates that Levitical singers from the city participated in the dedication of Jerusalem's new wall. We might assume, on the basis of this passage, that members of the Levitical order resettled their traditional city, if indeed they had abandoned it completely during the Exile.

The Persian period is a virtual Dark Age in biblical literature. Economic and political affairs apparently severely depressed Jewish culture and creativity, causing despair for many in the community. The prophets responded to this gloom with words of hope and new promise for Judah. It is not surprising, therefore, that the last we hear of Geba in the Bible is in the context of Zech. 14.10, an apocalyptic oracle dating to the third century.[72] There, an anonymous prophet predicts a Utopian wonder in which the Lord will defeat Jerusalem's enemies and level the whole land 'from Geba to Rimmon southwards'. It is possible to translate this phrase as 'from Geba southwards to Rimmon',[73] so that the saying functions as a postexilic equivalent to the monarchical description of Judah's northern and southern borders, 'Geba to Beersheba' (2 Kgs 23.8). Geba appears even in late times to have been regarded as the northern extremity of the Jewish patrimony and culture.

Summary Observations

The identification of Geba and Gibeah has made possible a fresh approach to the use of the Gibeah tradition in the prophet Hosea. Since 'Gibeah' was identical to the Judean border post of Geba, and since Ramah and Beth-Aven can be shown to have existed in close proximity to this fortress, we can now understand Hos. 5.8 as the prophet's warning to Judah of an imminent attack by Syro-Ephraimite forces. Furthermore, Hosea's use of a Gibeah tradition in 9.9 and 10.9 is not apparently merely an obscure, offhand reference to a vague event, but his deliberate choice of Israel's most shameful ancient tradition as an analogy for the imminent attack on its brother nation. As Israel once massacred Benjaminites at Gibeah in antiquity, so now it intended to repeat this murderous policy in the Syro-Ephraimite invasion.

There is also reason to believe that Isaiah responded to this same attack from a Judean perspective in an oracle now recorded in Isa. 10.27c-32. As the Jerusalem prophet observed the invading Syro-Ephraimite forces marching through Gibeah/Geba in their attempt to overthrow Ahaz, he alarmed the cities of Benjamin and Jerusalem with news of the invasion. The failure of the Geba fortress to hold the invading armies might have occasioned Isaiah's reference to another ancient Gibeah tradition in his statement, 'Gibeah of Saul has fled'.

Hosea's use of the Outrage of Gibeah tradition and Isaiah's reference to Saul's headquarters at the city occurred only because Gibeah/Geba briefly found itself at the center of a terrible moment in history: the outbreak of a fratricidal war. For most of the rest of its history, Gibeah/Geba seems to have served inconspicuously as a royal border fortress and sanctuary. After the Josian reform desecrated the sanctuary and gathered in the Levitical priests, on the one hand, and extended Judah's borders into Ephraim making the fortress unnecessary, on the other, Geba's importance diminished considerably. After the exile, it retained enough importance to accept returning Judean refugees and house a sizable Levitical community, yet it never again captured center stage in the events that shaped Jewish history.

125

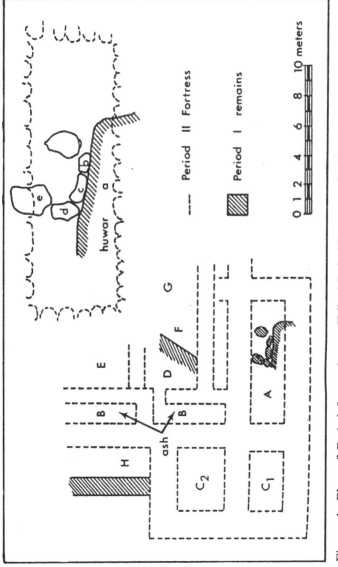

Figure 1. Plan of Period I remains at Tell el-Ful (Courtesy of ASOR)

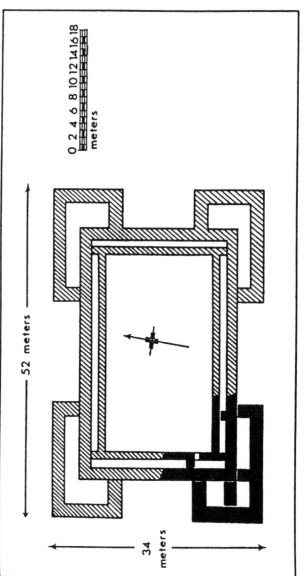

Figure 2. Albright's reconstruction of Fortresses I and II at Tell el-Ful (Courtesy of ASOR)

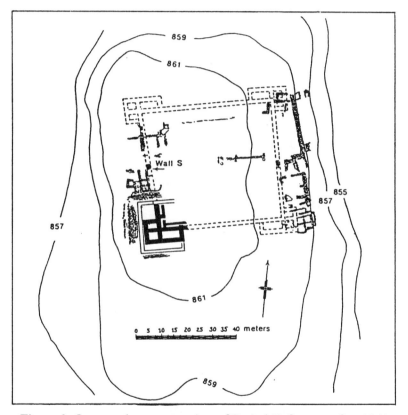

Figure 3. Suggested reconstruction of Period II fortress after 1964
campaign at Tell el-Ful (Courtesy of ASOR)

Plate 1: The village of Jeba, likely site of Gibeah/Geba, looking north. The biblical city existed on the crest of the hill overlooking the Wadi es-Swenit to the north.

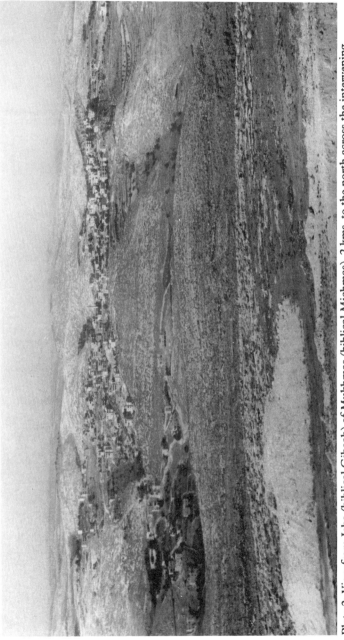

Plate 2: View from Jeba (biblical Gibeah) of Mukhmas (biblical Michmas), 2 kms. to the north across the intervening Wadi es-Swenit (the biblical Migron). Saul's men on the watch in Gibeah reportedly observed the confusion in Michmas caused by Jonathan's raid (1 Sam. 14.16).

Plate 3: The Wadi es-Swenit (biblical Migron) directly southeast of the Geba Pass area (foreground). The desert highway followed this canyon to the Wadi el-Qelt, and thence to Jericho and Gilgal. No north-south travel is possible east of the Geba Pass area because of the steep wadi walls.

131

Plate 4: A 'tooth of rock' (1 Sam. 14.4-5) in the Geba Pass region of the Wadi es-Swenit, looking northwest towards Mukhmas (Michmas) on the ridge. Jonathan reportedly passed such a formation during his raid on the Philistines.

Plate 5: The cave el-Jaia in the south wall of the Wadi es-Swenit (the Migron), 2 kms. east of Jeba (Gibeah). The pitted interior of the giant cave suggests that the feature may be the Pomegranate Rock where 600 Benjaminites fled after the Gibeah massacre (Judg. 20.45). Saul reportedly lodged with his 600 troops 'on the outskirts of Gibeah under the Pomegranate, which is in the Migron' (1 Sam. 14.2).

Appendix 1: גבע-Root Toponyms in Benjamin

Citation	Context	Provenance
	Gibeah (הגבעה)	
Judg. 19–20	rape/murder of concubine, retaliation on Gibeah by tribes of Israel	Ephraimite war story (1100) + Israelite edition (800) + Lev./Dtr redactions (500–300)
1 Sam. 10–14	Rise of Saul to Israelite Kingship at Gibeah	Benjaminite hero story (1000) + Dtr editing
1 Sam. 15–26	David's struggles with Saul at 'Gibeah of Saul'	Judean 'Rise of David' cycle (950)
2 Sam. 21	Extermination of Saulides at Gibeah	Judean Davidic court records (900)
2 Sam. 23	List of David's heroes	Judean Davidic court records (900)
= 1 Chron. 11, 12	List of David's supporters	postexilic copy (500) of Judean court record
Hos. 5–10	Prophetic oracles vs. Israel	Israelite prophetic indictment (735)
Isa. 10.29	Invasion route of Syro-Ephraimite army	Judean oracle (735)
	Geba (גבע)	
Josh. 18.24	Joshua's list of towns in Benjamin	Judean administrative list (900–600)
Josh. 21.17 = 1 Chron. 6.45	Joshua's list of Levitical cities = Benjaminite inheritance of Aaron	Judean monarchical list (900–600) = Chr copy of list (500)
1 Chron. 8.6	Towns of descendants of Benjamin	postexilic priestly list (500)
Judg. 20	Israel attacks Gibeah	Judean version?
1 Sam. 13–14	Jonathan's daring raid on Michmas	Judean pro-David cycle (900)
*2 Sam. 5.25 (MT)	David's victories over the Philistines	Judean Davidic court war summary (900)
1 Kgs 15.22	Asa fortifies northern border vs. Israel	Judean court records (900)

2 Kgs 23.8	Josiah's reform eliminates hill shrines	Judean court records (600)
Ezra 2.26 = Neh. 7.30	Returned Jewish exiles numbered in towns	Jewish list? Persian tax roll? (500)
Neh. 11.31	Nehemiah's list of Jewish towns	List of Jewish towns (500-400)
Neh. 12.29	Levitical list of cultic singers	Levitical list of singers (400)
Zech. 14.10	Zechariah's apocalyptic vision	Late postexilic addition to Zech. (300-200)

Gibeath Ha-Elohim (גבעת האלהים)

1 Sam. 10.5	Saul's mysterious mission to Gibeah	Benjaminite hero story (1000)

Gibeath Kiriath (גבעת קרית)

Josh. 18.28	Joshua's list of towns in Benjamin	Judean administrative list (900-600)

* toponym in text very uncertain; LXX reads 'Gibeon'

Appendix 2: The Reconstructed Core Narrative

(L indicates present Levitical/Priestly additions in text and D indicates present Deuteronomistic additions)

(19.1b) There was a man (L) who lived on the flanks of Mt Ephraim who took to himself a wife (L) from Bethlehem of Judah. (2) And she was unfaithful to him (L) and went home to her father in Bethlehem of Judah where she stayed four months. (3) The man went after her to speak to her heart and bring her back; he took with him a servant and two asses and went to the house of her father, who (L) rejoiced when he saw him. (4) His father-in-law (L) sat with him three days and they ate and drank and lodged together. (5) On the fourth day when they woke up in the morning, he got up to go and the father (L) said to his son-in-law, 'strengthen yourself, eat some bread—you can go later'. (6) So the two of them sat and ate and drank together, and the father (L) said to the man, 'stay for the night—enjoy yourself!' (7) The man got up to go but his father-in-law stopped him, so he settled down and stayed the night there. (8) When he got up on the fifth day to go, the father (L) said to him, 'strengthen yourself!' so the two of them ate and he stayed till late in the day. (9) When the man got up to go, (L) his father-in-law (L) said, 'Look, evening is coming on; stay here tonight and enjoy yourself! You can get up early tomorrow and be on your way back home'. (10) But the man would not stay the night, and he got up and left. When he arrived opposite Jebus (D) with his wife and laden asses, (D) (11) it was late in the afternoon. The boy said to his master, 'Let us turn into this city of the Jebusites and stay there for the night'. (12) And the man said to him, 'We are not going to turn into a foreign city'. (L) (13) And so he said to the boy, 'Let us go on and stay the night in either Gibeah or Ramah'. (14) So they went over and the sun was going down when they came to Gibeah of Benjamin. (15) They turned in there to stay the night in Gibeah, but when they sat in the square of the city no one would bring them home to stay the night. (16) Before long, an old man came from his evening field-work. Now the man himself was from Mt Ephraim, though he was living in Gibeah with Benjaminites. (17) When he looked up and saw the visitor in the town square, the old man said, 'Where have you been, and where are you going?' (18) The man replied, 'We are passing through from Bethlehem of Judah towards the flanks of Mt Ephraim—I am from there. We are on our way from Bethlehem of Judah (L) but no one will take me home. (19) I have fodder for the asses and even bread and wine for us and the boy—I've got all I need'. (20) The old man said to him, 'Peace be with you! I will take care of everything you need—just do not stay the night in the square!' 21) So they went to his house and he fed his asses, and they washed their feet, and ate and drank. (22) As they were enjoying themselves, some men of that city (D) suddenly surrounded the house and started beating on the door. They said to the old man in the house, 'Bring out the man who came to your house so that we can "get to know" him!' (23) Then the owner of the house went out to them and said, 'Do not do such an evil thing, my brothers! This man is my guest!(D) (24) Look, I have a virgin daughter, (L) I will bring her out to you. You can have sex with her and do whatever you want!' (25) But when the men would not listen to him, the man suddenly seized his (wife)(L) and pushed her out to them, and they had sex and abused her all night till the next morning, when they sent her back at dawn. (26) And the woman came back in the morning and fell at the gate of the house where her husband was staying. (27) When her husband got up in the morning and opened the doors of the house and went out to the road, he saw the woman (L) lying at the house gate, her hands on the threshold. (28) When he said to her, 'Get up, let us go', there was no answer. He then placed her on one of the asses and went back to his home. (29) When he came to his house he took a knife (L) and cut her up (D) in pieces, sending them into every territory of Israel. (30) So it was that everyone saw her. (D)

(20.11) (L,D) Then every man of Israel gathered against the city, united as one man. (L,D) (20) The men of Israel went out for war on Benjamin, and the men of Israel drew up for battle against Gibeah. (29) Now Israel had laid an ambush around Gibeah, (L) (31b) and when they came out from the city to begin the attack (L) they struck down in the field 30 men of Israel near the highways, one leading up to Bethel and the other to Gibeah. (L) (33) But when the men of Israel left the lines they had set up at Baal Tamar, the Israelite ambush burst out from its location in the Geba Pass. (34) As they came in from the east of Gibeah (L) heavy fighting broke out but (the Benjaminites) did not suspect the evil awaiting them. (L) (36b) The men of Israel gave way to Benjamin, for they trusted in the ambush which they had set for Gibeah. (37) Then the ambush swept out and made a dash on Gibeah, and the ambush struck down everyone in the city with the sword. (38) Now the ambushers had agreed on a smoke signal with the men of Israel in the town. (39) When the men of Israel began to retreat in the battle, Benjamin started to cut down the men of Israel, killing about 30 men. (L) (40) But when the column of smoke went up from the city, Benjamin turned around and saw total disaster in their city. (41) So the men of Israel turned and pursued the men of Benjamin, who saw at last the evil that had befallen them. (42) They turned and fled before the men of Israel on the desert road, but the fighting caught up with them and the men from the city joined in, cutting them down. (43) They hemmed in Benjamin and pursued him without respite east of Gibeah. (L) (47) They turned and fled to the desert to the Pomegranate Rock, and 600 of the men stayed at the Pomegranate Rock for four months. (48) The men of Israel then returned to deal with Benjamin, putting to the sword the cattle and everything they found in their cities, sending everything up in flames.

Appendix 3: The Reconstructed 'Rise of Saul' Narrative

(D indicates present Dtr intrusion)

(9.1) There was a man from Benjamin whose name was Kish son of Abiel, son of Zeror, son of Bechorath, son of Aphia; he was a brave fighting man. (2) He had a son named Saul, a good young man; there was no man among the Israelites better—he was even taller than everyone else. (3) One day some asses belonging to Saul's father Kish strayed, so Kish said to Saul, 'Take one of the servants, and go look for the asses'. (4) So they crossed the hills of Benjamin, through the land of Shalisha, but did not find them; then they traversed the land of Shaalim but they were not there; they even crossed through Benjamin but did not find them. (5) When they came to the land of Zuph, Saul said to the boy who was with him, 'Let us go back lest my father forget the asses and start worrying about us'. (6) But he replied, 'Look, there is a very important man of God in this city; everything he says comes true. Let us go there now—perhaps he will tell us which way to go'. (7) Saul said to the boy, 'if we go, what will we bring him? There is no bread in our sacks, and we have nothing to bring the man of God'. (8) The boy answered Saul, 'Look, I found a quarter-shekel of silver! I'll give it to the man of God so he will tell us what to do.' (9) (D) (10) Saul said, 'Good. Let us go'. So they went to the city where the man of God was.

(11) As they were going up the hill to the city, they met some young girls going out to draw water and said, 'Is the seer here?' (12) And they answered, 'He is right ahead of you... hurry now, it is growing late, he is sacrificing today at the hill-shrine. (13) As you go into the city you will meet him before he goes to the sanctuary to eat—the people won't eat until he comes and blesses the sacrifice; go right away and you will find him'. (14) So they went up to the middle of the city, and there (D) he was coming to meet them on the way to the sacrifice at the sanctuary. (D) (18) When Saul came to him (D) in the gate he said, 'Please tell me where the house of the seer is'. (19) The (D) man of God answered, saying, 'I am the seer. Go to the sanctuary and eat with me today, and I will send you away in the morning and tell you everything in your heart. (20) Do not worry about the asses lost three days ago—they have been found... but what is all Israel looking for? Is it not you and the whole house of your father?' (21) Saul answered, 'Am I not a Benjaminite—from the smallest of the tribes of Israel, and my family the smallest of all the families of Benjamin? Why do you say this to me?' (22) (D) Then the seer took Saul and the boy to the hall and gave them a place at the head of the group, numbering about thirty. (23) The man of God said to the cook, 'Give the portion which I gave you and told you to put aside'. (24) So the cook took the whole haunch and leg and set it before Saul and said, 'Here is the left-over for you. Eat it, for it is set apart for you from among the

people I called here'; Saul then ate. (D) (25) Then they came down from the sanctuary to the city, and Saul slept on the roof.

(26) At dawn, the seer called Saul on the roof, 'Up! I am sending you away'. Saul got up and the two of them went out into the street. (27) They went down to the outskirts of the city, and the man of God said to Saul, 'Tell the boy to go on'. After he did so, the seer he said, 'Stand and hear the word of God. (D) (10.2) When you leave me today, you will meet two men at Rachel's tomb in the territory of Benjamin at Zelah. They will say to you, "we found the asses you are looking for—your father is not concerned about them, he is worried about you saying, 'what have I done to my son?'" (3) Leave there, and when you come to the sacred tree of Tabor you will find three men going up to God at Bethel. One will be carrying three kids, one three loaves of bread, and one a jar of wine. (4) They will answer you, "Peace!" and give you two loaves of bread. You will take them from their hands. (5) After that, go to Gibeath Ha-Elohim, where the Philistine governor lives. As you go into the city, you will meet a band of prophets coming down from the sanctuary with harp, tambourine, flute, and lyre—all of them in ecstacy. (6) The spirit of the Lord will overpower you, and you will fly into ecstacy with them and become like another man. (7) When these signs happen to you, do whatever you must—God will be with you! (8) Then go down before me to Gilgal, and I will come down to you to burn holocausts and sacrifice offerings. In seven days I will join you and make known to you what you must do'.

(9) When (Saul) turned to leave (D) the seer, God changed him, giving him a whole new heart; and all these signs came true that day. (10) When he came to Gibeah, there truly was a band of prophets coming to meet him. And the spirit of God overpowered him and he fell into ecstacy in their midst. (11) Everyone who knew him saw that he really was ecstatic like a prophet. And the people said to themselves, 'What happened to the son of Kish? Is Saul one of the prophets, too?' (12) One of the men answered, 'And who is their "father?"' Hence the saying, 'Is Saul one of the prophets, too?' (13) Then all those prophesying came to the sanctuary.

(During the frenzy at the high-place, Saul strikes down the Philistine governor watching over the ceremony. Amidst the confusion and uproar, Saul escapes from Gibeah and proceeds immediately to Gilgal as commanded by the seer).

(13.3b) Then Saul sounded the trumpet throughout the whole land saying, 'Hear, O Hebrews!' (4) And all Israel heard, and said, 'Saul struck down the Philistine governor!' And Israel stank among the Philistines, and the people cried out and followed Saul to Gilgal. (5) Then the Philistines gathered to attack Israel, (D) and they camped at Michmas, east of Beth-Aven. (6) The men of Israel saw that they were in deep trouble, for the people were hard pressed, so they hid themselves in caves, amidst the thorn-trees, in the rocks, cisterns and wells. (7) Some Hebrews crossed the Jordan to the land of Gad and Gilead, but Saul remained at Gilgal, and the rest of the people flocked to him there. (D)

(The seer joins Saul, they offer sacrifice, and Saul and the Israelites are sent back to face the gathering Philistines.)

(13.15) Then (ר) Saul left Gilgal and went up to Gibeah of Benjamin along with about 600 men. (D) (14.2) And Saul set up camp on the outskirts of Gibeah, under the 'Pomegranate' which is in the Migron, with the 600 men who had joir d him. (D)

(Saul and his 600 men execute a daring raid on the Philistines in Michmas, and drive them off toward the west).

(Possibly located at this point: (13.2) Saul chose three thousand Israelites—two thousand to join him in Michmas and the hills of Bethel, and one thousand to stay with Jonathan in Gibeah of Benjamin.)

(10.26) Then Saul went back to his house in Gibeah, and took with him the warriors whose hearts God had touched. (11.1) Then Nahash the Ammonite attacked Jabesh Gilead, and they asked him to swear a treaty that they might serve him. (2) And Nahash said to them, 'I will only make a treaty with you if I can gouge out your right eyes and thus bring humiliation to Israel'. (3) The Jabeshite elders then said, 'Give us seven days to send messengers throughout the territory of Israel, and if no one rescues us, we will surrender to you'. (4) When the messengers come to Saul at Gibeah, their words caused the people to cry and lament. (5) But when Saul came with his oxen from the fields he said, 'Why are the people crying?' and they told him what the men of Jabesh had just said. (6) And the spirit of God overpowered Saul when he heard and he became extremely angry. (7) He took a pair of oxen, sliced them in pieces, and sent messengers with them to the whole territory of Israel saying, 'Whoever does not follow Saul (D) will suffer the fate of the oxen'; (D) and the people came out as one man. (8) He gathered (D) three (D) thousand Israelites at Bezek (D) (9) and said to the messengers, 'Tell the Jabeshites that they will be delivered tomorrow by the time the sun is hot', and they told the Jabeshites this and they rejoiced. (10) The Jabeshites said to Nahash, 'Tomorrow we will give up to you, and you can do to us whatever you want'. (11) The next day Saul put the people in three columns, and they went right into the enemy camp in the morning and struck down the Ammonites until the day grew hot, after which the survivors were so scattered that no two were left together.

(Possible conclusion: (12) Then the people said to the man of God, 'Who could say that Saul should not be king over us? Give us the men and we will kill them!' (13) But Saul replied, 'Kill no one on a day when the Lord has delivered Israel'. (D) (15) And the whole people went to Gilgal and there made Saul king before the Lord. They sacrificed offerings in the presence of the Lord, and Saul and all the men of Israel rejoiced greatly.)

NOTES

Notes to Chapter 1

1. See J.M. Miller, 'Site Identification: A Problem Area in Contemporary Biblical Scholarship', *ZDPV* 99 (1983), pp. 119-20.

2. Other names associated with more than one site include: Aphek, Aroer, Bethlehem, Carmel, Gath, Hazor, Jabneel, Kedesh, Mizpah, Rabbah, Ramah, Rechov, Rimmon and Zalmonah; see B.S. Isserlin, 'Israelite and Pre-Israelite Place-Names in Palestine: A Historical and Geographical Sketch', *PEQ* 89 (1957), pp. 133-44, who identified 21 variant גבע-root cognates in Palestine. Fortunately, Gibeah of Judah (Josh. 15.57) does not lend itself to confusion with Benjaminite sites since it is mentioned in a clearly distinct context.

3. Acceptance of the Gibeon/el-Jib equation is today unanimous to my knowledge. J.B. Pritchard's excavations (1956-60) discovered 31 jar handles inscribed with the Hebrew גבען ('Gibeon'); see F. Cross, 'The Inscribed Jar Handles from Gibeon', *BASOR* 168 (1962), pp. 18-23, and Pritchard, *Gibeon: Where the Sun Stood Still* (Princeton: University Press, 1962), which offers as strong a site identification for Gibeon as anyone ever is likely to find in biblical archaeology. For an interesting discussion of Gibeon and its place in biblical history and tradition, see J. Blenkinsopp, *Gibeon and Israel* (Cambridge: University Press, 1972). For an updated, shorter treatment, see my article 'Gibeon' in the forthcoming *Anchor Bible Dictionary*.

4. See the Benjaminite town-list (Josh. 18.21-28), the Levitical cities list (Josh. 21), genealogies in 1 Chron. 8, the list of returnees from Exile in Neh. 7.25-30, and the list of Benjaminite citizens active in the reconstruction of Jerusalem (Neh. 3.7 and 12.29).

5. See A. Demsky, 'Geba, Gibeah and Gibeon—an Historico-Geographic Riddle', *BASOR* 212 (Dec. 1973), pp. 26-31. Demsky distinguishes 'Geba' from 'Geba Benjamin' on the basis of a text (1 Samuel 13-14) which does not differentiate the two names, yet he identifies 'Gibeah' and 'Gibeah of Benjamin' despite the fact that both these toponyms also occur in that same passage. Demsky proceeds to identify (correctly) 'Geba Benjamin' with modern Jeba, yet strangely associates 'Geba' with 'Gibeon' (located at el-Jib) despite five separate biblical texts that clearly distinguish the two (see note 4).

6. *Ibid.*, p. 27. The context of the story in 1 Samuel 10 demands that if 'Gibeath Ha-Elohim' is to be identified with another toponym, 'Gibeah' and 'Geba' are logical alternatives for literary reasons, as we shall see below.

7. This position was first developed by Blenkinsopp, 'Did Saul Make Gibeon his Capital'? *VT* (1974), pp. 1-7.

8. Demsky, 'Historico-Geographic Riddle', p. 31.

9. M. Noth, *Das Buch Josua* (Tübingen: Mohr, 1953), p. 112.

10. K. Schunck, *Benjamin: Untersuchung zur Entstehung und Geschichte eines israelitischen Stammes*, BZAW 86 (Berlin: Töpelmann, 1963), p. 158.

11. W.F. Albright, 'Excavations and Results at Tell el-Ful (Gibeah of Saul)', AASOR 4 (1924), p. 32.

12. Y. Aharoni, *The Land of the Bible: A Historical Geography* (Philadelphia: Westminster, 1967), p. 301.

13. The original 'Yearim' was apparently omitted through haplography; for a more detailed discussion of emandation and literary issues here, see Miller, 'Geba/Gibeah of Benjamin', *VT* 25 (1975), pp. 145-66.

14. Y. Kaufmann, *The Biblical Account of the Conquest of Palestine* (Jerusalem, Magnes, 1953), pp. 97-98; Kaufmann regards the lists as stemming from the period of Judges under Joshua's authorship.

15. A. Alt, 'Judas Gaue unter Josia', *Kleine Schriften zur Geschichte des Volkes Israel*, vol. 2 (München: Beck, 1959), pp. 276-88.

16. Noth, *Josua*, p. 112.

17. S. Mowinckel, *Zur Frage nach Dokumentarischen Quellen in Joshua 13-19* (Oslo: Dybwald, 1946), pp. 26-27.

18. F. Cross and G. Wright, 'The Boundary and Province Lists of the Kingdom of Judah', *JBL* 75 (1956), pp. 202-26.

19. Z. Kallai-Kleinmann, 'The Town-Lists of Judah, Simeon, Benjamin, and Dan', *VT* 8 (1958), pp. 134-60.

20. Aharoni, *Land of the Bible*, p. 235, and 'The Province List of Judah', *VT* 9 (1959), pp. 225-46. Aharoni agrees with Kallai-Kleinmann that the 'Geba' in the list was in Ephraim, as does Schunck, *Benjamin*, p. 160.

21. For the original treatment of the now well-accepted DH hypothesis, see Noth, *Deuteronomistic History* (Sheffield: JSOT, 1981); and E.W. Nicholson, *Deuteronomy and Tradition* (Philadelphia: Fortress, 1967); for a briefer overview of the subject, see D.N. Freedman, 'The Deuteronomistic History', in *IDBS* (Nashville: Abingdon, 1976), pp. 226-28.

22. Kallai-Kleinmann, 'Town-Lists of Judah', pp. 138-40.

23. Kallai-Kleinmann proposed an Ephraimite Geba, located at Khirbet et-Tell, 2 kms. south-southeast of Sinjil, following a recommendation of B. Mazar (*Encyclopedia Biblica II*, 1954, p. 412). However, a surface survey at the site could identify only 3 possible Israelite sherds in a mass of Roman-Byzantine and Medieval remains; see Arnulf Kuschke, 'Historisch-topographische Beiträge zum Buche Josua', in *Gottes Wort und Gottes Land: Festschrift für Hans-Wilhelm Hertzberg zum 70. Geburtstag*, ed. H.G.

Reventlow (Göttingen: Vandenhoeck & Ruprecht, 1965), pp. 90-109.

24. According to the results of Kallai's archaeological survey; cf. 'The Land of Benjamin and Mt. Ephraim', in *Judea, Samaria, and the Golan: Archaeological Survey 1967-1968*, ed. M. Kochavi (Jerusalem: Carta, 1972), pp. 153-93. Jericho, Beth-Hoglah, Emek-keziz, and Beth-Arabah were probably cities in the Jordan Valley. Bethel (if Beitin) and Ophrah (if et-Taiyeh—cf. W. Morton, 'Ophrah', *IDB* 3, pp. 606-607) are east of the watershed. Kallai's 1967 survey suggested locations east of the watershed for Zemaraim (= Ras et-Tahuneh, p. 158) and Geba (= Jeba, p.183). Astride and west of the watershed are: Gibeon (el-Jib), Ramah (er-Ram), Beeroth (el-Bireh), Mizpah (Tell en-Nasbeh), Mozah (Qaluniya— cf. S. Cohen, 'Mozah', *IDB* 3, p. 455), and 'Gibeath Kiriath', which will be discussed below. We shall also propose that Tell el-Ful, now normally identified with Gibeah, actually is ancient Eleph.

25. Alt, 'Bemerkungen zu einigen judäischen Ortslisten des Alten Testaments', *KS* 2, pp. 289-305; and Albright, 'The List of Levitic Cities', in the *L. Ginzburg Jubilee Volume* (1945), pp. 49ff., both rightly considered the Chron. list to represent merely a shortened version of the original found in Joshua 21.

26. Kaufmann, *Biblical Account*, pp. 40-46, suggested that these lists derived from the time of Joshua's conquest.

27. A Davidic-era setting for the list was first proposed by Albright, *Archaeology and the Religion of Israel* (Baltimore: Johns Hopkins, 1942), pp. 121-25. In his view, these lists are thus related to Joshua 13-19, which Albright also dated to the time of David, and represent an actual, if 'ephemeral', attempt at central government planning. B. Mazar, 'The Cities of the Priests and Levites', *SVT* 7 (Leiden: Brill, 1960), pp. 193-205, included the notion that the cities were fortified settlements on newly conquered land. The Benjaminite sites were also believed to have served as places of residence for priests connected with the new temple in Jerusalem, a proposal advanced later by M. Haran, 'Studies in the Account of the Levitical Cities', *JBL* 80 (1961), pp. 45-54. This general approach has been incorporated by J. Miller and J. Hayes, *A History of Ancient Israel and Judah* (Philadelphia: Westminster, 1986) in their treatment of the Davidic period; see p. 172 and map on p. 181. Today, international law forbids the introduction of such settlements on occupied territory.

28. Alt, 'Bemerkungen zu einigen Judäischen Ortslisten des Alten Testaments', *KS* 2, pp. 289-305, explained that the great gaps between groupings of the cities gave evidence of Josiah's reform of Judean high-places 'from Geba to Beersheba' (2 Kgs 23.8).

29. Noth, *Josua*, pp. 127-132. Noth's assumptions about the relationships between Priests and Levites seem most determinative in arriving at this date.

30. For a discussion of pertinent literary and historical issues, see O.

Eissfeldt, *The Old Testament: An Introduction* (New York: Harper & Row, 1965), pp. 531-35. For other evaluations of this material, see Alt, 'Bermerkungen', *KS* 2, pp. 289-305; L. Watermann, 'Some Repercussions from Late Levitical Genealogical Accretions in P and the Chronicler', *AJSL* 58 (1941), pp. 49-56; and H. Williamson, *Israel in the Books of Chronicles* (Cambridge: University Press, 1977), pp. 71-82.

31. This genealogy is an important part of Blenkinsopp's proposed connection of Saul with Gibeon; cf. *Gibeon and Israel*, pp. 59-61, and 'Did Saul Make Gibeon His Capital', pp. 1-7. Blenkinsopp contended that the presence of Saul in this genealogy (8.33; 9.39) implies that Gibeon was Saul's birthplace. However, the genealogy does not actually associate Gibeon with Saul, but only Saul's grandfather Jehiel. Postexilic genealogies, moreover, are weak foundations on which to build an historical case relating to a period seven centuries earlier.

32. Variants based on the feminine גבעה appear 22 times in two distinct constructions: (a) the indefinite form גבעה occurs with various prepositional prefixes in 19.12, 13, 15, 16; 20.9, 13, 34 while its definite form הגבעה appears in the construct and with separate prepositions in 19.14; 20.5, 15, 19, 20, 21, 25, 29, 30, 36, 37, 43; and (b) the feminine directional form גבעתה appears in the definite in 20.4, 14 and in the indefinite in 20.31. None of these 22 feminine forms is textually problematic and each appears in regular grammatical form.

33. We know of one such 'Gibeah' in Judah (Josh. 15.57).

34. Scholars have taken one of two options with this reading. The first emends 'Geba' to read 'Gibeah'; for example, G. Moore, *The Book of Judges* (New York: Dodd, Mead, & Co., 1898), p. 40; A. Schulz, *Das Buch der Richter und das Buch Ruth*. HSAT (Bonn: Hanstein, 1926), p. 106; J. Martin, *The Book of Judges*. CBC (Cambridge: University Press, 1975), pp. 207ff; and R. Boling, *Judges*. AB (Garden City, N.Y.: Doubleday, 1975), p. 282. The Hebrew ממערה is either translated 'from the clearing', or emended to ממערבה 'the west'. The other group would retain 'Geba' and propose that the Gibeah ambush was launched from near Geba; for instance, M.J. Lagrange, *Le Livre des Juges* (Paris: Lecoffre, 1903), p. 318; J. Gray, *Joshua, Judges and Ruth* (Greenwood, S.C.: Attic, 1967), pp. 383 ff.; J.A. Soggin, *Judges: A Commentary*. OTL (Philadelphia: Westminster, 1981), p. 296; and A. Cundall, *Judges and Ruth* (London: Tyndale, 1968), pp. 204-207. To complicate matters, Burney, *The Book of Judges* (London: Rivingtons, 1930), p. 464 and Moore, *Judges*, p. 40, emended הגבעה in 20.43 to read 'Geba', and Burney, *Judges*, p. 479; Cundall, *Judges*, p. 204; and Soggin *Judges*, pp. 295-96, emended הגבעה in 20.31 to read 'Gibeon', though there is neither textual support nor topographical logic in either of these changes.

35. Wellhausen, *Prolegomena* (Gloucester, Mass.: Smith, 1973), p. 237, was among the first to claim this. For a review of critical commentary on Judges 19–21 before Wellhausen, cf. H.-W. Jüngling, *Richter 19: Ein Pläydoyer für*

das Königtum. Stylistische Analyse der Tendenz Erzählung Ri 19, 1-30a, 21, 25 (Rome: Biblical Institute, 1981), pp. 1-18. See also K. Budde, 'Die Anhänge des Richterbuchs', *ZAW* (1888), pp. 285-300; De Vaux, *Early Israel*, p. 684; Gray, *Joshua, Judges and Ruth*, pp. 237-43 (who saw Judges 19-21 as a device to cast aspersions on Gibeah, the home of Saul); J. Martin, *The Book of Judges*. CBC (Cambridge: University Press, 1975), pp. 181-82; A.D.H. Mayes, *Israel in the Period of the Judges* (Naperville, Ill.: Allenson, 1974), p. 42 (who regards Judges 19-21 as a tradition handed down separately from DH); Hertzberg, *Die Bücher Josua, Richter, und Ruth*, p. 141; and A. Cundall, *Judges and Ruth* (London: Tyndale, 1968), pp. 25-26.

36. Noth, *The Deuteronomistic History*, p. 121, n. 9, excluded these chapters from his reconstruction of DH.

37. See R. Boling, 'In Those Days There Was No King in Israel', in *A Light Unto My Path: Old Testament Studies in Honor of Jacob M. Myers* ed. H. Bream *et al.* (Philadelphia: Temple, 1974), p. 44; and T. Veijola, *Das Königtum in der Beurteilung der deuteronomistischen Historiographie: eine redaktionsgeschichtliche Untersuchung* (Helsinki: Suomalainen Tiedeakatemia, 1977). Veijola points to passages like Judg. 19.30, which seems to echo Deut. 9.7; 1 Sam. 8.8; 2 Sam. 7.6; 1 Kgs 8.16; 2 Kgs 21.15 and Jer. 7.25 and 11.7 (pp. 21-22). Further, Veijola considers the mention of the Ark in Bethel (Judg. 20.27-28) to be a Dtr notice designed to highlight the illegitimacy of Jereboam's Bethel shrine by mention of the past. Regarding the charge that Dtr was 'anti-monarchical' (Jüngling, *Richter 19*, pp. 59ff.), Veijola admits that, though Dtr's antipathy towards kingship may have existed regarding foreign threats, Judges 19-21 presupposes *interior* strife among the tribes. Thus, Dtr was only opposed to kingship as protection against foreign threats, not internal ones. For a recent summary judgment on this entire question, see Soggin, *Judges*, p. 263.

38. Eissfeldt, *Introduction*, pp. 261-67, argued that the chapters also underwent a P redaction. For a discussion of the 'Levite' as a later addition to the original story in Judges 19- 20, see H. Strauss, *Untersuchungen zu den Überlieferungen der vorexilischen Leviten*, Diss. Bonn, 1960, pp. 105ff. It is probably the presence of material from both Dtr and P redactions which causes mixed results in the attempt to determine the relationship between the 'main body' of Judges and chapters 17-21 by means of statistical linguistic analysis. According to Y. Radday, *et al.*, 'The Book of Judges Examined by Statistical Linguistics', *Bib* 58 (1977), pp. 469-99, statistical analysis reveals that Judges 17-18 and 19-21 are 'not dissimilar' and, in turn, show some differences from the 'main body' of Judges. If Veijola and Eissfeldt are correct, these differences derive from the distinct literary tradition that produced chapters 17-21, while their similarities are caused by common Dtr or P redactions.

39. Wellhausen, *Prolegomena*, pp. 245-72; Budde, *Richter und Samuel*, pp. 268-76, proposed a continuation in this chapter of the Pentateuchal J and

E sources, which were supposedly combined and edited by a Dtr redactor. Eissfeldt, *Introduction*, pp. 271-81, in addition to Budde's J and E sources, added his own Lay (L) source; the Dtr redaction was considered slight. See also H. Smith, *A Critical and Exegetical Commentary on the Books of Samuel*. ICC (New York: Scribner's, 1929), pp. xv-xxix.

40. H. Gressmann, 'Die älteste Geschichtsschreibung und Prophetie Israels (von Samuel bis Amos und Hosea)' in *Die Schriften des Alten Testaments* Part 2, Vol. 1 (Göttingen: Vandenhoeck & Ruprecht, 1910). In Gressmann's view, a great variety of independent narrative sources have been loosely combined here. See also A. Weiser, *Samuel: Seine geschichtliche Aufgabe und religiöse Bedeutung* (Göttingen: Vandenhoeck & Ruprecht, 1962), pp. 48-79.

41. Noth, *Deuteronomistic History*, pp. 47, 54.

42. For a survey of the history of scholarship on these questions, see B. Birch, *The Rise of the Israelite Monarchy: The Growth and Development of 1 Samuel 7-15*, Diss. Yale, 1970 (Ann Arbor: University Microfilms, 1971), pp. 1-10. See also F. Crüsemann, *Der Widerstand gegen das Königtum*. WMANT 40 (Neukirchen-Vluyn: Neukirchener, 1978), and Mayes, *The Story of Israel Between Settlement and Exile: A Redactional Study of the Deuteronomistic History* (London: SCM, 1983), pp. 85-86. Mayes sees the following pro/anti kingship pattern in 1 Sam. 8-12: 8 = anti; 9.1-10.16 = pro; 10.17-27 = critical; 11.1-15 = pro; and 12.1-25 = anti, but with a resolution of the tension. For Mayes, this pattern is a Dtr arrangement of old sources. Finally, see B. Childs, *Introduction to the Old Testament as Scripture* (Philadelphia: Fortress, 1979), pp. 277-78.

43. We shall see that Noth's unit 10.17-27a ought to end at v. 25, and that the mention of 'Gibeah' in 10.26 actually opens another unit (10.26-11.15).

44. Noth, *Deuteronomistic History*, pp. 47 and 54.

45. LXX takes both toponyms in 10.10 and 10.13 as appellatives.

46. See, for example, H. Stoebe, 'Noch einmal die Eselinnen des Kîs (1 Sam. 9)', *VT* (1957), pp. 362-70; Miller, 'Saul's Rise to Power: Some Observations Concerning I Sam. 9.1-10.16; 10.26-11.15 and 13.2-14.46', *CBQ* 36 (1974), pp. 171-73; Gressmann, 'Die Älteste', pp. 26-27; Mayes, 'The Rise of the Israelite Monarchy', *ZAW* 90 (1978), pp. 1-19; L. Schmidt, *Menschlicher Erfolg und Jahwes Initiative*. WMANT 38 (Neukirchen-Vluyn: Neukirchener, 1970), pp. 58-102; and H. Seebass, 'Die Vorgeschichte der Königserhebung Sauls' *ZAW* 79 (1967), pp. 155-171. Other scholars who find two narratives include Crüsemann, *Widerstand*, pp. 57 ff.; and van Seters, *Search*, pp. 254 ff.

47. So Mayes, *Story*, pp. 86-89; Miller, 'Saul's Rise', pp. 157-74; and D. Edelman, 'Saul's Rescue of Jabesh-Gilead (1 Sam. 11.1-11): Sorting Story from History', *ZAW* 96 (1984), pp. 195-209.

48. Noth, *Deuteronomistic History*, pp. 50-51. Birch, *Rise*, pp. 87-89,

regards W. 26-27 as a 'transition to the next pericope'. Scholars who would unite W. 26-27 with 10.17-25 in agreement with Noth include Hertzberg, *I and II Samuel: A Commentary*. OTL (Philadelphia: Westminster, 1964), pp. 79-95; Mayes, *Story*, pp. 85-86; van Seters, *Search*, p. 252; and C. Hauer, 'Does 1 Sam. 9.1-11.15 reflect the extension of Saul's dominions?' *JBL* 86 (1967), pp. 306-310. Weiser, *Samuel*, pp. 48-79, includes v. 26 but assigns v. 27 to the next unit. But see Miller, 'Saul's Rise', pp. 165-67, who regarded vv. 25-26a as part of a Dtr redaction.

49. Wellhausen, *Die Composition Hexateuchs und der Historischen Bücher des Alten Testaments*, 2nd edn (Berlin: Reimer, 1889), is followed by Noth, *History*, pp. 167-68; Weiser, *Samuel*, p. 69; and H. Wildberger, 'Samuel und die Entstehung des israelitischen Königtums', *TZ* 13 (1957), pp. 442-69, among others. Van Seters, *Search*, p. 256, will only allow that it is the 'oldest' account of Saul's rise.

50. The word נציב is variously translated 'garrison', 'governor', or 'pillar'. Since either Saul or Jonathan individually 'struck down' the נציב in Geba (1 Sam. 13.3-4), the translation 'garrison' is unlikely here. We have adopted the translation 'governor' on the theory that an assassination is the most probable activity of a single individual, and more likely to have provoked the Philistine response indicated in 13.5ff than the destruction of a 'pillar', though the latter translation can not be excluded. Note that LXX merely transliterated the word as in 13.3. See Miller, 'Saul's Rise', p. 159, n. 8.

51. Noth, *The History of Israel*, 2nd edn (New York: Harper and Row, 1960), p. 173; S. Hermann, *A History of Israel in Old Testament Times*, 2nd edn (Philadelphia: Fortress, 1980), p. 138; Bright, *A History of Israel* (Philadelphia: Westminster, 1959), p. 168; van Seters, *In Search of History*, p. 257, and Miller and Hayes, *HAIJ*, pp. 120-48.

52. As recognized by Noth, *History*, p. 173; Hermann, *History*, p. 138; Mayes, 'The Period of the Judges and the Rise of the Monarchy' in *Israelite and Judean History*, ed. John H. Hayes and J. Maxwell Miller (Philadelphia: Westminster, 1977), pp. 326-28; and Miller and Hayes, *HAIJ*, pp. 127-28.

53. Noth, *History*, p. 173 n. 1.

54. For example, see Albright, *Excavations and Results at Tell el-Ful (Gibeah of Saul)*. AASOR 4 (New Haven: Yale, 1924), p. 38.

55. So Mayes, 'The Period of the Judges and the Rise of the Monarchy', *IJH*, p. 327; and H. Stoebe, 'Zur Topographie und Überlieferung der Schlacht von Mikmas, 1 Sam. 13 und 14', *TZ* 21 (1965), pp. 269-80.

56. Miller, 'Saul's Rise', pp. 162-65.

57. *Ibid.*, p. 161; Miller describes this placement of the outcome before the battle as a literary technique also employed in Isa. 7.1.

58. Birch, *Rise*, p. 124, and Schunck, *Benjamin*, pp. 107-108.

59. For a survey of scholars viewing 14.1-46 as a unity, see Birch, *Rise*, p. 141. But see also F. Schicklberger, 'Jonatans Heldtat. Textlinguistische Beobachtungen zu 1 Sam. xiv 1-23a', *VT* 24 (1974), pp. 324-33, for a

discussion of the raid narrative in 14.1-23 as an originally independent entity. Birch himself regards the piece as a typical 'battle report', following the analysis of W. Richter, *Traditionsgeschichtliche Untersuchungen zum Richterbuch* (Bonn: Hanstein, 1966), p. 263.

60. J. Blenkinsopp, 'Jonathan's Sacrilege: 1 Sam. 14.1-46. A Study in Literary History', *CBQ* 26 (1964), pp. 423-49, detects elements of the Judean Yahwistic corpus in the story, while D. Jobling, 'Saul's Fall and Jonathan's Rise: Tradition and Redaction in 1 Sam. 14.1-46', *JBL* 95 (1976), pp. 367-76, has claimed that the literary purpose of the story is to provide the basis for Jonathan's transference of the Saulide monarchical claims to David.

61. Placing the narratives in David's own reign are H.U. Nubel, *Davids Aufstieg in der frühen israelitischen Geschichtsschreibung* (Diss. Bonn, 1959); and J. Flanagan, 'Judah in all Israel', in *No Famine in the Land: Studies in Honor of John L. McKenzie* (Missoula: Scholars, 1975), pp. 101-16. Favoring a Solomonic setting are: G. von Rad, *Der Heilige Krieg im Alten Israel* (Zurich: Zwingli, 1951), p. 41; A. Weiser, 'Die Legitimation des Königs David. Zur Eigenart und Entstehung der sogenannten Geschichte von Davids Aufstieg', *VT* 16 (1966), pp. 325-54; and R. Ward, *The Story of David's Rise: A Traditio-Historical Study of 1 Sam. 16.14-2 Sam. 5* (Diss. Vanderbilt, 1967) (Ann Arbor: University Microfilms, 1972). Those placing the narratives after the division of the kingdoms include J. Grønbaeck, *Die Geschichte vom Aufstieg Davids (1 Sam. 15-2 Sam. 5): Tradition und Komposition*. ATD 10 (Copenhagen, 1971); and F. Schicklberger, 'Die Davididen und das Nordreich. Beobachtungen zur sogenannten Geschichte vom Aufstieg Davids', *BZ* 18 (1974), pp. 255-63.

62. See Noth, *Deuteronomistic History*, p. 124, n. 3; Eissfeldt, *Intro.*, pp. 269-70; and Childs, *Intro.*, p. 273.

63. So Mayes, 'The Period of the Judges and the Rise of the Monarchy', *IJH*, p. 348; and Bright, *History*, p. 187. See also Miller and Hayes, *HAIJ*, p. 156, and p. 176, where 2 Sam. 16.5-14 is linked to this incident.

64. LXX reads 'Gibeon of Saul'. These textual problems are significant, since the LXX reading is taken by Blenkinsopp as evidence that Gibeon was Saul's capital, cf. 'Did Saul Make Gibeon His Capital', pp. 1-7. Yet LXX's 'Gibeon' probably derives from a scribal error under the influence of the other appearances of 'Gibeon' in the story. The MT 'Gibeah of Saul' is therefore preferable.

65. LXX's 'every hill of Benjamin', of course, is an unlikely reading. 2 Chron. 16.6 also retains 'Geba' in the MT.

66. See H. Donner, 'The Separate States of Israel and Judah', *IJH*, p. 390.

67. For a recent discussion of the Josian Reform, see Miller and Hayes, *HAIJ*, pp. 397-401. See also Aharoni, 'Arad: Its Inscription and Temple', *BA* 31 (1968), pp. 2-32; B. Oded, 'Judah and the Exile', *IJH*, p. 465; and Gray, *I and II Kings*, 2nd edn, OTL (Philadelphia: Westminster, 1969), p. 735.

68. For a discussion of the literary problems in Ezra-Nehemiah, see J. Myers, *Ezra and Nehemiah*. AB (Garden City, N.Y.: Doubleday, 1965), esp. pp. xix-lxxvii; R. Coggins, *The Book of Ezra and Nehemiah*. CBC (Cambridge: University Press, 1976), pp. 1-8; F. Fensham, *The Books of Ezra and Nehemiah*. NIC (Grand Rapids, Mich.: Eerdmans, 1982), pp. 1-19; Childs, *Intro.*, pp. 626-38; G. Widengren, 'The Persian Period', *IJH*, pp. 490-93; Eissfeldt, *Intro.*, pp. 541-57; and H.G.M. Williamson, *Ezra-Nehemia* (Waco: Word Books, 1985).

69. For a discussion of the priority of Ezra 2 over Nehemiah 7, cf. Myers, *Ezra and Nehemiah*, pp. 14-22. However, W. Rudolph, *Esra und Nehemia*. HAT (Tübingen: Mohr, 1949), p. 13, considers Nehemiah 7 the original version.

70. See G. Hölscher in *Die Heilige Schrift des Alten Testaments*, ed. E. Kautzsch, p. 504; Alt, *KS* II, pp. 334-35; K. Galling, 'The "Gola List" According to Ezra 2, Nehemiah 7', *JBL* 70 (1951), pp. 149-58; W. Rudolph, *Esra und Nehemiah*, p. 17; and Widengren, 'Persian Period', *IJH*, p. 491.

71. See Widengren, 'Persian Period', *IJH*, pp. 491-92; and Eissfeldt, *Intro.*, p. 350, who suggests that too much Jewish territory is described for the lists to have originated so soon after the return from Exile; see also Myers, *Ezra*, p. 192.

72. Eissfeldt, *Intro*, p. 542; and Myers, *Ezra*, p. 202.

73. Throughout Hosea, LXX mistakes 'Gibeah' for an appellative, an unacceptably vague rendering in view of the specificity of other cities mentioned in 5.8, and Hosea's references to the sins of antiquity in 9.9 and 10.9.

74. Alt, 'Hosea 5.8-6.6. Ein Krieg und seine Folgen in prophetischen Beleuchtung', *KS* 2, pp. 163-87.

75. For example, J. Mays, *Hosea: A Commentary*. OTL (Philadelphia: Westminster, 1969), pp. 67-68; H.W. Wolff, *Hosea. A Commentary on the Book of the Prophet Hosea*. Hermeneia (Philadelphia: Fortress, 1974), pp. 111-13; Bright, *History*, p. 256; and W. Rudolph, *Hosea*. KAT (Gerd Mohn: Gütersloher, 1966), pp. 125-26. Those dissenting from the prevailing view, and finding liturgical roots to the passage are E. Good, 'Hosea 5.8-6.6: An Alternative to Alt', *JBL* 85 (1966), pp. 276-86; and G.A. Danell, *Studies in the Name Israel* (Uppsala, 1946), p. 138.

76. Wolff, *Hosea*, p. 157 rightly considers 9.8a to be one of the most difficult passages in Hosea.

77. So, for example, J. Ward, *Hosea: A Theological Commentary* (New York: Harper and Row, 1966), pp. 169-70; and N. Gottwald, *The Hebrew Bible: A Socio-Literary Introduction* (Philadelphia: Fortress, 1985), p. 361.

78. Thus, for example, Wolff, *Hosea*, p. 158; Mayes, *Hosea*, p. 131; and J. Jeremias, *Der Prophet Hosea* (Göttingen: Vandenhoeck & Ruprecht, 1983), pp. 118-19.

79. See F. Andersen and D. Freedman, *Hosea*. AB (New York: Doubleday, 1980), pp. 534-35.

80. LXX mistranslates, 'fear shall seize Ramah, city of Saul', an unlikely and otherwise unattested association of Saul with Ramah.

81. For example: J. Mauchline, *Isaiah 1-39* (New York: Macmillan, 1962), pp. 125-256; O. Kaiser, *Isaiah 1-12: A Commentary*. OTL (Philadelphia: Westminster, 1972), p. 151; and A. Fernández, 'El Paso difícil del ejercito asirio (Is. 10,28)', *EstE* 10 (1931), pp. 339-48.

82. See A. Herbert, *The Book of the Prophet Isaiah: Chapters 1-39* (Cambridge: Cambridge University, 1973), p. 88; Donner, *Israel unter den Völkern*. VTS 11 (Leiden: Brill, 1964), pp. 30-38; R. Scott, 'Isaiah', *IB* 5 (New York: 1956), pp. 245-46; and J. Hayes and S. Irvine, *Isaiah: The Eighth-Century Prophet* (Nashville: Abingdon, 1987), pp. 206-10.

83. So, for example, L. Federlin, 'A propos d'Isaie 10.29- 31', *RB* 3 (1906), p. 266; Albright, 'The Assyrian March on Jerusalem: Isa. 10.28-32', AASOR 4 (1924), pp. 134-40; and D.L. Christensen, 'The March of Conquest in Isaiah 10.27c-34', *VT* 26 (1976), pp. 385-99.

84. W. Neil, 'Zechariah', *IDB* 4, pp. 943-47; G. Widengren, 'The Persian Period', *IJH*, pp. 520-21; and Herrmann, *History*, pp. 520ff.

85. For a detailed study of Zechariah 9-14, see I. Willi- Plein, *Prophetie am Ende. Untersuchungen zu Sacharja 9-14* (Köln: Hanstein, 1974). For a review of scholarly research on these chapters, cf. B. Otzen, *Studien über Deutero-sacharja* (Copenhagen: Munksgaard, 1964); and P. Hanson, *The Dawn of Apocalyptic* (Philadelphia: Fortress, 1975), pp. 287-90. Neil, 'Zechariah', *IDB* 4 (Nashville: Abingdon, 1962), pp. 943-47, and Childs, *Intro.*, pp. 472-87, similarly suppose that Zechariah 9-14 did not originate with Zechariah but was composed at a much later date.

Notes to Chapter 2

1. Robinson, *Biblical Researches in Palestine* II (Jerusalem: Universitas, 1970), pp. 11-12, reasoned that the Arabic name Kuryet el-Enab retains the Hebrew 'Kiriath', and that the location of the village close to Gibeon (el-Jib) accords with Josh. 9.17 and Ezra 2.25. See also S. Lauffs, 'Zur Lage und Geschichte des Ortes Kirjat-jearim', *ZDPV* 38 (1915), pp. 249ff; P. Cooke, 'The Site of Kiryat-jearim', AASOR 5 (1923/24), pp. 105ff; R. de Vaux and A. Steve, *Fouilles à Qaryet el Enab–Abu Ghosh, Palestine* (Paris: Gabalda & Cie, 1950); Blenkinsopp, 'Kiriath-Jearim and the Ark', *JBL* 88 (1969), pp. 143-56; and Gold, 'Kiriath-Jearim', *IDB* 3, pp. 37-38.

2. Since Gibeon (el-Jib) also lies on the slopes of this important peak and since its famous sanctuary was never found, it is possible that Nebi Samwil is the 'hill' of Kiriath-Jearim as well as the hill-shrine from which the village of Gibeon derived its name. For a discussion of this possibility, see R. Brinker, *The Influence of Sanctuaries in Early Israel* (Manchester, 1946), p. 160; Pritchard, *Gibeon*, p. 39; and Blenkinsopp, *Gibeon*, pp. 65-83. Earlier works which had proposed that the hill-shrine of Gibeon rested on Nebi Samwil

include Dalman, 'Die Schalensteine Palästinas in ihrer Beziehung zu alter Kultur und Religion', *PJB* (1908), p. 32; A. Bruno, *Gibeon* (Leipzig: Deichert, 1923), p. 59, and H.W. Hertzberg, 'Mizpa', *ZAW* 47 (1929), p. 177.

3. See A. Demsky, 'Historico-Geographic Riddle', pp. 26-31; Schunck, *Benjamin*, pp. 131-38; Edelman, 'Saul's Rescue of Jabesh-Gilead', pp. 204-205, or *The Rise of the Israelite State Under Saul* (Diss. Chicago, 1986) (Ann Arbor: University Microfilms, 1987), pp. 202-12; and Blenkinsopp, 'Did Saul Make Gibeon His Capital?' pp. 1-7; or *Gibeon*, p. 59, where Blenkinsopp regards the term Gibeath Ha-Elohim as a 'covert reference' to the famous cult center at Gibeon.

4. Wellhausen, *Prolegomena*, pp. 17-22.

5. Pritchard, *Gibeon*, makes no mention of any Philistine archaeological remains discovered at el-Jib.

6. See Miller, 'Saul's Rise', pp. 157-74.

7. Edward Robinson, *Biblical Researches in Palestine*, 11th edition, (Boston: Crocker and Brewster, 1874), pp. 440-42.

8. See Kallai, 'The Land of Benjamin and Mt Ephraim', in *Judea, Samaria, and the Golan*, ed. M. Kochavi, p. 183.

9. An account of these journeys can be found in the first edition of Robinson's *Biblical Researches* (Boston: Crocker and Brewster, 1941), pp. 111-17; 315-17.

10. See Gross's review of Robinson's *Biblical Researches* in *Theologische Studien und Kritiken* (1843), p. 1082.

11. See Robinson, *Biblical Researches*, 2nd and later editions, p. 600.

12. C.R. Conder, 'Gibeah of Saul', *PEFQS* (1877), pp. 104-105.

13. See Birch, 'Gibeah at Adaseh' *PEFQS* (1913), pp. 38-42 and 'The Site of Gibeah', *PEFQS* (1914), pp. 42-44; and the reply of E.W.G. Masterman, 'Tell el-Ful and Khirbet Adaseh', *PEFQS* (1913), pp. 132-37, who found only Byzantine sherds at Adaseh.

14. See Albright, *Excavations and Results at Tell el-Ful (Gibeah of Saul)*. AASOR 4 (New Haven: Yale, 1924); and 'A New Campaign of Excavations at Gibeah of Saul', *BASOR* 52 (1933), pp. 6-13.

15. L. Sinclair, 'An Archaeological Study of Gibeah (Tell el-Ful)', AASOR 34-35 (New Haven: ASOR, 1960), pp. 1-52.

16. H.J. Franken and C.A. Franken-Batterschild, *A Primer in Old Testament Archaeology* (Leiden: Brill, 1963), p. 85.

17. P. Lapp, 'Tell el-Ful', *BA* 28 (1965), pp. 2-10.

18. Miller, 'Geba/Gibeah', pp. 145-66.

19. J. Graham in N. Lapp, ed., *The Third Campaign at Tell el-Ful: The Excavations of 1964*. AASOR 45 (Cambridge, Mass.: ASOR, 1981), p. 17.

20. Albright, AASOR 4, p. 32.

21. As shown long ago by R.A.S. Macalister, 'The Topography of Rachel's Tomb', *PEFQS* (1912), pp. 74-82. See also Miller, 'Geba/Gibeah', p. 159.

22. Albright, AASOR 4, p. 33.

23. Against Albright, AASOR 4, p. 38. That Tell el-Ful even possessed a watchtower at this time is also unlikely; Albright had assumed a fortress with tower at the end of the 12th century. Lapp's 1964 investigation moved the dates to 1025-950 which, even if correct, seemingly jeopardizes the assumption that Saul operated from such a building at the time of the Battle of Michmas; see p. xvii in N. Lapp, AASOR 45.

24. See my article 'Rimmon' in the forthcoming *ABD*.

25. See my article 'Migron' in the forthcoming *ABD*.

26. Josephus, *Antiquities of the Jews* V, 2:8.

27. Jerome, *Epistolae S. Hieronymi* ed. J.P.Migne, vol. 22, Epistle CVIII, col. 883.

28. Josephus, *Antiquities of the Jews*, Book VI, 6, 1, p. 180. There may have been a site named 'Gilgal' in the Benjaminite hill-country.

29. Josephus, *Wars of the Jews*, Book V, 2, 1, p. 775.

30. See Miller, 'Geba/Gibeah', p. 161; and C.R. Conder, 'Gibeah of Saul', *PEFQS* (1877), pp. 104-105.

31. Note especially the 20-30 stadia discrepancy if only one 'Gibeah' were intended. If Albright intended to argue that these figures were 'a careless estimate of distance' (AASOR 4, pp. 41-42), then he could not logically also rely on them so heavily in his own topographical arguments.

32. Miller, 'Geba/Gibeah', p. 162.

33. Albright, AASOR 4, pp. 7-8; 49.

34. See Albright, *BASOR* 52, p. 7, and Sinclair, AASOR 34-35, pp. 6-11.

35. Graham, AASOR 45, pp. 6-7, reports that 'substantially more evidence for a 12th century occupation was unearthed', but then claims that the subsequent fortress destroyed most of this evidence.

36. Albright, *BASOR* 52, p. 7.

37. Graham, AASOR 45, pp. 24-26. See also Sinclair, AASOR 34-35, p. 13; and Nancy Lapp, 'Casemate Walls in Palestine and the Late Iron II Casemate at Tell el-Ful (Gibeah)', *BASOR* 223 (1976), pp. 25-42, where the casemate wall is dated to the 'second half of the 7th Century B.C.'

38. Graham, AASOR 45, p. 26.

39. *Ibid.*, pp. 25-26.

40. P. Lapp, 'Tell el Ful', p. 4.

41. See Albright, *BASOR* 52, pp. 6-7, and Sinclair, AASOR 34-35, p. 8.

42. See chart in N. Lapp, AASOR 45, p. xvii; and P. Lapp, 'Tell el-Ful, p. 3.

43. N. Lapp, AASOR 45, p. xvii.

44. For example, Gibeon (el-Jib), Ramah (er-Ram), Bethel (Beitin), Geba (Jeba), Michmas (Mukhmas), Azemoth (Hizmeh), and Anatoth (Anata).

45. The word מערה would mean 'an open clearing', while the reading מערב would mean 'from the west'. See Gray, *Joshua, Judges, and Ruth*,

pp. 383 ff; Soggin, *Judges*, pp. 290-96; and Cundall, *Judges*, pp. 204-207.

46. The term for 'ford' or 'pass' appears both in the masculine (e.g. Gen. 32.23) and the feminine (e.g. 1 Sam. 14.4) forms; we could thus also emend the phrase to read מעברת־נבע.

47. See Rawnsley, 'The Rock of Pomegranate', *PEFQS* (1879), pp. 118-26.

48. See my article 'Migron' in the forthcoming *ABD*. The name Migron is similar in form to other toponyms designating wadis, e.g. Kidron, Arnon, Kishon, etc.

49. LXX's 'Aggai' in place of MT's 'Geba' probably transliterates a Hebrew version which described the army crossing the 'Valley' (הגי); namely, the Wadi es-Swenit.

50. 'Zion' is paralleled with 'Jerusalem' in Isa. 2.3; 4.3- 4; 10.12; 10.32; 24.23; 30.19; 31.9; 33.20; 37.22, 32; 'Jacob' is paralleled with 'Israel' in 10.20; 14.1; and 27.6; 'Ariel' is paralleled with 'City of David' in 29.1.

51. See Kallai, 'Notes on the Topography of Benjamin', *IEJ* 6 (1956), pp. 180-87.

52. Dialectical differences among the ancient Hebrew tribes are a difficult phenomenon to study. One well-known example is the different pronunciations of the Ephraimites and the Gileadites (Judg. 12.5-6). Yet the 'shibboleth' example only survived in the literature because it was a famous folk-tale exemplifying dialect differences with mortal consequences. Tribal dialect differences were probably largely dissolved in biblical literature under the influence of official national editing of the Hebrew scriptures. However, differences in official orthography may have influenced the variant Gibeah-Geba spellings. Northern versions spelled the name of the city הגבעה while Judean works spelled it גבע. It is unclear whether this difference was phonological, or merely orthographical. After the fall of Israel in 721, the 'Geba' spelling of the Judeans became standard in the surviving contemporary writings from Jerusalem; 'Gibeah' never appeared again in contemporary writings. Later editors, however, held tenaciously to sources which gave both spellings. For a discussion of dialectical differences in OT literature, cf. E. Ullendorff, 'The Knowledge of Languages in the Old Testament', *BJRL* 44 (1961-62), pp. 455-65. See also Rudolph, *Hosea*, pp. 20-21, for a discussion of peculiarities of northern speech as observed in the prophet Hosea.

53. Kallai, 'The Land of Benjamin and Mt Ephraim', in *Judea, Samaria, and the Golan*, ed. M. Kochavi, p. 183. Recently supportive of Gibeah's location at Jeba (and also critical of the archaeological case for Tell el-Ful), is Israel Finkelstein, *The Archaeology of the Israelite Settlement* (Jerusalem: Israel Exploration Society, 1988), pp. 56-60.

Notes to Chapter 3

1. Along with Judges 17-18. See Budde, 'Anhange', pp. 285-300; de Vaux, *Early History*, p. 68 ; Gray, *Joshua, Judges and Ruth*, pp. 237-43; Martin, *Judges*, pp. 181-82; Mayes, *Israel in the Period of the Judges*, p. 42; Herzberg, *Josua, Richter und Ruth*, p. 141; Cundall, *Judges and Ruth*, pp. 25-26; and Noth, *Dtr History*, p. 121, n. 29.

2. For example, Boling, 'In those days', p. 44; Veijola, *Das Königtum*, pp. 15-22; and Soggin, *Judges*, p. 263.

3. See the discussion of Miller, 'Jebus and Jerusalem: a Case of Mistaken Identity', *ZDPV* 90 (1974), pp. 115-27.

4. 'Sons of Belial' occurs in Deut. 13.14 and 15.9, 1 Sam. 1.16; 2.12; 10.27; 25.17; 2 Sam 20.1; 22.5; 1 Kgs 21.10, 13. For a discussion of the term, cf. Burney, *Judges*, pp. 467-69.

5. The word נבלה ('outrage, folly') is often found in the context of a sexual crime: Deut. 22.21; 2 Sam. 13.12; Jer. 29.23, but is also used in Josh. 7.5 to describe Achan's defiance of the ban, and 1 Sam. 25.25 to explain Nabal's name. Outside of a Dtr context, it is used in Gen. 34.7 to describe the rape of Dinah.

6. Veijola, *Das Königtum*, pp. 21-22. The phraseology recalls Deut. 9.7; 1 Sam. 8.8; 2 Sam. 7.6; 1 Kgs 8.16; 2 Kgs 21.15; Jer. 7.25; 11.7. See Childs, 'A Study of the Formula "Until This Day"', *JBL* 82 (1963), pp. 279-92.

7. The word שבט occurs over 18 times in Deuteronomy and only once in Leviticus

8. The phrase 'the whole people' appears in Deut. 16 times and in Lev. only twice.

9. Luther, 'Kahal', pp. 44-63. The term appears in Judg. 20.2; 21.5,8.

10. Veijola, *Das Königtum*, pp. 21-22.

11. As argued recently by Jüngling, *Richter 19*, pp. 59ff.

12. Veijola, *Das Königtum*, pp. 27-29. This same theme has been intruded into Judges 17-18 (17.6, 18.1), likewise altering the original meaning of these chapters.

13. Eissfeldt, *Introduction*, pp. 261-67.

14. For a discussion of the Levite as an addition to the story, cf. A. Gunneweg, 'Jdc. 19 und 20' in *Leviten und Priester* (Göttingen: Vandenhoeck & Ruprecht, 1965), pp. 23-26.

15. Levites were described as possessing no territory (Deut. 18.1), and were equated with strangers, the fatherless, and widows in Israelite law (Deut. 14.27-29; 16.11,14; 26.12). In Judges 17-18, Levitical characters also appear, suggesting that this story also underwent a Levitical redaction like 19-21 before final incorporation into the DH (cf. esp. Judg. 17.7-9).

16. For a treatment of the long-standing dispute between the Levites and the Zadokites, cf. R. Abba, 'Priests and Levites', *IDB* 3 (Nashville: Abingdon, 1962), pp. 876-89. See also Jüngling, *Richter 19*, p. 315.

17. LXX reads 'and she became angry', suggesting a mere argument. Soggin, *Judges*, p. 284, suggests that the Hebrew verb originally meant 'to quarrel'.

18. Lev. 20.10. Though Israelite law prescribed death for adultery, considerable doubt exists as to whether this sanction was carried out, since no instance of this penalty is recorded in the Hebrew Bible. For a discussion of the problem of the inapplicability of Israelite law to actual conditions, cf. H. McKeating, 'Sanctions Against Adultery in Ancient Israelite Society, with some reflections on Methodology in the study of Old Testament Ethics', *JSOT* 11 (1979), pp. 57-72.

19. For example, Bertheau, *Richter und Ruth*, pp. 265-74, who found an 'A source' with the term 'sons of Israel' and 'B source' with the 'man of Israel' idiom; Budde, *Richter und Samuel*, pp. 149-55, largely followed Bertheau's delineations, and noticed that the A and B sources mentioned Mizpah and Bethel, respectively, which he regarded as clues as to their origins; Burney, *Judges*, pp. 442-58, found another source, 'C', which identified the Israelite forces as 'the people'; Moore, *Judges*, pp. 36-42, believed that a E fragments supplemented a basic J narrative; Simpson, *Composition*, pp. 74-92, believed secondary J additions supplemented the basic J narrative; Gray, *Joshua, Judges, and Ruth*, pp. 239-43, preferred the relative simplicity of Burney's analysis, adding that Dtr had redacted the piece; and Besters, 'Sanctuaire', pp. 34-37, also largely followed Burney.

20. Judg. 20.1; 21.10, 13, 16; see B. Luther, '*Kahal* and *edah* als Hilfsmittel in der Quellenscheidung im Priesterkodex und in der Chronik', *ZAW* 56 (1938), pp. 44-63.

21. See Besters, 'Israel', p. 8. 'Sons of Israel' is a frequent term in Priestly materials, appearing, for example, 54 times in Leviticus and 171 times in Numbers versus only 21 times in Deuteronomy.

22. See J. Muilenberg, 'Mizpah', *IDB*, 407-409; 'Mizpah of Benjamin', *ST* 8 (1955), pp. 25-42; or my article on Mizpah in the forthcoming *ABD*.

23. See R. Smend, *Yahweh War and Tribal Confederation* (Nashville: Abingdon, 1970), p. 93.

24. Luther, 'Kahal', pp. 44-63.

25. The word שלמים occurs 27 times in Leviticus and never in Deuteronomy.

26. For a discussion of these changes, cf. Trible, 'An Unnamed Woman', p. 82; Niditch, 'Sodomite Theme', p. 371; and Lasine, 'Guest and Host', pp. 48-50.

27. Schunck, *Benjamin*, p. 63; Burney, *Judges*, p. 454; Bertheau, *Richter und Ruth*, pp. 267-68; Moore, *Judges*, p. 432; and Simpson, *Composition*, p. 85.

28. Gray, *Joshua, Judges and Ruth*, pp. 241-42.

29. The term איש ישראל here (20.1) might suggest that the tradition of refusing to marry a Benjaminite traces to the original written narrative.

30. The folk-tale behind this account undoubtedly preserves the memory of close connections between the tribe of Benjamin and Jabesh-Gilead, as is shown in 1 Samuel 11 when the Benjaminite strong-man Saul rescued the city from Ammonite attack.

31. For a full discussion of this approach, cf. Robert Alter, *The Art of Biblical Narrative* (New York: Basic Books, 1981); and Robert Culley, *Studies in the Structure of Hebrew Narrative* (Philadelphia: Fortress, 1976).

32. Walter Ong, *Orality and Literacy: The Technologizing of the Word* (New York: Methuen, 1982), especially pp. 31-77.

33. Mt Ephraim is probably Jebel Asur, the highest mountain in central Ephraim (Miller, 'Geba/Gibeah', p. 153). The notion that the story is Judean in origin (Burney, *Judges*, p. 443) on the basis of this geographical information is unsound. Even if the man's home is on the 'other side' of Mt Ephraim, this does not necessarily place the writer's viewpoint in Judah. Still less tenable is Trible's identification of these stories as 'Benjaminite' (Trible, 'An Unnamed Woman', pp. 65-91). The location of the action in Benjamin hardly implies the story's origin there, especially since the stories are so strongly anti-Benjaminite in tendency.

34. MT: 'committed adultery', LXX: 'became angry'. For a discussion of this discrepancy, see Trible, 'An Unnamed Woman', pp. 66-67.

35. For a discussion of two hospitality scenes, cf. Culley, *Studies*, pp. 54-55.

36. See Alter, *Art*, pp. 49-51, for a thorough discussion.

37. Burney, *Judges*, pp. 442-43; Simpson, *Composition*, pp. 74-81; Gray, *Joshua, Judges and Ruth*, p. 372. Against the argument that singular and plural verb forms are another indication of multiple sources, cf. Trible, 'An Unnamed Woman', p. 68, and Soggin, *Judges*, p. 285.

38. See Alter, *Art*, pp. 88-113; Hammond, 'The Bible and Literary Criticism—Part I', *CQ* 25 (1983), pp. 5-20; and S. Niditch, 'The "Sodomite" Theme in Judges 19–20: Family, Community, and Social Disintegration', *CBQ* 44 (1982), pp. 365-78. For a typical example of the multiple source theory, cf. Simpson, *Composition*, pp. 120-21.

39. Niditch, 'Sodomite Theme', pp. 366-67; Trible, 'An Unnamed Woman', pp. 65-66; and Martin, *Judges*, p. 200.

40. Trible, 'An Unnamed Woman', pp. 67-69; and Hammond, 'Bible—Part II', pp. 9-10.

41. For a discussion of this Jebus's probable identification and location, cf. Miller, 'Jebus and Jerusalem', pp. 115-27. As shown earlier in chapter 2, Ramah and Gibeah were not cities along the same route, but on two different routes running north from Jebus/Jerusalem, both roughly the same distance away.

42. See Alt, *Essays on Old Testament History and Religion* (Garden City, N.J.: Doubleday, 1967), p. 251, and Noth, *History*, p. 105, who thought the

account underwent only slight literary elaboration. Neither Alt nor Noth proved why the account was historical, and not fictional.

43. Wellhausen, *Prolegomena*, pp. 236-37, regarded the tales as fictional. Alter, *Art*, p. 24, suggested the term 'historicized prose fiction' for this sort of narrative.

44. Burney, *Judges*, pp. 442-44; Moore, *Judges*. ICC (New York: Scribner's, 1895), p. 405; Budde, *Richter und Samuel*, p. 150; and Gray, *Joshua, Judges and Ruth*, p. 240. Soggin, *Judges*, p. 282, claims that the author of Judges 19 has 'drawn considerably on Genesis 19'. Simpson, *Composition*, pp. 74-80, assigned virtually every verse with a Genesis parallel to 'J' authorship. Trible, 'An Unnamed Woman', pp. 74-75, thought the story would surface in the audience 'terrible memories' of the Sodom tragedy. Lasine, 'Guest and Host', p. 38, claimed that 'Judges 19 presupposes the reader's awareness of Genesis 19 in its present form, and depends on that awareness in order to be properly understood'. Finally, Hammond, 'Bible—Part II', p. 11, believed that the 'narrator is playing off the Book of Genesis with great care'.

45. See M. Pope, 'Homosexuality', *IDBS*, pp. 415-17. No homosexual interpretation of the Sodom tradition exists in any other references to it in the Old Testament: Deut. 29.23; Isa. 1.9; 13.19; Jer. 49.18; 50.40; Ezek. 16.46; Amos 4.11; Zeph. 2.9; Ps. 11.6; Lam. 4.6.

46. Lasine, 'Guest and Host', pp. 38-39: 'the events described in Judges 19 must be viewed together with Genesis 19 for the intended contrast between the two situations to make the reader aware of the topsy-turvy nature of the 'hospitality' in Gibeah'. Lasine and Hammond ('Bible—Part II', p. 11) both make ʼne critical mistake of interpreting the story only in its final, Dtr frame—a valid canonical-literary technique, but an unsound procedure for determining the literary intent of the original story.

47. So, for example, Simpson, *Composition*, pp. 74-80.

48. Niditch, 'Sodomite Theme', p. 375.

49. For an excellent discussion of this technique, see Ong, *Orality and Literacy*, pp. 31-77.

50. By 'type-story' I mean a basic progression of scenes or events which bring events to a resolving climax or outcome. A 'type-story' could function in larger frameworks and yet keep its narrative elements intact. It need never have existed in only one form, but the progression of events remained the same, and was utilized in varying contexts.

51. Von Rad, *Genesis*, pp. 218-21.

52. D.S. Bailey, *Homosexuality and the Western Tradition* (New York: Longmans, 1955), pp. 2-3, suggested that the term ידע ('to know') should not be interpreted sexually, a view adopted by J. Boswell, *Christianity, Tolerance, and Homosexuality* (Chicago: University Press, 1980), pp. 93-94. This view appears somewhat disingenuous, since in both stories virgins are offered who have not 'known' man. The demand to 'bring them out that we may know them' appears to be a highly ironic euphemism, couched in mock innocence,

which underscores the unspeakably vicious intent of the town's citizens.

53. For the classic treatment of this position, see Gottwald, *Tribes of Yahweh*. Many other modern studies reinforce this view, including, for example, Miller and Hayes, *HAIJ*, pp. 80-107.

54. G. Wallis, 'Die Stadt in den Überlieferungen der Genesis', *ZAW* 78 (1966), pp. 133-48.

55. The concern for hospitality appears in legal form in all the major legal codes of Israel; Covenant Code: Exod. 22.20; 23.9; Ritual Decalogue: Exod. 23.12; Twelve Curses: Deut. 27.19; Deuteronomistic Code: Deut. 14.29; 16.11; 18.19; Holiness Code: Lev. 19.33-34; 23.22; 25.36; and the Priestly Code: Num. 9.14; 15.14-16. Furthermore, the care of strangers is emphasized in many 'motive clauses' in ancient Israelite law; e.g. Exod. 23.9.

56. Homosexual behaviour is clearly proscribed in the OT only in duplicate passages in the Holiness Code, i.e. Lev. 18.22; 20.13. This legal code represents a limited Priestly circle of experience, is fraught with arcane ritualistic and taboo practices, and hardly represents general Israelite mores.

57. For a discussion of homosexual rape as a tool of class oppression, cf. Arno Karlen, *Sexuality and Homosexuality* (London, 1971), p. 414.

58. T. Gasten, *Myth, Legend, and Custom in the Old Testament* (New York: Harper and Row, 1909), p. 158, writes: 'the notion that itinerant strangers may be gods in disguise reappears in many other cultures. . . gods. . . often wander through cities in the guise of strangers in order to see for themselves the *hubris* of men on the one hand, and their decency of conduct on the other'. On p. 157: 'Buddhist legend relates similarly that once, when a wandering saint visited the city of Holaolakia, everyone rebuffed him except one man. The city was destroyed, but that man was spared'. The blinding of men of the city in Gen. 19.11 appears to have been an original ending to the supernatural version of the story. Its later attachment to the Sodom tradition then justified the destruction of the whole city.

59. Niditch, 'Sodomite Theme', pp. 367-69, overstresses the homosexual theme in the Judges version, emphasizing as she does its threat to 'proper family concepts'. As we have suggested above, the story must be understood through the aspect of the gang-rape, both in the threat to the man and the actual deed done to his wife. Niditch is on more solid ground in realizing that our Levitical version views the rape as an attack on the whole 'family' of Israel, not just one Ephraimite family.

60. The cruelty and misogyny of this act is starkly developed in Trible's treatment of the story ('An Unnamed Woman', pp. 73-79).

61. The troubling insensitivity of the story to its characters belies Niditch's assessment of Judges 19 as a 'beautifully crafted tale' ('Sodomite Theme', p. 377). The inconsistency of portraying a male who travels across

foreign territory to reconcile himself to his wife, but only hours later tosses her out to rapists like meat to dogs, cannot really be harmonized and remains the most unsatisfactory feature of the story; see Trible, 'An Unnamed Woman', pp. 65-91, who rightly points out the story's cold insensitivity to the woman in the story and, as such, the lack of profundity and humanity in the narrative. However, since the story is essentially a creation of political propaganda, it should be no wonder that the woman—and the man for that matter—are used like mere one-dimensional fictional props in a larger nationalistic scheme.

62. As noticed, for example, by Burney, *Judges*, p. 444; Budde, *Richter und Samuel*, p. 150; Schunck, *Benjamin*, p. 64; Soggin *Judges*, p. 282; Martin, *Judges*, p. 206; and Gray, *Joshua, Judges and Ruth*, p. 378.

63. Wallis, 'Eine Parallele zu Richter 19.29ff und 1 Sam. 11.5ff aus den Briefarchiv von Mari', *ZAW* 64 (1952), pp. 57-61.

64. So Mayes, *Israel in the Period of the Judges*, p. 80; Schunck, *Benjamin*, pp. 63-64; and Martin, *Judges*, p. 206. This totemistic 'call to war' ritual is meant to speak for itself in the story. The explanation accompanying Saul's oxen pieces ('the same will be done to the oxen of any man who does not follow Saul'—1 Sam. 11.7) is probably a late literary explanation of the bloodcurdling rite. Lasine's elaborate explanation that the Judges story 'presupposes' the account in 1 Sam. 11 is an overly rationalistic treatment which fails to let the Judges text speak for itself ('Guest and Host', pp. 41-43).

65. Judg. 20.11, 20, 22, 33, 36, 38, 39, 41, 42, 48.

66. The term is used in the account of Joshua's attack on the central hill country (Josh. 9.6, 7; 10.24). Note especially its use in the accounts of Gideon's attack on Midian (Judg. 7.8,14,23; 8.22) where the 'men of Israel' were called out from Naphtali, Asher, and Manasseh (7.23). The phrase is also used to describe the Israelites who saw that Abimelech of Shechem had died (Judg. 9.55).

67. Various terms for 'Israelites' including איש ישראל appear to be early, whereas the term 'sons of Israel' is usually late. For a full discussion of this phenomenon, cf. A. Besters, '"Israel" et "Is d'Israel" dans les livres historiques (Genèse-2 Rois)', *RB* 74 (1967), pp. 5-23.

68. As was partially recognized by Rösel, 'Studien zur Topographie der Kriege (II)', p. 34. Rösel believed that the battle reports in Judges 20 and Joshua 7-8 are derived from a single, earlier source.

69. F.M. Abel, 'Les strategèmes dans le livre de Josué', *RB* 56 (1949), pp. 321-39. Accounts of this basic ambush strategy as used by the Romans and Carthaginians can be found on pp. 331-32.

70. For a thorough, annotated discussion of historical and archaeological problems related to the conquest narratives, see Miller, 'The Israelite Occupation of Canaan', *IJH*, pp. 213-84. For a discussion of archaeological and historical problems related to Ai, see J.A. Callaway, 'New Evidence on the Conquest of Ai', *JBL* 87 (1968), pp. 312-20.

71. As proposed by Roth, 'Hinterhalt und Scheinflucht', pp. 296-304, who argues that the Judges 20 ambush recalls an actual defeat inflicted on Benjamin by Ephraim. In turn, Roth proposes that the Ai ambush account developed as a Benjaminite answer to their ethnic shame. The same story was applied to a local ruin in order to praise the imaginary Benjaminite defeat of the Canaanite city of Ai. De Vaux, *Early History*, pp. 618-19, believed that the 'Bethel source' was responsible for the account of the ambush of Gibeah. We propose that his so-called 'Bethel source' actually represents the final Dtr redaction.

72. Alt, 'Josua', *KS* I, pp. 176-89; and Noth, *Josua*, pp. 11ff., argued that the conquest traditions of Joshua 1-12 were Benjaminite stories which did not originally contain the figure of Joshua.

73. Gottwald, *Tribes*, pp. 748-49, n. 249.

74. O. Eissfeldt, 'Der geschichtliche Hintergrund der Erzählung von Gibeas Schandtat (Richter 19-21)', *Kleine Schriften II* (Tübingen: Mohr, 1963), pp. 64-80, suggested that Judges 20 reflected a genuine historical memory. B. MacDonald, *Benjamin*, pp. 66-72, proposed that southern tribes broke off from Ephraim, giving rise to Gen. 35.18-19, the account of Benjamin's tragic birth from Rachel; see also Schunck, *Benjamin*, pp. 57-79. Benjamin's name, 'son of the south', would derive by way of reference to its origin in Ephraim to the north. S. Talmon, 'In Those Days There Was No King In Israel', *Immanuel* 5 (1975), pp. 27-36, theorized that a land dispute caused the rift between the tribes. Gottwald, *Tribes*, pp. 748-49, n. 249, blamed Benjamin's raiding proclivities. See also de Vaux, *Early History*, p. 706; Soggin, *Judges*, pp. 282-83; Budde, *Richter und Samuel*, p. 147; and Mayes, *Israel in the Period of the Judges*, p. 83.

Notes to Chapter 4

1. For a discussion of this overall theological design, cf. especially Mayes, *Story*, pp. 81-105, or 'Rise', pp. 1-19 and Childs, *Introduction*, pp. 277-78, which contains an analysis of theological implications. A treatment of the contrasting views of kingship as a problem in Israel can be found in D. McCarthy, 'The Inauguration of Monarchy in Israel: A Form-Critical Study of 1 Samuel 8-12', *Int* 27 (1973), pp. 401-12.

2. See Chapter 1, section 6; our identification of the Dtr additions follows Noth, *Deuteronomistic History*, pp. 47, 54, except for the versification of the Mizpah episode (1 Sam. 10.17-25). This particular account of Saul's rise to kingship is suggestive of popular folklore. Questions have been raised as to whether this tale is perhaps a conflation of two tales—one in which Saul is selected by lot (10.20-21b), and one in which he is designated king by Samuel's prophetic oracle because of his height (10.21b-24); cf. Eissfeldt, *Komposition der Samuelbücher*, p. 7; Noth, *Deuteronomistic History*, pp. 49-

50; and Birch, 'Rise', pp. 72-90. The tale's comic tone suggests an anti-Saul tendency, as if the king achieved his office only through luck. This motif might have suited DH well; for a discussion of the Dtr editing of 1 Sam. 10.16-27 see Mayes, 'Rise', pp. 285-331; see also Noth, *Deuteronomistic History*, pp. 47-49, 51; Schunck, *Benjamin*, pp. 81-82. But see also Birch, 'Choosing of Saul', pp. 447-57, who finds no Dtr influence. For the theory that the tale may have originated as a 'sanctuary legend' of Mizpah, see Weiser, *Samuel*, p. 63, and my discussion of Mizpah in the forthcoming *ABD*.

3. See, for example, Lods, *Israel*, p. 354; Schunck, *Benjamin*, pp. 110-12; Wildberger, 'Samuel', pp. 442-69; Mayes, *Story of Israel*, p. 89; Miller, 'Saul's Rise', pp. 157-74; Tryggve Mettinger, *King and Messiah*, CBOTS 8 (Lund: Gleerup, 1976), p. 97; Edelman, 'Saul's Rescue of Jabesh-Gilead', pp. 195-209; and Baruch Halpern, *The Constitution of the Monarchy in Israel*, HSM 25, 1981 (Chico, Calif: Scholars, 1982), pp. 155-56.

4. Miller, 'Saul's Rise', pp. 162, 171; Mettinger, *King and Messiah*, p. 97. See also Halpern, *Constitution*, pp. 155-56.

5. See Edelman, *Rise of the Israelite State*, pp. 206-207, who does not find cogent reasons for such a Dtr literary move.

6. For a discussion of this folktale, see Gressmann, 'Die Älteste', pp. 26-27; Weiser, *Samuel*, pp. 48-61; Seebass, 'Vorgeschichte', pp. 155-71. See Birch, 'The Development of the Tradition of the Anointing of Saul in 1 Sam. 9.1-10.16', *JBL* 90 (1971), pp. 55-68 for a careful delineation of the original folktale.

7. Birch, 'Anointing', p. 58, follows Gressmann's suggestions.

8. Lods, *Israel*, p. 353, had suggested that the tale was entirely fictional, a suggestion Birch, 'Anointing', pp. 67-68, rejects.

9. See Miller, 'Saul's Rise', pp. 171-73. Miller considers the seer's subsequent identification as Samuel, and the account of Saul's anointment as prince, to be later additions to the folktale; indeed, the Samuel accounts in general may be additions to the Saul stories. Among other scholars who envision such Samuel additions in 9.1-10.16 are Seebass, 'Vorgeschichte', pp. 157-58; Hauer, 'Does 1 Samuel', p. 306; Hertzberg, *Samuel*, pp. 78-80; Crüsemann, *Widerstand*, pp. 57ff.; Weiser, *Old Testament*, pp. 157-69; Schmidt, *Menschliche*, pp. 58-102; and Van Seters, *Search*, pp. 254-56.

10. Mayes, 'Rise', pp. 17-18.

11. For example, John Sturdy, 'The Original Meaning of "Is Saul also among the Prophets?" (1 Sam. 10.11, 12; 19.24)', *VT* 20 (1970), pp. 206-13. Also regarding the saying as secondary to the original context: V. Epstein, 'Was Saul also among the Prophets?', *ZAW* 81 (1969), pp. 287-304, and J. Lindblom, 'Saul inter Prophetas', *ASTI* 9 (1973), pp. 30-41.

12. Edelman, *Rise of the Israelite State*, p. 209.

13. *Ibid.*, pp. 208-209. The suggestion was originally advanced by D.R. Ap-Thomas, 'Saul's "Uncle"', *VT* 11 (1961), pp. 241-45, and adopted by

P. Ackroyd, *The First Book of Samuel*, CBC (Cambridge: Cambridge University Press, 1971), p. 86. Against the claim that Saul's meeting with his uncle belonged to an early version of the folktale (Schmidt, *Menschlicher Erfolg*, pp. 58-102), Miller, 'Saul's Rise', p. 160, argued that 1 Sam. 10.13-16 is a Dtr addition intended to allow for the transition to the account of Saul's election at Mizpah which follows in DH since 10.16-25 necessitates Saul's secrecy concerning his pre-selection as Israel's king. Miller also points out that Saul's conversation with his uncle rather than his father in the addition supposes the editor's awareness that Saul and his father Kish were not residents of Gibeah.

14. E.g. Hertzberg, *Samuel*, pp. 75, 80, who follows Wellhausen's conjecture and places Kish's home in Gibeah, identified with Tell el-Ful. Likewise, Noth, *History*, p. 168, states, 'Saul, son of Kish, was a Benjaminite from the Benjaminite village of Gibeah (modern Tell el-Ful)'. Edelman, *Rise of the Israelite State*, pp. 213-16, argues that Saul belonged to the landed gentry of Gibeon. The tradition which remembers Saul's slaughter of the inhabitants of Gibeon (2 Sam. 21.1) makes such a proposal unlikely.

15. Khirbet es-Salah (g.n. 169134) would retain the Hebrew toponym. Saul was buried in Zela in his father's grave (2 Sam. 21.14), which would imply a family-owned plot; see Schunk, *Benjamin*, p. 118 n. 41; Blenkinsopp, *Gibeon*, pp. 59-60; Seebass, *David, Saul und das Wesen des biblischen Glaubens* (Neukirchen-Vluyn: Neukirchener Verlag, 1980), p. 70 n. 33; and M. Tsevat, 'Studies in the Books of Samuel, part II', *HUCA* 33 (1962), pp. 107-18. Miller, 'Sauls Rise', pp. 159-60, also suggests that the 'Zelzah' of 1 Sam. 10.2 is a corruption of 'Zela', and thus, the two men who informed him that the asses had been found were fellow villagers.

16. 1 Sam. 13.5 reads '30,000 chariots, 6,000 horses, and infantry as countless as the sands of the seashore'. These figures are recognized as exaggerated even by Hauer, 'The Shape of Saulide Strategy', *CBQ* 31 (1969), p. 153-67, in his otherwise traditional discussion of the battle. These are inflated figures typical of late editorial work.

17. See Birch, *Rise*, p. 124; Noth, *Deuteronomistic History*, p. 54, and Schunck, *Benjamin*, pp. 107-108, who thinks it is from Dtr. Gunn, *Fate of King Saul*, pp. 40, 66-67, reading the story in its final form, interprets Saul's rejection as a punishment for his failure to proceed to Gilgal as commanded after his prophetic ecstasy at Gibeah (1 Sam. 10.8). The arbitrary quality of Samuel's judgment is a very unsatisfying feature of the canonical version and points to the artificiality of its arrangement.

18. The fact that both stories envision 600 Benjaminite soldiers hiding out at the Pomegranate Rock (Rock of Rimmon) probably indicates that a local oral tradition has been incorporated in both stories. Rawnsley, 'The Rock of Pomegranate', p. 119, reported in the 19th century that a contemporary Arab tradition held that the cave at his proposed 'Pomegranate Rock' (Mugharet el-Jai) could hold 600 men. See my article on Rimmon in the forthcoming *ABD*.

19. See my article on Migron in the forthcoming *ABD*.

20. Miller, 'Saul's Rise', p. 161, and H. Stoebe, 'Zur Topographie und Überlieferung der Schlacht von Mikmas, 1 Sam. 13 und 14', *TZ* 21 (1965), pp. 269-80.

21. Gottwald, *Tribes*, pp. 420-25. Gottwald's analysis of the Hebrew tribes is a major step toward understanding the social condition of the early Israelites. However, the catalyst which united them would not seem to be ideological so much as military. T. Ishida, *Royal Dynasties in Ancient Israel*, BZAW 142 (New York: de Gruyter, 1977), pp. 26-54, sees Saul as a שׁפט (judge) style deliverer who acceded to the popular call for a stronger royal institution in order to face the threatening Philistines. See also W. Evans, 'An Historical Reconstruction of the Emergence of Israelite Kingship and the Reign of Saul', in *Scripture in Context II. More Essays in Comparative Method*, ed. W. Hallo *et al.* (Winona Lake, Ind.: Eisenbraun's, 1983), pp. 61-77.

22. See McCarthy, 'Inauguration', p. 409; Weiser, *Samuel*, pp. 46-94; and G. Wallis, 'Die Anfänge des Königtums in Israel', pp. 45-66.

23. Jabesh-Gilead is usually identified with Tell Abu Kharaz on the Wadi Yabis in Jordan; cf. N. Glueck, *Explorations in Eastern Palestine IV*, pp. 261-75.

24. Among historians regarding the account as historical: Noth, *History*, pp. 169-71; Herrmann, *History*, pp. 133-34; Bright, *History*, p. 167; de Vaux, *History*, p. 788; Mettinger, *King and Messiah*, p. 86; W. Beyerlin, 'Das Königscharisma bei Saul', *ZAW* 73 (1961), pp. 187-201; F. Langlamet, 'Les récits de l'institution de la royauté israélite (1 Sam. vii-xii)', *RB* 77 (1970), pp. 161-200; P. Kyle McCarter, *1 Samuel*, AB (Garden City, N.Y.: Doubleday, 1980), p. 207; Wildberger, 'Samuel', pp. 442-68; Boecker, 'Beurteilung', p. 59; Mayes, 'Rise', pp. 1-19; Fritz, 'Deutungen', pp. 346-62; and Miller, 'Saul's Rise', pp. 157-74.

25. Following the initial suggestion of Lods, *Israel*, p. 354, are: Schunck, *Benjamin*, pp. 110-12; Wildberger, 'Samuel', pp. 442-69; Mayes, *Story of Israel*, p. 89; Miller, 'Saul's Rise', pp. 157-74; and Edelman, *Rise of the Israelite State*, pp. 261-65. Other scholars who retain the traditional chronology are, for example: Noth, *History*, pp. 164-74; Hauer, 'Saulide Strategy', pp. 153-67; Seebass, 'Vorgeschichte', pp. 155-71; and Blenkinsopp, 'Historical Saul', pp. 75-99.

26. Schunck, *Benjamin*, pp. 110-12.

27. Miller, 'Saul's Rise', pp. 167-68.

28. Edelman, *Rise of the Israelite State*, pp. 261-62.

29. Miller, 'Saul's Rise', pp. 165-67, would begin the Jabesh-Gilead account with 1 Sam. 10.26b; other scholars regard all of the vv. 26-27 as editorial transitions: Noth, *Deuteronomistic History*, pp. 50-51; Birch, *Rise*, pp. 87-89; and Van Seters, *Search*, pp. 256-57. While v. 26 now appears to connect with the preceding account, there is no reason why the Jabesh-

Gilead account would not have begun with the notice of Saul's going to Gibeah, presumably after already having chased the Philistines from the region.

30. See Edelman, *Rise of the Israelite State*, p. 264, or 'Saul's Rescue', pp. 206-207.

31. The cultic nature of this act as a 'call to war' would suggest that the explanation in 1 Sam. 11.7b that Saul would 'do the same to the oxen of any man who did not follow him' might merely be an aetiological explanation of the rite. Note also that Samuel has been subsequently intruded into this context.

32. See Seebass, 'Vorgeschichte', pp. 165-69; Wildberger, 'Samuel', pp. 466-69; Boecker, 'Beurteilung', p. 59n 2; and Budde, *Richter und Samuel*, p. 173 n. 1. Mayes, 'Rise', pp. 1-19, and *Story of Israel*, p. 167 n. 19, rejects the theory that vv. 12-15 are additions, but Van Seters, *Search*, p. 256, views vv. 12-14 as redactional. Miller, 'Saul's Rise', pp. 169-71, argues that the verses contain the memory of Saul's overcoming factional hostility (10.27) with the account of popular acclamation.

33. Miller, *HAIJ*, pp. 138-39.

34. See Blenkinsopp, 'Did Saul Make Gibeon his Capital?', pp. 1-7; and Edelman, *Rise of the Israelite State*, esp. pp. 202-12, who holds that Dtr suppressed the fact that Gibeon served as Saul's base. While Edelman convincingly demonstrates the presence at Gibeon in this era of a major high-place, she by no means proves it was the sole 'national sanctuary' for Israel, or that Saul was in any way connected to it.

35. See J. Flanagan, 'Judah in All Israel', in *No Famine in the Land. Studies in Honor of John L. MacKenzie* (Missoula: Scholars, 1975), pp. 101-16. Blenkinsopp, 'Historical Saul', p. 97 n. 44, questions Saul's Transjordan conquests. Hauer, 'Does 1 Samuel 9.1–11.15 reflect the Extension of Saul's Dominions?', *JBL* 86 (1967), pp. 306-10, building on Hertzberg's theory (*Samuel*, pp. 78-91) that three accounts of Saul's rise derive from three sanctuaries, proposes that each account reflects the extension of Saul's control over the surrounding areas, with Gibeah in the center. See also Mayes, 'Period of the Judges', *JH*, p. 329; and Wallis, *Geschichte und Überlieferung*, pp. 63-66.

36. For example, see Mayes, 'Period of the Judges', *IJH*, p. 326; Morton, 'Gibeah', *IDB* 2, p. 390; and Demsky, 'Geba, Gibeah, and Gibeon', p. 28. An even more questionable development is the way in which the report of simple foundations of a tower at Tell el-Ful became the description of 'Israel's first capitol building'; cf. Mauchline, *Samuel*, p. 104.

37. Much of the debate regarding the substantiality of Saul's kingdom turns on the length of his reign. The MT of 1 Sam. 13.1 reads 'two years', not impossible in view of the fact that the Michmas battle and the Ammonite rescue seem to have taken place within a month of each other (11.1), and that little else of Saul's campaigns is preserved. This short reign would make the

formation of a royal government nearly impossible; cf. Noth, *History*, pp. 176-77, and Mayes, 'Period of the Judges', *IJH*, p. 329. For an emendation of the text creating a longer reign, cf. for example, Blenkinsopp, 'Historical Saul', pp. 75-99.

38. For detailed discussions of the stories of David's rise to power, see the following titles, grouped according to their conclusions regarding the era in which the stories were written. Time of David: Nubel, *David Aufstieg in der frühen israelitischen Geschichtsschreibung*; Flanagan, 'Judah in All Israel', pp. 101-16. Time of Solomon: Ward, *Story of David's Rise*; Weiser, 'Die Legitimation', pp. 325-54; von Rad, *Der Heilige Krieg*, p. 41. After the Division of the Kingdom: Grønbaeck, *Die Geschichte vom Aufstieg Davids*; Schicklberger, 'Die Davididen und das Nordreich', pp. 255-63. For a theory that places these stories in the reign of Jehu, see J. Conrad, 'Zum geschichtlichen Hintergrund der Darstellung von Davids Aufstieg', *ThLZ* 5 (1972), pp. 322-32.

39. See Blenkinsopp, 'Historical Saul', pp. 81-82.

40. Ward, *Story of David's Rise*, pp. 13-18.

41. So Soggin, 'The Davidic-Solomonic Kingdom', *IJH*, p. 326; and von Rad, *Der Heilige Krieg*, p. 41, who links the projection to the Solomonic court.

42. The 'Gibeah Complex', with its imaginary court scenes, was probably unconsciously influential in the assumption that the excavations at Tell el-Ful had uncovered the remains of an impressive 'fortress'; cf. Albright, *BASOR* 52, pp. 6-13.

43. The MT places the tamarisk 'in Ramah', but the LXX reading 'at the high place' ought to be preferred since the scene just mentioned Saul at Gibeah.

44. H. Cazelles, 'David's Monarchy and the Gibeonite Claim', *PEQ* 87 (1955), pp. 165-75. See also Blenkinsopp, 'Historical Saul', esp. pp. 88-89.

45. Reading the MT. LXX's 'Gibeon of Saul' is unlikely since the name is unattested elsewhere. The reading is probably a scribe's accidental reading of 'Gibeon', which occurs six times in the same passage.

46. David's sparing of Mephibaal (2 Sam. 21.7) is reported as an act of mercy, but in fact the crippled grandson of Saul was probably kept in virtual house-arrest in Jerusalem, cf. 2 Sam. 4.4; 9.1-13.

47. These texts are problematical. LXX reads 'Gabeah son of Benjamin' in 2 Sam. 23.29 and 'from the hill of Benjamin' in 1 Chron. 11.31.

48. Albright, *Archaeology and the Religion of Israel*, pp. 121-25.

49. Mazar, 'Cities of the Priests and Levites', pp. 193-205.

50. In 1 Sam. 11.4, the MT reads 'Gibeah of Saul'.

51. See H. Stoebe, 'Zur Topographie', pp. 269-80; Miller, 'Saul's Rise', esp. 162-65; F. Schicklberger, 'Jonatan's Heldentat', pp. 324-33; Jobling, 'Saul's Fall and Jonathan's Rise', pp. 367-76 and 'Jonathan', in *The Sense of Biblical Narrative: Three Structural Analyses in the Old Testament*, JSOTS 7 (Sheffield: JSOT, 1978), pp. 4-25.

52. As recognized by Budde, *Richter und Samuel*, p. 206.

53. For a full treatment of holy war elements in this story, cf. Blenkinsopp, 'Jonathan's Sacrilege', pp. 427-36. See also P. Davies, 'Ark or Ephod in 1 Sam. xiv.18?', *JTS* 26 (1975) pp. 82-87.

54. See Blenkinsopp, 'Jonathan's Sacrilege', pp. 444-49.

55. This basic approach to the Jonathan narratives has also been taken by Jobling, 'Saul's Fall and Jonathan's Rise', pp. 367-76. For a treatment of the structure of the Jonathan narratives, see Jobling, 'Jonathan: A Structural Study in 1 Samuel', in *SBL 1976 Seminar Papers*, ed. George MacRae, pp. 15-32. For two rather literal renditions of Jonathan's deference to David, cf. for example J. Morgenstern, 'David and Jonathan', *JBL* 78 (1959), pp. 322-25, and T. Horner, *Jonathan Loved David: Homosexuality in Biblical Times* (Philadelphia: Westminster, 1977).

56. See Blenkinsopp, 'Jonathan's Sacrilege', esp. pp. 427-31.

57. David's lament over Saul and Jonathan's death (2 Sam. 1.19-27) probably derives from the same circles of Davidic literature which produced the account of Jonathan's raid. This literature thus attempted to portray David as the gracious successor to Saul, while re-emphasizing the David-Jonathan relationship. For two detailed analyses of the piece which accept Davidic authorship, see D. Freedman, 'The Refrain in David's Lament over Saul and Jonathan', in *Ex Orbe Religionem I* (Leiden: Brill, 1972), pp. 115-26; W. Holladay, 'Form and Word-play in David's Lament over Saul and Jonathan', *VT* 20 (1970), pp. 153-89. Except for the final defeat at Gilboa (1 Sam. 31.2), where he was killed, Jonathan is not mentioned in other military feats of Saul. The mention of Jonathan among the three sons of Saul killed in the battle may, in fact, be the only other occurrence of his name in Israelite story telling (except for 1 Sam. 13.2) before the activities of the pro-Davidic literary sphere in late tenth-century Jerusalem.

58. Dalman, 'Der Pass von Michmas', prefers to locate Bozez on the south, and Seneh on the north; the text is not clear on this point.

59. Josephus, *Jewish War*, 5, 2.1. See Conder, 'Gibeah of Saul', *PEFQS* (1877), pp. 104-105.

60. Dalman, 'Der Pass von Michmas', pp. 161-79.

61. For discussions of 1 Samuel 13-14 which regard Geba and Gibeah as separate places and which are forced to emend the text, see Hertzberg, *Samuel*, pp. 101-13; Ackroyd, *1 Samuel*, pp. 101-107; Mauchline, *1 & 2 Samuel*, pp. 111-17; Driver, *Samuel*, pp. 98-108; Hauer, 'Saulide Strategy', pp. 153-67; Albright, 'Excavations at Tell el-Ful', esp. pp. 28-43; Noth, *History*, pp. 173-74 (though Noth adds that 'the similarity between the two names and the fact that they can be easily confused makes it impossible to come to a definite decision', cf. note 1); Bright, *History*, p. 168; Schunck, *Benjamin*, p. 110 n. 6, who suggests that 'Gibeah' was changed to 'Geba' in order deliberately to hide the fact that the first Israelite capital also housed the Philistine governor; Birch, *Rise*, pp. 129-31; Budde, *Richter und Samuel*,

pp. 204-206; Blenkinsopp, 'Jonathan's Sacrilege', pp. 431-36, who connects all these events with the *Gibeon* high place.

Notes to Chapter 5

1. H. Donner, 'The Separate States of Israel and Judah', *IJH*, pp. 390-91.

2. The location of Mizpah was once much disputed. Robinson, *Biblical Researches*, p. 460, originally suggested Nebi Samwil because of its impressive panoramic view and its proximity to Ramah some 6 kms. to the northeast. This view won wide acceptance; see Albright, 'Mizpah and Beeroth', AASOR 4 (1924), esp. pp. 90-92; and James Muilenberg, 'Survey of the Literature on Tell en-Nasbeh' in *Tell en-Nasbeh: Excavated under the Direction of the Late W.F. Badé*, ed. C.C. McCown (New Haven: ASOR, 1947), pp. 13-22. Nebi Samwil has since proved archaeologically unacceptable; see C. McCown, 'The Archaeological Problem' in *Tell en-Nasbeh*, pp. 55-56; and Kochavi, *Judea, Samaria, and the Golan*, p. 186. Alt's suggestion of Tell en-Nasbeh, a mound located on the watershed highway 3 kms. north of Ramah, however, proved fruitful; see 'Mizpah in Benjamin', *PJB* 6 (1910), pp. 46-62. Tell en-Nasbeh not only retains the Hebrew toponym Mizpah, but exhibits archaeological features which closely match the requirements for biblical Mizpah; see McCown, *Tell en-Nasbeh*, 189-203; Muilenberg, 'Literary Sources', pp. 43-44, and 'Mizpah of Benjamin', *ST* 8 (1965), pp. 25-42. Muilenberg shows that Mizpah's so-called role in pre-monarchical times (1 Sam. 7; 10.17 and Judges 20-21) actually represents the retrojection into ancient times of its acknowledged religious significance after the fall of Jerusalem. See my article on Mizpah in the forthcoming *ABD*.

3. Josephus mentions this route in the description of Titus' invasion of Jerusalem in 70 AD.

4. Donner, 'Separate States', *IJH*, p. 391, contends that this boundary between Judah and Israel remained basically unchanged from the time of Asa to the fall of Samaria. Aharoni, *Land of the Bible*, pp. 282-83; and Schunck, *Benjamin*, p. 155, also place the border in the Wadi el-Qelt and the Wadi es-Swenit, as do Kallai-Kleinmann, 'Notes on the Topography of Benjamin', *IEJ* 6 (1956), pp. 180-87 and Dalman, 'Palästinische Wege und die Bedrohung Jerusalems nach Jes. 10', *PJB* 12 (1916), pp. 37-57.

5. Since both the watershed and eastern highways converge in Israel at Bethel, the northern kingdom probably needed only one border fortress at this location.

6. Aharoni, 'Arad: Its Inscriptions and Temple', *BA* 31 (1968), pp. 2-32.

7. This view was expressed to the author by Aharoni at Beer-Sheva in 1974. In the northern kingdom, Dan and Bethel served as the north and south border sanctuaries. For other possible Judean border-sanctuary locations, cf. Aharoni, *Land of the Bible*, p. 351.

8. Aharoni, 'The Horned Altar of Beer-Sheba', *BA* 37 (1974), pp. 2-6.

9. The MT reads רמה, but LXX more plausibly suggests an original במה, or 'high-place'; there is no tradition linking Saul to Ramah as a headquarters.

10. Mizpah likewise served as a border-sanctuary, as is suggested by its cultic significance as a successor to Jerusalem after the destruction of the temple (cf. Jer. 41 which seems to mention a 'house of the Lord' there.)

11. Donner, 'Separate States', *IJH*, p. 391.

12. J. Begrich, 'Der Syrische-Ephraimitische Krieg und seine weltpolitischen Zusammenhänge', in *Gesammelte Studien zum Alten Testament*, ed. Walther Zimmerli, *TB* 21 (München: Kaiser, 1964), pp. 99-120, views the war as an attempt by Syria and Israel to force Judah into a coalition to block Tiglath-Pileser's advance on the eve of his invasion of Philistia. Begrich has been followed in the view by, e.g. Albright, 'The Son of Tabeel (Isaiah 7.6)', *BASOR* 140 (1955), pp. 34-35; Noth, *History*, pp. 259-60; Hermann, *History*, p. 247; and Bright, *History*, pp. 256-57. For a recent summary of these positions and a fresh treatment of the war, see Michael Thompson, *Situation and Theology. Old Testament Interpretations of the Syro-Ephraimite War* (Sheffield: Almond, 1982).

13. See B. Oded, 'The Historical Background of the Syro-Ephraimite War Reconsidered', *CBQ* 34 (1972), pp. 153-65.

14. See Oded, 'Syro-Ephraimite War Reconsidered', pp. 162- 65. For a new estimation of Rezin's designs and strategy, see Miller and Hayes, *HAIJ*, 323-26; and John Hayes and Stuart Irvine, *Isaiah: The Eighth Century Prophet* (Nashville: Abingdon, 1987), pp. 42-46.

15. For evidence of Rezin's connections with Tyre, cf. D.J. Wiseman, 'A Fragmentary Inscription of Tiglath-Pileser III from Nimrud', *Iraq* 18 (1956), pp. 117-29. Line 5 of the Assyrian fragments ND 4301 + 4305 reads: '[H]iram of Tyre who with Rezin of [Damascus]'; Wiseman dates this reference to Tiglath-Pileser's campaign of 734-32 (p. 120). Concerning Rezin's relations with Philistia, see I. Eph'al, *The Ancient Arabs* (Jerusalem: Magnes, 1982), p. 24, for a reference to an Assyrian fragment (Lay. 29b) which associates Rezin with Mitinti of Ashkelon, who was killed in the aftermath of the latter's defeat. Eph'al sees a connection between the removal of Mitinti from kingship and the defeat of Rezin (p. 27, n. 70, and p. 84).

16. 2 Kgs 15.37; 16.5; Isa. 7.1,4,5,8; 2 Chron. 28.5-6. Oded, 'Syro-Ephraimite War Reconsidered', pp. 162-63, suggests that Pekah was placed on the throne in Samaria by Rezin.

17. The account of the Syro-Ephraimite War in 2 Chron. 28 mentions attacks by the Philistines on Judah which appear to be coordinated with attacks by Aram, Israel, and Edom.

18. Albright, 'The Son of Tabeel', pp. 34-35, identified this figure as Ayanur from the land of Tab'el; but the Assyrian text in which this name was found referred to the period after the fall of Damascus in 732. See also Oded, 'Syro-Ephraimite War Reconsidered', pp. 161-62.

19. See L. Levine, 'Menachem and Tiglath-Pileser: A New Synchronism', *BASOR* 206 (1972), pp. 40-42.

20. Asurmendi, *La Guerra Siro-Efraimita*, pp. 51-54; see also Miller and Hayes, *HAIJ*, p. 236, and Hayes and Irvine, *Isaiah*, p. 46.

21. Against Donner, 'Separate States', *IJH*, p. 429; Noth, *History*, pp. 258ff; and Herrmann, *History*, pp. 246ff., who would place the invasion of Judah in 734 while Tiglath-Pileser campaigned in Philistia. Thompson, *Situation and Theology*, pp. 111-12, more plausibly places the invasion in 735, early in the reign of Pekah. This chronology is also suggested by Cazelles, 'Problèmes de la guerre Syro-Ephraimite', *Eretz Israel* 14 (Jerusalem: IES, 1978), pp. 70-78, though he has Jotham as king at this time.

22. See Bright, *History*, p. 272; and Gottwald, *All the Kingdoms of the Earth. Israelite Prophecy and International Relations in the Ancient Near East* (New York: Harper and Row, 1964), p. 149. Thompson, *Situation and Theology*, p. 111, considers this possibility an 'open question'.

23. Wolff's translation, *Hosea*, p. 104, suggests 'terrify Benjamin' based on LXX.

24. For example, E. Good, 'Hosea 5.8-6.6: An Alternative to Alt', *JBL* 85 (1966), pp. 273-86; and G.A. Danell, *Studies in the Name Israel* (Uppsala, 1946), p. 138.

25. So Alt, 'Hosea 5.8: Ein Krieg und seine Folgen in prophetischer Beleuchtung', in *KS* II (München: Beck, 1959), pp. 163-87; Wolff, *Hosea*, pp. 110-12; Mays, *Hosea*, pp. 86-87; Bright, *History*, p. 256; Asurmendi, *La Guerra Siro-Efraimita*, pp. 111-16; Noth, *History*, pp. 259-60; Herrmann, *History*, p. 247; Gottwald, *All the Kingdoms of the Earth*, p. 129; W. Rudolph, *Hosea*. KAT (Gerd Mohn: Gütersloher, 1966), pp. 125-26; J. Ward, *Hosea: A Theological Commentary* (New York: Harper and Row, 1966), pp. 106-108; J. Jeremias, *Der Prophet Hosea*. ATD (Göttingen: Vandenhoeck & Ruprecht, 1983), pp. 80-81; and Thompson, *Situation and Theology*, pp. 66-67. F. Andersen and D. Freedman, *Hosea*. AB (New York: Doubleday, 1980), pp. 399-410, find no definite historical setting for the passage, but allow that it represents some Judean invasion of Ephraim.

26. So Thompson, *Situation and Theology*, p. 19, and Andersen/Freedman, *Hosea*, pp. 399-410.

27. The Assyrian invasion of Tiglath-Pileser III or Sargon II cannot be the background for the passage. The Benjaminite towns alerted to battle are all south of Ephraim, an unlikely direction for an Assyrian onslaught, and one for which there is no evidence.

28. Alt, 'Hosea 5.8', pp. 163-87.

29. *Ibid.*, pp. 170ff.

30. Alt, *ibid.*, p. 168, assumes that after Asa's counter attack (1 Kgs 15.16-22), the border between Israel and Judah moved back and forth across Benjamin so that, by Hosea's time, Gibeah (Tell el-Ful) constituted Israel's southern border. Wolff, *Hosea*, p. 113, assumes that the three cities fell into

Israel's hands during Jehoash's attack on Jerusalem at the beginning of the eighth century (2 Kgs 14.8-14), an hypothesis endorsed by Asurmendi, *La Guerra Siro-Efraimita*, p. 114.

31. Alt, 'Hosea 5.8', pp. 166ff; and Wolff, *Hosea*, pp. 111-13. Procksch (*Die Kleinen prophetischen Schriften vor dem Exil*, p. 37) had taken this so-called northerly advance as partial evidence of an Egyptian invasion, similarly expecting an enemy from the south.

32. Among those who accept Alt's thesis: Wolff, *Hosea*, pp. 111-13; Mays, *Hosea*, pp. 86-87; Bright, *History*, p. 256; Cazelles, 'Problèmes de la guerre Syro-Ephraimite', p. 72; H. Donner, *Israel unter den Völkern*. VTS 11 (Leiden: Brill, 1964), p. 47; Asurmendi, *La Guerra Siro-Efraimita*, pp. 111-16; Gottwald, *All the Kingdoms*, p. 126, n. 46; Ward, *Hosea*, pp. 106-108; Rudolph, *Hosea*, pp. 125-26; Herrmann, *History*, p. 247; and Thompson, *Situation and Theology*, pp. 66-67.

33. See Lapp, 'Tell el-Ful', p. 3.

34. Alt, 'Hosea 5.8', p. 166; Wolff, *Hosea*, p. 113, n. 34; and Schunck, *Benjamin*, pp. 155ff. Rudolph, *Hosea*, p. 123, for example, does not view this appearance of 'Beth-Aven' as a slighting reference to Bethel.

35. R.B. Coote, 'Hosea XII', *VT* 21 (1971), pp. 389-402. See also M. Buss, *Semeia* 32, p. 78.

36. A parallel text describing the Ephraimite border, Josh. 16.1-2, makes no mention of the 'wilderness of Beth-Aven'. For an early treatment of this issue which associates Beth-Aven closely with Bethel, see Noth, 'Bethel und Ai', *PJB* 31 (1935), p. 13.

37. Albright, 'The Israelite Conquest of Canaan in the Light of Archaeology', *BASOR* 74 (1939), pp. 11-23.

38. See Kallai-Kleinmann, 'Notes on the Topography of Benjamin', pp. 180-87.

39. *Ibid.*, pp. 180-84.

40. See J.M. Grintz, '"Ai which is Beside Beth-Aven". A re-examination of the identity of Ai', *Biblica* 42 (1961), pp. 201-16. Grintz's proposal to find Beth-Aven at et-Tell is highly unlikely since 1 Sam. 13.5 locates Michmas to the *east* of Beth-Aven, while Mukhmas is almost directly *south* of et-Tell.

41. The first modern proposal for Ai's location was Deir Diwan—see Robinson, *Biblical Researches*, pp. 574-75; but et-Tell soon became a leading candidate; see C. Wilson, 'On the Site of Ai and the Position of the Altar which Abraham Built between Bethel and Ai', *PEFQS* 4 (1869), pp. 123-26. The next suggestion was Khirbet Haiyan—see C.R. Conder, 'On Some of the Gains to Biblical Archaeology Due to the New Survey', *PEFQS* 16 (1881), pp. 34-56. However, a surface survey could find no pottery earlier than Roman, cf. J. Callaway, 'A Sounding at Khirbet Haiyan', *BASOR* 183 (1966), pp. 27-29. H.H. Kitchener, 'The Site of Ai', *PEFQS* 13 (1878) pp. 194-96, contributed yet another candidate, Khirbet Hai, one mile east of Mukhmas, but a recent survey could find no evidence of occupation there

before the Middle Ages; cf. Kallai, 'The Land of Benjamin and Mt Ephraim', in *Judea, Samaria and the Golan*, ed. Kochavi, p. 182. The archaeological investigations of Judith Marquet-Krause, *Les Fouilles de Aij (et-Tell) 1933-35* (Paris: Guethner, 1949), caused even greater debate since she determined that the favorite site of et-Tell had been abandoned (except for a brief period c. 1200 BC) after a great destruction there c. 2200 BC. For a recent discussion of Ai's location, see Z. Zevit, 'The Problem of Ai', *BAR*, Vol. 11 (1985), pp. 58-59. D. Livingston, 'Location of Biblical Bethel and Ai Reconsidered', *WTJ* 33 (1970-71), pp. 20-44, and 'Traditional Site of Bethel Questioned', *WTJ* 34 (1971-72), pp. 39-50, suggests reasons for locating Bethel at el-Bireh. The usual identification of Bethel was defended by Anson Rainey, 'Bethel is still Beitin', *WTJ* 33 (1971), pp. 175-88. Also preferring to retain Beitin, but still distinguishing Beth-Aven from Bethel, is Jacques Briend, 'Bethel et Beth-Aven', in *Escritos de Biblia et Oriente*. BS 38 (Salamanca, 1981), pp. 65-70.

42. See Kallai-Kleinmann, 'Notes on the Topography of Benjamin', pp. 180-83; Kallai's survey agreeably showed both Iron I and II sherds at Tell Maryam; see *Judean, Samaria, and the Golan*, ed. Kochavi, p. 183.

43. Noth, *History*, pp. 259-60, hints at this interpretation of Hos. 5.8. Wellhausen, 'Die Kleinen Propheten übersetzt und erklärt', p. 114, also appears to view the passage as an invasion of Judah—though by the Assyrians. Jeremias, *Hosea*, pp. 80-81, offers the suggestion that Gibeah and Ramah were being called to attack the northern kingdom through the border post of Bethel (Beth-Aven). Such an event is unattested, and the notion that cities were ever called to attack an army is most unlikely. For a complete discussion of these issues, see my recent article, 'Hosea and the Sin of Gibeah', *CBQ* 51 (1989), pp. 447-60.

44. See Martin Buss, *The Prophetic Word of Hosea: A Morphological Study*. BZAW 111 (Berlin: Töpelmann, 1969), p. 37; and H.L. Ginsberg, 'Hosea', in *Encyclopedia Judaica* 8, columns 1010-1024 (Jerusalem: Macmillan, 1975).

45. A recently discovered Assyrian inscription reveals that Menachem paid tribute to Tiglath-Pileser around 737, two or three years before the Syro-Ephraimite invasion; see Levine, 'Menachem and Tiglath-Pileser', pp. 40-42.

46. Wolff, *Hosea*, p. 152, regards Hos. 9.9 as clearly Hosean with its characteristic four-line strophe; cf. also Buss, *The Prophetic Word of Hosea*, p. 39.

47. So Ward, *Hosea*, p. 160. Among those who also take the verses as a description of Ephraim's hostility to Hosea are Jeremias, *Hosea*, pp. 117-18, and Rudolph, *Hosea*, pp. 179-80.

48. Translation and interpretation of R. Dobbie, 'The Text of Hosea 9.8', *VT* 5 (1955), pp. 199-203. For a similar usage of צָפָה, see Ps. 37.32, 'the wicked *lie in wait* for the righteous man'. Wolff, *Hosea*, p. 151; Mays, *Hosea*,

p. 128; and Andersen/Freedman, *Hosea*, pp. 533-34, translate the phrase as 'the watchman of Ephraim'. This translation yields the interpretation that the *prophet* is the one who sets traps and causes hostility in Israel. Yet the sense of the passage is just the opposite: Ephraim is the sinister one who sets traps.

49. For example, Ward, *Hosea*, pp. 169-70; and Gottwald, *The Hebrew Bible: A Socio-Literary Introduction* (Philadelphia: Fortress, 1985), p. 361.

50. See Wolff, *Hosea*, p. 184. Hos. 7.7; 8.4, 10; 10.3; 13.10 seem to refer to the perversion of the office of king in Hosea's day. The tendency to take Hos. 9.9 as a reference to Saul is probably unconsciously influenced by the anti-Saul programme of Davidid literature with which Hosea probably would have been unaware. Ward, *Hosea*, pp. 169-70, also contended that Hosea might have in mind Saul's opposition to Samuel in this passage. This interpretation is untenable for two reasons. First, such a 'conflict' between Saul and Samuel is probably a late editorial creation, and second, Saul, in any case, is pictured as being rather obedient to Samuel in these stories.

51. Wolff, *Hosea*, p. 158; Mays, *Hosea*, p. 131; and Jeremias, *Hosea*, pp. 118-19, relate this passage to Judges 19-20 through the unsatisfactory comparison of Hosea himself with the Levite victim at Gibeah. This analogy breaks down because, in the Levitical version of the story, it is *Benjamin* which committed the evil and *Ephraim* which punished the crime, thus avenging the Levite. In Hos. 9.9, however, it is surely Ephraim which the prophet wishes to indict.

52. The event to which this passage refers is difficult to identify historically. Against suggestions that the passage points to any of the Assyrian kings named Shalmaneser, Gottwald marshals impressive evidence; cf. *All the Kingdoms*, p. 128, n. 49. With Wolff, *Hosea*, p. 188, and others, Gottwald suggests that the allusions refer to an otherwise unknown atrocity committed by the contemporary Moabite king Salamanu, mentioned in a tributary list of Tiglath-Pileser III (*ANET*, p. 282).

53. Jeremias, *Hosea*, p. 133, recognized 10.9-15 as a unity in that it envisioned the punishment of Israel by 'war,' the only occurrence of the word in Hosea. Jeremias, however, imagined these battles as occurring after Tiglath-Pileser's invasion in 727. 2 Kgs 16.5 and Isa. 7.1 report that the Syro-Ephraimite forces were not opposed in their invasion, or in their seige of Jerusalem (cf. also Isa. 10.27c-32), through a decision of Ahaz. The prophet Isaiah appears to have counselled this approach (Isa. 7.4-9), and Ahaz appears to have followed his advice. The account in 2 Chron. 28.5-8 mentioning Judean losses of 120,000 dead and 200,000 captured is a late invention with typically inflated figures.

54. Hosea chose the harnessed heifer as a metaphor for this productive but passive obedience. For a discussion of this 'training', cf. M. Goshen-Gottstein, 'Ephraim is a well-trained heifer' and Ugaritic *mdl*', *Biblica* 41 (1960), pp. 64-66. See also M. Kockert, 'Prophetie und Geschichte im

Hoseabuch', *ZTK* 85 (1987), pp. 3-30, who demonstrates that Hosea proclaimed that contemporary Israel was responsible for its past sins from the earliest days.

55. Regarding Hos. 10.13, Y. Kaufmann, *The Religion of Israel* (New York: Schocken, 1972), p. 375, stated, 'The first biblical author, indeed the first man in history, to condemn militarism as a religious-moral sin was Hosea'. See also Hos. 8.14. Andersen/Freedman, *Hosea*, pp. 562-65, also agree that this unit condemns military strength, as illustrated by the 'bloodbath' at Gibeah (Judges 19-20).

56. See R. Wilson, *Prophecy and Society in Ancient Israel* (Philadelphia: Fortress, 1980), pp. 130-31. Several texts suggest that the Hebrew root עדר may be an archaic term for 'prophet'; see Iddo the 'seer' (2 Chron. 12.15) or 'prophet' (2 Chron. 13.22), and the prophet Azariah, son of Oded (2 Chron. 15.1). See B.Z. Luria, 'A Prophet of the Lord Named Oded', *BethMikra* 30 (1984/85), pp. 413-15.

57. Among those regarding Isa. 10.27ff. as stemming from the Assyrian invasion of 701 are, Mauchline, *Isaiah 1-39*, pp. 125-26; Kaiser, *Isaiah 1-12*, p. 151; and R.E. Clements, *Isaiah and the Deliverance of Jerusalem: A Study in the Interpretation of Prophecy in the Old Testament*. JSOTS 13 (Sheffield, 1980), p. 111, n. 5.

58. See N. Na'aman, 'Sennacherib's "Letter to God" on His Campaign to Judah', *BASOR* 214 (1974), pp. 25-39. Analysis of Assyrian records reveals this plan of attack on Judah, according to Na'aman: 'Penetration through the central region and conquest of two key cities in the Shephelah, thus opening the route into the heart of the land, between the two principal centers of Jerusalem and Lachish'. W. Shea, 'Sennacherib's Second Palestinian Campaign', *JBL* 104 (1985), pp. 401-18, argues that Sennacherib campaigned against Palestine in 689 as well as 701. That Isa. 10.29-32 is related to neither of these campaigns is probable since both appear to have followed a similar strategy: invasion from the Palestinian coast. No evidence of a northern approach to Jerusalem is apparent in either of Shea's proposed campaigns.

59. H. Wildberger, *Jesaja 1-12*. BKAT (Neukirchen-Vluyn: Neukirchener, 1972), pp. 423-33.

60. Among those seeing Isa. 10.27ff as a visionary prediction are: L. Federlin, 'A propos d'Isaie 10.29-31', *RB* 3 (1906), p. 266; Dalman, 'Palästinische Wege', pp. 37-57; Albright, *AASOR* 4, pp. 134-40; and D.L. Christensen, 'The March of Conquest in Isaiah X 27c-34', *VT* 26 (1976), pp. 385-99. For a review of commentaries which see the passage as imaginary, cf. Donner, *Israel*, pp. 31-32.

61. *Ibid.*, pp. 32-33.

62. Among those viewing the passage as belonging to the Syro-Ephraimite war are: Donner, *Israel*, pp. 30-38, and 'Der Feind aus dem Norden: Topographische und archäologische Erwägungen zu Jes. 10.27b-34', *ZDPV* 84 (1968), pp. 46-54; R. Scott, 'Isaiah', *IB* 5, pp. 245-46; Herbert, 'Isaiah',

p. 88; G. Wright, *Isaiah*. LBC (London: SCM Press, 1964), pp. 48-49; Hermann, *History*, p. 253 n.16; Childs, *Isaiah and the Assyrian Crisis*. SBT (Naperville, Ill.: Allenson, 1967), pp. 61-63; and Hayes and Irvine, *Isaiah*, pp. 206-10. Dalman, 'Palästinische Wege', p. 42, allows for this interpretation.

63. See G. Shepard, 'The Anti-Assyrian Redaction and the Canonical Context of Isaiah 1-39', *JBL* 104 (1985), pp. 193-216, for a thorough discussion of possible anti-Assyrian editing in Isaiah 1-39; and H. Barth, *Die Jesaja-Worte in der Josiazeit: Israel und Assur als Thema einer produktiven Neuinterpretation der Jesajaüberlieferung*. WMANT 48 (Neukirchen-Vluyn: Neukirchener, 1977).

64. See Donner, *Israel*, p. 30, and Albright, 'Assyrian March', p. 135.

65. Dalman, 'Palästinische Wege', p. 45, entertained the possibility of reading 'Samaria', but adopted 'Bethel' without textual support. The 'Samaria' reading is favored by Kaiser, *Isaiah*, p. 150; see also Donner, *Israel*, p. 30.

66. This same locale apparently was also known as the 'Michmas Pass' in 1 Sam. 13.23. 'Geba Pass' is also the probable reading for Judg. 20.33, as we have seen. The MT reading here acquired a directional ה, i.e. 'through the Geba Pass'. LXX's reading 'he shall arrive at Aggai' probably witnesses to an underlying Hebrew text reading הגי ('the Valley'). This version would be equivalent to the MT text since the Valley is undoubtedly the Wadi es-Swenit, known in 1 Sam. 14.2 as the Migron.

67. Donner, 'Der Feind', p. 47, and *Israel*, p. 36.

68. Josephus, *Wars of the Jews*, V, 2.1.

69. The account of 2 Chron. 28.6-8 mentioning 120,000 Judean deaths apparently contradicts 2 Kgs 16.5 and Isa. 7.1 and appears to be a late, imaginary, interpolation. The lack of Judean military response might also indicate significant Judean support for Rezin in opposition to Ahaz; see Isa. 8.5.

70. For a more detailed discussion of these border changes under Josiah, see Oded, 'Judah and the Exile', *IJH*, pp. 463-67; see Alt, 'Judas Gaue unter Josia', pp. 276-88, and Noth, *Josua*, p. 112.

71. W. Rudolph, *Esra und Nehemiah*, p. 17, plausibly dates this list to the 539-515 period. One notes that in this list, Ramah is associated with Geba as it was throughout biblical history (Judg. 19.13; 1 Kgs 15.17-22; Hos. 5.8; Isa. 10.29).

72. A wide consensus of biblical scholarship dates Zechariah 9-14 much later than the original corpus of the pre-exilic prophet; see, for example, Hanson, *The Dawn of Apocalyptic*, pp. 287-90; Neil, 'Zechariah', pp. 943-47; and Childs, *Intro.*, pp. 472-87.

73. Dalman, 'Palästinische Wege', pp. 43-44, places Rimmon near Geba (at Rammun), but Sellin, *Zwölfprophetenbuch*, pp. 582ff., identifies the city with the Rimmon in the Negev, a more probable interpretation in light of the literary context suggesting a great deal of land. See my article on Rimmon in the forthcoming *ABD*.

BIBLIOGRAPHY

Abba, Raymond, 'Priests and Levites', *IDB* 3, pp. 876-89. Nashville: Abingdon, 1962.

Abel, F.-M, 'Les strategèmes dans le livre de Josué', *RB* 56 (1949), pp. 321-39.

Ackroyd, Peter, *The First Book of Samuel*, CBC; Cambridge: University Press, 1971.

Aharoni, Yochanan, 'Arad: Its Inscriptions and Temple', *BA* 31 (1968), pp. 2-32.

—'The Horned Altar at Beersheba', *BA* 37 (1974), pp. 2-6.

—*The Land of the Bible: A Historical Geography*, Trans. A.F. Rainey; Philadelphia: Westminster, 1967.

—'The Northern Boundary of Judah', *PEQ* 90 (1958), pp. 27-31.

—'The Province-Lists of Judah', *VT* 9 (1959), pp. 225-46.

Albright, William F. *Archaeology and the Religion of Israel*, Baltimore: Johns Hopkins, 1942.

—*Excavations and Results at Tell el-Ful (Gibeah of Saul)*, AASOR 4; New Haven: Yale University Press, 1924.

—'Gibeah of Saul and Benjamin', *BASOR* 6 (1922), pp. 8-11.

—'The Israelite Conquest of Canaan in the Light of Archaeology', *BASOR* 74 (1939), pp. 11-23.

—'A New Campaign of Excavation at Gibeah of Saul', *BASOR* 52 (1933), pp. 6-13.

—'The Son of Tabeel (Isaiah 7.6)', *BASOR* 140 (1955), pp. 34-35.

Alt, Albrecht, 'Bemerkungen zu einigen Judäischen Ortslisten des Alten Testaments', in *Kleine Schriften zur Geschichte des Volkes Israel*, Vol. 2, pp. 289-305. München: Beck, 1959.

—'The Formation of the Israelite State in Palestine', in *Essays on Old Testament History and Religion*, pp. 171-237. Garden City, N.Y.: Doubleday, 1967.

—'Hosea 5.8-6.6. Ein Krieg und seine Folgen in prophetischer Beleuchtung', in *KS*, Vol. 2, pp. 163-87. München: Beck, 1959.

—'Judas Gaue unter Josiah', in *KS*, Vol. 2, pp. 276-88. München: Beck, 1959.

—'Mizpah in Benjamin', *PJB* 6 (1910), pp. 46-62.

—'Neue Erwägungen über die Lage von Mizpa, Ataroth, Beeroth, und Gibeon', *ZDPV* 69 (1953), pp. 1-27.

Alter, Robert, *The Art of Biblical Narrative*, New York: Basic Books, 1981.

Andersen, Francis and David Freedman, *Hosea*. AB; New York: Doubleday, 1980.

Anderson, B.W. and W. Harrelson, eds., *Israel's Prophetic Heritage: Essays in Honor of James Muilenberg*, New York: Harper Bros., 1962.

Ap-Thomas, D.R, 'Saul's "Uncle"', *VT* 11 (1961), pp. 241-45.

Arnold, Patrick, 'Hosea and the Sin of Gibeah', *CBQ* 51 (1989), pp. 447-60.

Asurmendi, Jesus, *La Guerra Siro-Efraimita: Historia y Profetas*, Valencia: San Jeronimo, 1982.

Auld, A, 'The "Levitical Cities:" Texts and History', *ZAW* 91 (1979), pp. 194-206.

Bächli, Otto, 'Von der Liste zur Beschreibung. Beobachtungen und Erwägungen zu Jos. 13-19', *ZDPV* 89 (1973), pp. 1-14.

Bailey, D.S., *Homosexuality and the Western Tradition*, New York: Longmans, 1955.
Begrich, Joachim, 'Der syrisch-ephraimitische Krieg und seine weltpolitischen Zusammenhänge', in *Gesammelte Studien zum Alten Testament*, ed. W. Zimmerli, pp. 99-120. *TB* 21; München: Kaiser, 1964.
Bertheau, E., *Das Buch der Richter und Ruth*, 2nd edition, Leipzig: Hirzel, 1883.
Besters, André, '"Israel" et "Fils d'Israël" dans les livres historiques (Genèse-2 Rois)', *RB* 74 (1967), pp. 5-23.
—'Le Sanctuaire central dans Jud. XIX-XXI', *ETL* 41 (1965), pp. 20-41.
Beyerlin, W., 'Das Königscharisma bei Saul', *ZAW* 73 (1961), pp. 187-201.
Bic, M., 'Saul sucht die Eselinnen, 1 Sam. ix', *VT* 7 (1957), pp. 92-97.
Birch, Bruce, 'The Choosing of Saul at Mizpah', *CBQ* 37 (1975), pp. 447-57.
—'The Development of the Tradition on the Anointing of Saul in I Sam. 9.1-10.16', *JBL* 90 (1971), pp. 55-68.
—*The Rise of the Israelite Monarchy: The Growth and Development of I Sam. 7-15*, Dissertation: Yale University, 1970; Ann Arbor: University Microfilms, 1971.
Birch, W.F., 'Gibeah at Adaseh', *PEFQS* 1913, pp. 38-42.
—'Gibeah of Saul and Zela: The Site of Jonathan's Home and Tomb', *PEFQS* 1911, pp. 101-109.
—'The Rock of Rimmon and Gibeah', *PEFQS* 1880, pp. 236-37.
—'The Site of Gibeah', *PEFQS* 1914, pp. 42-44.
Blenkinsopp, Joseph, 'Are there Traces of the Gibeonite Covenant in Deuteronomy?' *CBQ* 28 (1966), pp. 207-19.
—'Did Saul make Gibeon his Capital?' *VT* 24 (1974), pp. 1-7.
—*Gibeon and Israel. The role of Gibeon and the Gibeonites in the political and religious history of early Israel*, SOTS 2; Cambridge: University Press, 1972.
—'Jonathan's Sacrilege: 1 Sam. 14.1-46. A Study in Literary History', *CBQ* 26 (1964), pp. 423-49.
—'Kiriath-Jearim and the Ark', *JBL* 88 (1969), pp. 143-56.
—'The Quest of the Historical Saul', in *No Famine in the Land. Studies in Honor of John L. McKenzie*, ed. James W. Flanagan, pp. 75-99. Missoula: Scholars, 1975.
Blizzard, R.B., 'Intensive Systematic Surface Collection at Livingston's Proposed Site for Biblical Ai', *WTJ* 36 (1973-74), pp. 221-30.
Boecker, Hans, *Die Beurteilung der Anfänge des Königtums in den Deuteronomistischen Abschnitten des I Samuelbuches*, WMANT 31; Neukirchen-Vluyn: Neukirchener Verlag, 1969.
Böhme, W., 'Richter c. 21', *ZAW* 1885, pp. 30-36.
Boling, Robert and G. Ernest Wright, *Joshua*, AB; Garden City, N.Y.: Doubleday, 1982.
Boling, Robert 'In Those Days There Was No King In Israel', in *A Light Unto My Path. Studies in Honor of Jacob M. Myers*, ed. H. Bream, pp. 33-48. Philadelphia: Temple University, 1974.
—*Judges*, AB; Garden City, N.Y.: Doubleday, 1975.
Boswell, John, *Christianity, Social Tolerance, and Homosexuality. Gay People in Western Europe from the Beginning of the Christian Era to the Fourteenth Century*, Chicago: University of Chicago, 1980.
Briend, Jacques, 'Bethel et Beth-Aven', in *Escritos de Biblia et Oriente*. BS 38, pp. 65-70. Salamanca, 1981.
Bright, John, *A History of Israel*, Philadelphia: Westminster, 1959.
Brockington, L., *Ezra, Nehemiah, and Esther*, Greenwood, S.C.: Attic, 1969.
Brueggeman, Walter, 'Yahwist', *IDBS*, pp. 971-75. Nashville: Abingdon, 1976.

Bruno, Arvid, *Gibeon*, Leipzig: Deichert, 1923.
Budde, Karl, *Die Bücher Richter und Samuel. Ihre Quellen und ihr Aufbau*. Giessen: Ricker, 1890.
—'Die Anhänge des Richterbuches', *ZAW* 1888, pp. 285-300.
Burney, C.F., *The Book of Judges*, London: Rivingtons, 1930.
Buss, Martin, *The Prophetic Word of Hosea. A Morphological Study*, BZAW 111; Berlin: Töpelmann, 1969.
Callaway, Joseph, 'A Sounding at Khirbet Haiyan', *BASOR* 183 (1966), pp. 27-29.
Cazelles, Henri, 'David's Monarchy and the Gibeonite Claim', *PEQ* 87 (1955), pp. 165-75.
—'Problèmes de la guerre Syro-Ephraimite', *Eretz Israel* 14 (1978), pp. 70-78. Jerusalem: Israel Exploration Society, 1978.
Childs, Brevard, *Introduction to the Old Testament as Scripture*, Philadelphia: Fortress, 1979.
—*Isaiah and the Assyrian Crisis*, SBT; Naperville, Ill.: Allenson, 1967.
—'A Study of the Formula "Until This Day"', *JBL* 82 (1963), pp. 279-92.
Christensen, D.L., 'The March of Conquest in Isaiah 10.27c-34', *VT* 26 (1976), pp. 385-99.
Clements, R.E., *Isaiah and the Deliverance of Jerusalem: A Study in the Interpretation of Prophecy in the Old Testament*, JSOTS 13; Sheffield: JSOT, 1980.
Coggins, R.J., *The Books of Ezra and Nehemiah*, CBC; Cambridge: University Press, 1976.
Conder, C.R., 'Gibeah of Saul', *PEFQS* 1877, pp. 104-105.
—'Notes on a Disputed Point—Gibeah of Saul', *PEFQS* 1881, p. 89.
—'Rimmon', *PEFQS* 1879, pp. 170-71.
—'On Some of the Gains to Biblical Archaeology due to the New Survey', *PEFQS* 16 (1881), pp. 34-56.
Conrad, Joachim, 'Zum geschichtlichen Hintergrund der Darstellung von Davids Aufstieg', *TLZ* 5 (1972), pp. 322-32.
Coote, R.B., 'Hosea xii', *VT* 21 (1971), pp. 389-402.
Cross, Frank M. and G.E. Wright, 'The Boundary and Province Lists of the Kingdom of Judah', *JBL* 75 (1956), pp. 202-26.
Cross, Frank M., *Canaanite Myth and Hebrew Epic. Essays in the History of the Religion of Israel*, Cambridge, Mass.: Harvard University, 1973.
Crüsemann, F., *Der Widerstand gegen das Königtum*, WMANT 40; Neukirchen-Vluyn: Neukirchener Verlag, 1978.
Culley, Robert, *Studies in the Structure of Hebrew Narrative*, Philadelphia: Fortress, 1976.
Cundall, A.E., 'Judges—An Apology for the Monarchy?' *ET* 81 (1969-70), pp. 178-81.
—*Judges and Ruth*, London: Tyndale, 1968.
Dalgish, E.R., 'Jonathan Son of Saul', *IDB* 2, pp. 968-70. Nashville: Abingdon, 1962.
Dalman, G., 'Die Nordstrasse Jerusalems', *PJB* 21 (1925), pp. 58-89.
—'Palästinische Wege und die Bedrohung Jerusalems nach Jesaja 10', *PJB* 12 (1916), pp. 37-57.
—'Der Pass von Michmas', *ZDPV* 27 (1904), pp. 161-73.
—'Das Wadi es-Suwenit', *ZDPV* 28 (1905), pp. 161-75.
Danell, G.A., *Studies in the Name Israel*, Uppsala, 1946.
Davies, P.R., 'Ark or Ephod in 1 Sam. xiv 18?' *JTS* 26 (1975), pp. 82-87.
Demsky, A., 'Geba, Gibeah, and Gibeon—an Historico-Geographic Riddle', *BASOR* 212 (1973), pp. 26-31.

Dobbie, R., 'The Text of Hosea 9.8', *VT* 5 (1955), pp. 199-203.

Donner, Herbert, 'Der Feind aus dem Norden: Topographische und archäologische Erwägungen zu Jes. 10, 27b-34', *ZDPV* 84 (1968), pp. 46-54.

—*Israel unter den Völkern*, VTS 11; Leiden: Brill, 1964.

—'The Separate States of Israel and Judah', in *IJH*, eds. John H. Hayes and J. Maxwell Miller, pp. 381-434. Philadelphia: Fortress, 1977.

Driver, G.R., 'Problems in Judges newly Discovered', *ALUOS* 4 (1962-63), pp. 6-25.

Driver, S.R., *Notes on the Hebrew Text and the Topography of the Books of Samuel*, 2nd edition, Oxford: Clarendon, 1913.

Dus, Jan, 'Die altisraelitische amphiktyonische Poesie', *ZAW* 75 (1963), pp. 45-54.

—'Bethel und Mispa in Jdc. 19-21 und Jdc. 10-12', *OrAnt* 3 (1964), pp. 227-43.

—'Gibeon—eine Kultstätte des SMS und die Stadt des Benjaminitischen Schicksals', *VT* 10 (1960), pp. 353-85.

Edelman, Diana, *The Rise of the Israelite State under Saul*, Dissertation: University of Chicago, Ann Arbor: University Microfilms, 1987.

—'Saul's Rescue of Jabesh-Gilead (1 Sam. 11.1-11): Sorting Story from History', *ZAW* 96 (1984), pp. 195-209.

Eissfeldt, Otto, 'Der geschichtliche Hintergrund der Erzählung von Gibeas Schandtat (Richter 19-21)', in *KS* Vol. 2, pp. 64-80. Tübingen: Mohr, 1963.

—*Die Komposition der Samuelbücher*, Leipzig: J.C. Hinrichs, 1931.

—'Levitische Traditionen in Gen 34, Gen 49.5-7, Dt 33.8-11, Ri 17-18, Ri 19-21', in *Erwägungen zur Herkunft der Josianischen Tempelurkunde*, ed. J. Lindblom; Lund: Gleerup, 1971.

—*The Old Testament: An Introduction*, trans. Peter Ackroyd. New York: Harper and Row, 1965.

—*Die Quellen des Richterbuchs*, Leipzig: J.C. Hinrichs, 1925.

Elliger, Karl, 'Beeroth und Gibeon', *ZDPV* 73 (1957), pp. 125-32.

Eph'al, Israel, *The Ancient Arabs: Nomads on the Borders of Fertile Crescent 9th-5th Centuries B.C.*, Jerusalem: Magnes, 1982.

Eppstein, V., 'Was Saul also among the Prophets', *ZAW* 81 (1969), pp. 287-304.

Evans, William, 'An Historical Reconstruction of the Emergence of Israelite Kingship in the Reign of Saul', in *Scripture in Context II. More Essays in Comparative Method*, ed. William Hallo *et al.*, pp. 61-77. Winona Lake: Eisenbraun's, 1983.

Farr, George, 'The Concept of Grace in the Book of Hosea', *ZAW* 70 (1958), pp. 98-107.

Federlin, L, 'A propos d'Isaïe 10.29-31', *RB* 3 (1906), pp. 266ff.

Fensham, F.C. *The Books of Ezra and Nehemiah*, Grand Rapids: Eerdmans, 1982.

—'The Treaty between Israel and the Gibeonites', *BA* 27 (1964), pp. 96-100.

Fernandez, A. 'El atendado de Gabaa (Iud 19-21)', *Biblica* (1931), pp. 297-315.

—'El Paso dificil del ejercito asirio (Is 10.28)', *EstE* 10 (1931), pp. 339-48.

Finkelstein, Israel. *The Archaeology of the Settlement*, Jerusalem: Israel Exploration Society, 1988.

Flanagan, James, 'Judah in all Israel', in *No Famine in the Land. Studies in Honor of John L. McKenzie*, ed. J. Flanagan, pp. 101-16. Missoula: Scholars, 1975.

Franken, H.J. and C.A. Franken-Batterschild, C.A. *A Primer in Old Testament Archaeology*, Leiden: Brill, 1963.

Freedman, D.N., 'The Refrain in David's Lament over Saul and Jonathan', in *Ex Orbe Religionem*, pp. 115-26. Leiden: Brill, 1972.

Fritz, Volkmar, 'Die Deutungen des Königtum Sauls in den Überlieferungen von seiner Entstehung. I Sam. 9-ll', *ZAW* 88 (1976), pp. 346-62.

Garstang, John, *Joshua and Judges.*, London: Constable, 1931.

Galling, K., 'The "Gola List" According to Ezra 2, Nehemiah 7', *JBL* 70 (1951), pp. 149-58.

Gaster, Theodore, *Myth, Legend, and Custom in the Old Testament*, New York: Harper and Row, 1969.

Ginsberg, H.L., 'Hosea', *Encyclopedia Judaica* 8, cols. 1010-1024. Jerusalem: Macmillan, 1975.

Good, E.M., 'Hosea 5.8–6.6: An Alternative to Alt', *JBL* 85 (1966), 273-86.

Gordis, Robert, 'Democratic Origins in Ancient Israel—the Biblical *edah*', in *Alexander Marx Jubilee*, Vol. 1, pp. 369-88. New York: Jewish Theological Seminary, 1950.

Goshen-Gottstein, M., '"Ephraim is a well-trained heifer" and Ugaritic *mdl*', *Biblica* 41 (1960), pp. 64-66.

Gottwald, Norman, *All the Kingdoms of the Earth. Israelite Prophecy and International Relations in the Ancient Near East*, New York: Harper and Row, 1964.

—*The Hebrew Bible: A Socio-Literary Introduction*, Philadelphia: Fortress, 1985.

—*The Tribes of Yahweh. A Sociology of the Religion of Liberated Israel 1250-1050 BCE*, Maryknoll, N.Y.: Orbis, 1970.

Graesser, G., 'Gibeah', *IDBS*, pp. 363-64. Nashville: Abingdon, 1976.

Graham, W.C., 'Isaiah's Part in the Syro-Ephraimite Crisis', *AJSL* 50 (1933/34), pp. 201-16.

Gray, John, *Joshua, Judges, and Ruth*, Greenwood, S.C.: Attic, 1967.

—*I & II Kings*, 2nd edition, OTL; Philadelphia: Westminster, 1969.

Greenspahn, Frederick, 'An Egyptian Parallel to Judg. 17.6 and 21.25', *JBL* 101 (1982), pp. 129-30.

Gressmann, Hugo, '"Die älteste Geschichtsschreibur und Prophetie Israels (von Samuel bis Amos und Hosea)', in *Die Schriften des Alten Testaments*, Vol. 1, Part 2. Göttingen: Vandenhoeck & Ruprecht, 1910.

Grintz, Jehoshua, 'Ai which is beside Beth-Aven'. A reexamination of the identity of Ai', *Biblica* 42 (1961), pp. 201-16.

—'The Treaty of Joshua with the Gibeonites', *JAOS* 86 (1966), pp. 113-26.

Gronbaeck, Jacob, 'Benjamin und Juda. Erwägungen zu 1 Kon. 12.21-24', *VT* 15 (1965), pp. 421-36.

—*Die Geschichte vom Aufstieg Davids (1 Sam. 15-2 Sam. 5): Tradition und Komposition*, ATD 10; Copenhagen, 1971.

Gunkel, Hermann, *The Legends of Genesis: The Biblical Saga and History*, New York: Schocken, 1966.

Gunn, David, *The Fate of King Saul. An Interpretation of a Biblical Story*, JSOTS 14; Sheffield: JSOT, 1980.

—'Narrative Patterns and Oral Tradition in Judges and Samuel', *VT* 24 (1974), pp. 286-317.

—*The Story of King David. Genre and Interpretation*, JSOTS 6; Sheffield: JSOT, 1978.

Gunneweg, A.H., *Leviten und Priester*, FRLANT 89; Göttingen: Vandenhoeck & Ruprecht, 1965.

Halpern, Baruch, *The Constitution of the Monarchy in Israel*, HSM 25; Chico, Calif.: Scholars, 1982.

Hammond, Gerald, 'The Bible and Literary Criticism—Part I', *CQ* 25, (1983), pp. 5-20.

—'The Bible and Literary Criticism—Part I', *CQ* 25 (1983), pp. 3-15.

Haran, Menachem, 'The Gibeonites, the Nethinim, and the Sons of Solomon's Servants', *VT* 11 (1961), pp. 159-69.

—'Studies in the Account of the Levitical Cities', *JBL* 8 (1961), pp. 45-54.
Hauer, Christian, 'Does 1 Sam. 9.1-11-11.15 reflect the extension of Saul's dominions?' *JBL* 86 (1967), pp. 306-10.
—'The Shape of Saulide Strategy', *CBQ* 31 (1969), pp. 153-67.
Hauser, Alan, *A Study of Representative Approaches to the Historical Question of Saul's Rise to the Monarchy*, Dissertation: University of Iowa, 1972. Ann Arbor: University Microfilms, 1973.
Hayes, John H. and Stuart Irvine, *Isaiah: The Eighth-century Prophet*, Nashville: Abingdon, 1987.
Hayes, John H. and J. Maxwell Miller, eds., *Israelite and Judean History*, Philadelphia: Fortress, 1977.
Herbert, A.S., *Book of the Prophet Isaiah. Ch. 1-39*, CBC; Cambridge: Cambridge University Press, 1973.
Herrmann, Siegried, *A History of Israel in Old Testament Times*, 2nd edition, Philadelphia: Fortress, 1980.
—'Die Königsnovelle in Ägypten und Israel', *WZKMU* (1953-54), pp. 51-62.
Hertzberg, Hans, *I & II Samuel. A Commentary*, OTL; Phildelphia: Westminster, 1964.
—*Die Bücher Josua, Richter, und Ruth*, Göttingen: Vandenhoeck & Ruprecht, 1954.
—'Mizpa', *ZAW* 47 (1929), pp. 161-96.
Holladay, W.L., 'Form and Word-play in David's Lament over Saul and Jonathan', *VT* 20 (1970), pp. 153-89.
Irvin, Dorothy, *Mythyrion. The Comparison of Tales from the Old Testament and the Ancient Near East*, Neukirchen-Vluyn: Neukirchener Verlag, 1978.
Ishida, Tomoo, *The Royal Dynasties in Ancient Israel*, BZAW 142; New York: de Gruyter, 1977.
Isserlin, B.S., 'Israelite and Pre-Israelite Place-Names in Palestine: A Historical and Geographical Sketch', *PEQ* 89 (1957), pp. 133-44.
Jenks, Alan, *The Elohist and North Israelite Traditions*, SBLMS 22; Missoula, Mont.: Scholars, 1977.
Jeremias, Jörg, *Der Prophet Hosea*, ATD; Göttingen: Vandenhoeck & Ruprecht, 1983.
Jirku, A., 'Die Zwölfzahl der Städte in Jes. 10.28-32', *ZAW* 48 (1930), p. 230.
Jobling, David, 'Jonathan: a Structural Study in 1 Samuel', in *SBL 1976 Seminar Papers*, ed. G. Macrae, 1976, pp. 15-32.
—'Saul's Fall and Jonathan's Rise: Tradition and Redaction in 1 Sam. 14.1-46', *JBL* 95 (1976), pp. 367-76.
—*The Sense of Biblical Narrative: Three Structural Analyses in the Old Testament (1 Sam. 13-31, Numbers 11-12, 1 Kings 17.18)*, JSOTS 7; Sheffield: JSOT, 1978.
Josephus, Flavius, *The Life and Works of Flavius Josephus*, Trans. William Whiston; Philadelphia: Winston, 1957.
Jungling, Hans-Winfried, *Richter 19: Ein Playdoyer für das Königtum. Stylistische Analyse der Tendenz Erzählung Ri 19, 1-30a, 21, 25*, Rome: Biblical Institute, 1981.
Kaiser, Otto, *Isaiah 1-12. A Commentary*, OTL; Philadelphia: Westminster, 1972.
Kallai, Z., 'The Land of Benjamin and Mt. Ephraim', in *Judea, Samaria, and the Golan: Archaeological Survey 1967-68*, ed. M. Kochavi, pp. 153-93. Jerusalem: Carta, 1972.
—'Notes on the Topography of Benjamin', *IEJ* 6 (1956), pp. 180-87.
Kallai-Kleinmann, Z., 'The Town-Lists of Judah, Simeon, Benjamin, and Dan', *VT* 8 (1958), pp. 134-60.

Bibliography 181

Bibliography 181

Kaufmann, Yehezkel, *The Biblical Account of the Conquest of Palestine*, Jerusalem: Magnes, 1953.

—*The Religion of Israel. From its Beginnings to the Babylonian Exile*, New York: Schocken, 1972.

Kearney, P.J., 'The Role of the Gibeonites in the Deuteronomistic History', *CBQ* 35 (1973), pp. 1-19.

Kellermann, U. 'Die Listen in Nehemia 11. Eine Dokumentation aus den letzten Jahren des Reiches Juda'? *ZDPV* 82 (1966), pp. 209-27.

Kennedy, A.R.S., *Samuel*, New York: Frowde, 1898.

Kitchener, H.H., 'The Site of Ai', *PEFQS* (1878), pp. 194-96.

Kochavi, Moshe, *Judea, Samaria, and the Golan: Archaeological Survey 1967-68*, Jerusalem: Carta, 1972.

Kockert, Matthias, 'Prophetie und Geschichte im Hoseabuch', *ZTK* 85 (1987), pp. 3-30.

Kraus, Hans-Joachim, *Worship in Israel*, Richmond: Knox, 1966.

Kuschke, A., 'Historisch-topographische Beiträge zum Buche Josua', in *Gottes Wort und Gottes Land: Festschrift für Hans-Wilhelm Hertzberg zum 70. Geburtstag*, ed. H.G. Reventlow, pp. 90-109. Göttingen: Vandenhoeck & Ruprecht, 1965.

Lagrange, M.J., *Le Livre des Juges*, Paris: Lecoffre, 1903.

LaMarche, Paul, *Zacharie IX–XIV*, Paris: Librairie Lecoffre, 1961.

Langlamet, F., 'Les Récits de l'institution de la royauté. I Sam. 7–12', *RB* 77 (1970), pp. 161-200.

Lapp, Nancy, 'Casemate Walls in Palestine and the Late Iron II Casemate at Tell el-Ful (Gibeah)', *BASOR* 223 (1976), pp. 25-42.

—*The Third Campaign at Tell el-Ful: The Excavations of 1964*, AASOR 45; Cambridge, Mass.: ASOR, 1981.

Lapp, Paul, 'Tell el-Ful', *BA* 28 (1965), pp. 2-10.

Lasine, Stuart, 'Guest and Host in Judges 19: Lot's Hospitality in an Inverted World', *JSOT* 29 (1984), pp. 37-59.

Levine, Louis, 'Menachem and Tiglath-Pileser: A New Synchronism', *BASOR* 206 (1972), pp. 40-42.

Levine, M. Herschel, 'A Biblical Protest against the Violation of Women (Jg. 19.27)', *DorLeDor* 8 (1979), pp. 194-96.

Lindblom, Johannes, 'Saul inter Prophetas (1 Sam. 10.12 und 19.24)', *ASTI* 9 (1973), pp. 30-41.

Linder, Sven, 'Sauls Gibeah—Tell el-Ful', *PJB* 18/19 (1922/23), pp. 89-99.

Liver, Jacob, 'The Literary History of Joshua IX', *JSS* 8 (1963), pp. 227-43.

Liverani, M., 'Messaggi, donne, ospitalita; communicazione inter-tribale in Giud. 19-21', *SMSH* 3 (1979), pp. 303-41.

Livingston, D., 'Location of Biblical Bethel and Ai Reconsidered', *WTJ* 33 (1970-71), pp. 20-44.

—'Traditional Site of Bethel Questioned', *WTJ* 34 (1971-72), pp. 39-50.

Lods, Adolphe, *Israel*, Trans. S.H. Hooke; New York: Knopf, 1932.

Luria, B.Z., 'A Prophet of the Lord Named Oded', *Beth Mikra* 30 (1983/85), pp. 413-15 (Hebrew).

Luther, B., '*Kahal* und *edah* als Hilfsmittel der Quellenscheidung im Priesterkodex und in der Chronik', *ZAW* 56 (1938), pp. 44-63.

Macalister, R., 'The Topography of Rachel's Tomb', *PEFQS* (1912), pp. 74-82.

MacDonald, B., *The Biblical Tribe of Benjamin: Its Origins and its History during the Period of the Judges in Israel*, Dissertation: Catholic University, 1974; Ann Arbor: University Microfilms, 1975.

182   *Gibeah—The Search for a Biblical City*

Mangan, Celine, *1-2 Chronicles, Ezra, and Nehemiah*, Wilmington: Glazier, 1982.
Marquet-Krause, Judith, *Les Fouilles de Aij (et-Tell) 1933-35)*, Paris: Geuther, 1949.
Martin, J.D., *The Book of Judges*, CBC; Cambridge: Cambridge University, 1975.
Mason, Rex, *The Books of Haggai, Zechariah, and Malachi*, CBC; Cambridge: Cambridge University, 1977.
Masterman, E.W., 'Tell el-Ful and Khirbet Adaseh', *PEFQS* (1913), pp. 132-37.
Mauchline, John, *Isaiah 1-39*, New York: Macmillan, 1962.
—*1 and 2 Samuel*, NCB; London: Oliphants, 1971.
Mayes, A.D.H., *Israel in the Period of the Judges*, Naperville, Ill.: Allenson, 1974.
—'Israel in the pre-monarchy period', *VT* 23 (1973), pp. 151-70.
—'The Period of the Judges and the Rise of the Monarchy', in *IJH*, ed. J.H. Hayes and J.M. Miller, pp. 285-331. Philadelphia: Westminster, 1977.
—'The Rise of the Israelite Monarchy', *ZAW* 90 (1978), pp. 1-19.
—*The Story of Israel Between Settlement and Exile. A Redactional Study of the Deuteronomic History*, London: SCM, 1983.
Mays, J., *Hosea. A Commentary*, OTL; Philadelphia: Westminster, 1969.
Mazar, Benjamin, 'The Cities of the Priests and Levites', *SVT* 7 (1959); Leiden: Brill, 1960.
McCarter, P.K., *1 Samuel*, AB; Garden City, N.Y.: Doubleday, 1980.
McCarthy, Dennis, 'The Inauguration of Monarchy in Israel. A Form- Critical Study of 1 Sam. 8-12', *Int* 27 (1973), pp. 401-12.
McCown, C.C., *Tell en-Nasbeh: Excavated under the Direction of the late William Frederic Bade*, New Haven: AASOR, 1947.
McKane, William, *I & II Samuel*, London: SCM, 1963.
McKenzie, John L., 'The Four Samuels', *BR* 7 (1962), pp. 3-18.
Mendenhall, G.E., 'The Monarchy', *Int* 29 (1975), pp. 155-70.
Mettinger, Tryggve, *King and Messiah*, CBOTS 8; Lund: Gleerup, 1976.
Michaeli, F., *Les Livres des Chroniques, d'Esdras, et de Néhémie*, Neuchâtel: Delachaux et Niestlé, 1967.
Miller, J. Maxwell and John H. Hayes, *A History of Ancient Israel and Judah*, Philadelphia: Westminster, 1986.
Miller, J. Maxwell and Gene Tucker, *The Book of Joshua*, CBC; London: Cambridge University, 1974.
Miller, J. Maxwell, 'Geba/Gibeah of Benjamin', *VT* 25 (1975), pp. 145-66.
—'Jebus and Jerusalem: a Case of Mistaken Identity', *ZDPV* 90 (1974), pp. 115-27.
—'Saul's Rise to Power: Some Observations Concerning I Sam. 9.1-10.16; 10.26-11.15 and 13.2-14.46', *CBQ* 36 (1974), pp. 157-74.
Moller, C. and G. Schmitt, *Siedlungen Palästinas nach Flavius Josephus*. BTAVO, Reihe B, 14, Wiesbaden: Reichert, 1976.
Moller, H., 'Die Lage von Gibea Benjamin', *ZDPV* 38 (1915), pp. 49-53.
Moore, G., *The Book of Judges*, New York: Dodd, Mead, 1898.
—*Judges*, New York: Scribner's, 1895.
Morgenstern, J., 'David and Jonathan', *JBL* 78 (1959) pp. 322-25.
Morton, W., 'Gibeah', *IDB* 2, pp. 390-91. Nashville: Abingdon, 1962.
—'Ramah', *IDB* 4, pp. 7-9. Nashville: Abingdon, 1962.
Mowinckel, Sigmund, *Zur Frage nach dokumentarischen Quellen in Josua 13-19*, Oslo: Dybwad, 1946.
Muilenberg, J., 'The Birth of Benjamin', *JBL* 75 (1956), 194-201.
—'Mizpah', *IDB* 3, pp. 407-409. Nashville: Abingdon, 1962.
—'Mizpah of Benjamin', *ST* 8 (1965), pp. 25-42.

Myers, Jacob M., *Ezra and Nehemiah*, AB; Garden City, N.Y.: 1965.

Na'aman, N., 'The Brook of Egypt and Assyrian Policy on the Border of Egypt', *Tel-Aviv* 6 (1979), pp. 68-90.

—'Sennacherib's "Letter to God" on His Campaign to Judah', *BASOR* 214 (1974), pp. 25-39.

Neil, William, 'Zechariah', *IDB* 4, pp. 943-47. Nashville: Abingdon, 1962.

Niditch, Susan, 'The "Sodomite" Theme in Judges 19-20: Family, Community, and Social Disintegration', *CBQ* 44 (1982), pp. 365-78.

Noth, Martin, 'The Background of Judges 17-18', in *Israel's Prophetic Heritage. Essays in Honor of James Muilenberg*, ed. B.W. Anderson, pp. 68-85. New York: Harper, 1962.

—*Das Buch Josua*, 2nd edition, Tübingen: Mohr, 1953.

—*The Deuteronomistic History*, Sheffield: JSOT, 1981.

—*The History of Israel*, 2nd edition, New York: Harper and Row, 1960.

—*Das System der Zwölf Stämme Israels*, Darmstadt: Wissenschaftliche Buchgesellschaft, 1966.

Nubel, H.-U., *Davids Aufstieg in der frühen israelitischen Geschichtsschreibung*, Dissertation: Bonn, 1959.

Oded, B., 'The Historical Background of the Syro-Ephraimite War Reconsidered', *CBQ* 34 (1972), pp. 153-65.

—'Judah and the Exile', in *IJH*, eds. J.H. Hayes and J.M. Miller, pp. 435-88. Philadelphia: Fortress, 1977.

Orlinsky, H., 'The Tribal System of Israel and Related Groups in the Period of the Judges', *OrAnt* 1 (1962), pp. 11-20.

Otzen, Benedikt, *Studien über Deuterosacharja*, Copenhagen: Munksgaard, 1964.

Pritchard, J., *Gibeon: Where the Sun Stood Still. The Discovery of the Biblical City*, Princeton: Princeton University 1962.

Rad, Gerhard von. *Genesis, A Commentary*, OTL; Philadelphia: Westminster, 1972.

—*Der Heilige Krieg im alten Israel*, Zürich: Zwingli, 1951.

—'Zwei Überlieferungen von König Saul', *Gesammelte Studien*, Vol. 2, pp. 199-211. München: Kaiser, 1958.

Radday, Y., *et al.*, 'The Book of Judges Examined by Statistical Linguistics', *Biblica* 58 (1977), pp. 469-99.

Rainey, A., 'Bethel is still Beitin', *WTJ* 33 (1971) pp. 175-88.

Rawnsley, H., 'The Rock of Pomegranate', *PEFQS* (1879) pp. 118-26.

Reider, J., 'Etymological Studies: ידע or ירע and ירעע', *JBL* 66 (1947), pp. 315-17.

Reventlow, H. Graf, 'Kultisches Recht im Alten Testament', *ZTK* 60 (1963), pp. 267-304.

Revell, E.J., 'The Battle with Benjamin (Judges xx.29-48) and Hebrew Narrative Techniques', *VT* 35 (1985), pp. 417-33.

Reviv, H., 'The Pattern of the Pan-Tribal Assembly in the Old Testament', *JNSL* 8 (1980), pp. 85-94.

Richter, Wolfgang, *Die Bearbeitungen des 'Retterbuches' in der deuteronomistischen Epochs*, Bonn: Hanstein, 1964.

—*Traditionsgeschichtliche Untersuchungen zum Richterbuch*, Bonn: Hanstein, 1966.

Ritterspach, A., *The Samuel Traditions: An Analysis of the Anti-monarchical Sources in 1 Samuel 1-15*, Dissertation: Graduate Theological Union, 1967; Ann Arbor: University Microfilms, 1972.

Robertson, David, *The Old Testament and the Literary Critic*, Philadelphia: Fortress, 1977.

Robinson, Edward, *Biblical Researches in Palestine*, 11th edition, Boston: Crocker and Brewster, 1874.

Rosel, Hartmut, 'Studien zur Topographie der Kriege in den Büchern Josua und Richter', (I) *ZDPV* 91 (1975), pp. 159-90 and "Studien zur Topographie der Kriege in den Büchern Josua und Richter", (II) *ZDPV* 92 (1976), pp. 10-46.

Rost, Leonhard, *Die Überlieferung von der Thronnachfolge Davids*, Stuttgart: Kohlhammer, 1926.

Roth, Wolfgang, 'Hinterhalt und Scheinflucht', *ZAW* 75 (1963), pp. 296-304.

Rudolph, Wilhelm, *Der 'Elohist' von Exodus bis Josua*, Berlin: Töpelmann, 1938.

—*Esra und Nehemia*, HAT; Tübingen: Mohr, 1949.

—*Hosea*, KAT; Gütersloh Gerdmohn: Gutersloher, 1966.

Saebo, Magne, *Sacharja 9-14*, WMANT 34; Neukirchen-Vluyn: Neukirchener Verlag, 1969.

Schicklberger, F., 'Die Davididen und das Nordreich. Beobachtungen zur sogenannten Geschichte vom Aufstieg Davids', *BZ* 18 (1974), pp. 255-63.

—'Jonatans Heldentat. Textlinguistische Beobachtungen zu 1 Sam. xiv 1-23a', *VT* 24 (1974), pp. 324-33.

Schmidt, Ludwig, *Menschlicher Erfolg und Jahwes Initiative. Studien zu Tradition, Interpretation, und Historie in Überlieferungen von Gideon, Saul, und David*, WMANT 38; Neukirchen-Vluyn: Neukirchener Verlag, 1970.

Schunck, Klaus-Dietrich, 'Bemerkungen zur Ortsliste von Benjamin (Jos. 18.21-28)', *ZDPV* 78 (1962), pp. 143-58.

—*Benjamin. Untersuchung zur Entstehung und Geschichte eines israelitischen Stammes*, BZAW 86; Berlin: Töpelmann, 1963.

Schulz, Alfons, *Das Buch der Richter und das Buch Ruth*, Bonn: Hanstein, 1926.

Scott, R.B.Y., 'Isaiah', *IB*, Vol. 5, pp. 151-381. New York: Abingdon, 1956.

Seebass, H., *David, Saul, und das Wesen des biblischen Glaubens*, Neukirchen-Vluyn: Neukirchener Verlag, 1980.

—'Die Vorgeschichte der Königserhebung Sauls', *ZAW* 79 (1967), pp. 155-171.

Sellin, E., *Das Zwölfprophetenbuch*, KAT 12; Leipzig, 1929.

Seters, John Van, *In Search of History. Historiography in the Ancient World and the Origins of Biblical History*, New Haven: Yale University, 1983.

Shea, William, 'Sennacherib's Second Palestinian Campaign', *JBL* 104 (1985), pp. 401-18.

Sheppard, Gerald, 'The Anti-Assyrian Redaction and the Canonical Context of Isaiah 1-39', *JBL* 104 (1985), pp. 193-216.

Simons, J., '"Een opmerking over het "Aj-probleem"', *Ex Oriente Lux* 9 (1944), pp. 157-62.

Simpson, C.A., *Composition of the Book of Judges*, Oxford: Blackwell, 1958.

Sinclair, L., 'An Archaeological Study of Gibeah (Tell el-Ful)', *AASOR* 34-35 (1960), pp. 1-52. New Haven: ASOR, 1960.

—'An Archaeological Study of Gibeah (Tell el-Ful)', *BA* 27 (1964), pp. 52-64.

Smend, Rudolph, *Yahweh War and Tribal Confederation*, Nashville: Abingdon, 1970.

Smith, H., *A Critical and Exegetical Commentary on the Books of Samuel*, ICC; New York: Scribner's, 1929.

Smitten, Wilhelm in der, *Esra*, Assen: Van Gorcum, 1973.

Soggin, J. Alberto. *Judges, A Commentary*, OTL; Philadelphia: Westminster, 1981.

Stoebe, Hans, *Das erste Buch Samuelis*, Gütersloh: Gütersloher Verlagshaus, 1973.

—'Noch einmal die Eselinnen des Kis (1 Sam. ix)', *VT* 7 (1957), pp. 362-70.

—'Zur Topographie und Überlieferung der Schlacht von Mikmas, I Sam. 13 und 14', *TZ* 21 (1965), pp. 269-80.

Sturdy, J., 'The Original Meaning of "Is Saul also among the prophets?" (1 Sam. 10.11,12; 19.24)', *VT* 20 (1970), pp. 206-13.

Tadmor, Hayim and Mordechai Cogan, 'Ahaz and Tiglath-Pileser in the Books of Kings: Historiographic Considerations', *Biblica* 60 (1979), pp. 491-508.

Tadmor, Hayim, 'Azriyau of Yaudi', *SH* 8, pp. 232-71. Jerusalem: Magnes, 1962.

Talmon, S., 'In Those Days There Was No King In Israel', *Immanuel* 5 (1975), pp. 27-36.

Tate, M.E., 'The Whirlwind of National Disaster: A Disorganized Society. (Hos. 7-10)', *RExp* 72 (1975), pp. 449-63.

Thompson, J., 'The Significance of the Verb "Love" in the David-Jonathan Narratives in 1 Samuel', *VT* 24 (1974), pp. 334-38.

Thompson, Michael, *Situation and Theology. Old Testament Interpretations of the Syro-Ephraimite War*, Sheffield: Almond, 1982.

Trible, P., 'An Unnamed Woman: The Extravagance of Violence', pp. 65-91, in *Texts of Terror. Literary-Feminist Readings of Biblical Narratives*, Philadelphia: Fortress, 1984.

Tsevat, M., 'Studies in the Book of Samuel, part II', *HUCA* 33 (1962), pp. 107-18.

Ullendorff, E., 'The Knowledge of Languages in the Old Testament', *BJRL* 44 (1961-62), pp. 455-65.

Vaux, Roland de, *The Early History of Israel*, Philadelphia: Westminster, 1978.

Veijola, T., *Das Königtum in der Beurteilung der deuteronomistischen Historiographie (Jdc. 17-21, I Sam. 7-12). Eine redaktionsgeschichtliche Untersuchung*, Helsinki: Suomalainen Tiedeakatemia, 1977.

Vollmer, J., *Geschichtliche Rückblicke und Motive in der Prophetie Amos, Hosea, und Jesaja*, Berlin: de Gruyter, 1971.

Wallis, G., 'Die Anfänge des Königtums in Israel', in *Geschichte und Überlieferung*, pp. 45-66. Stuttgart: Calwer, 1968.

—'Eine Parallele zu Richter 19.29ff und I Sam. 11.5ff aus den Briefarchiv von Mari', *ZAW* 64 (1952), pp. 57-61.

—'Die Stadt in der Überlieferungen der Genesis', *ZAW* 78 (1966), pp. 133-48.

Ward, James, *Hosea: A Theological Commentary*, New York: Harper and Row, 1966.

Ward, R. *The Story of David's Rise: A Traditio-Historical Study of 1 Sam. 16.14-2 Sam. 5*, Dissertation: Vanderbilt, 1967. Ann Arbor: University Microfilms, 1972.

Watermann, L., 'Some Repercussions from Late Levitical Genealogical Accretions in P and the Chronicler', *AJSL* 58 (1941), pp. 49-56.

Weinfeld, M., 'The Period of the Conquest and of the Judges as seen by the Earlier and the Later Sources', *VT* 17 (1967), pp. 93-113.

Weingreen, J., 'Saul and the Habiru', *Fourth World Congress of Jewish Studies I*, pp. 63-66. Jerusalem: World Union of Jewish Studies, 1967.

Weiser, A., 'Die Legitimation des Königs David. Zur Eigenart und Entstehung der sogenannten Geschichte von Davids Aufstieg', *VT* 16 (1966), pp. 325-54.

—*The Old Testament: Its Formation and Development*, New York: Association, 1961.

—*Samuel. Seine geschichtliche Aufgabe und religiöse Bedeutung*, Göttingen: Vandenhoeck & Ruprecht, 1962.

Wellhausen, J., *Die Composition des Hexateuchs und der historischen Bücher des Alten Testaments*, 2nd edition Berlin: Reimer, 1889.

—*Prolegomena to the History of Israel*, Gloucester, Mass.: Smith, 1973.

Westermann, Claus, *Genesis*, Vol. 2, Neukirchen-Vluyn: Neukirchener Verlag, 1981.

Wildberger, Hans, *Jesaja 1-12*, BKAT; Neukirchen-Vluyn: Neukirchener Verlag, 1972.

—'Samuel und die Entstehung des israelitischen Königtums', *TZ* 13 (1957), pp. 442-69.

Willi-Plein, Ina, *Prophetie am Ende. Untersuchungen zu Sacharja 9-14*, Köln: Hanstein, 1974.

Williamson, H., *Israel in the Books of Chronicles*, Cambridge: Cambridge University, 1977.

Wilson, C., 'On the Site of Ai and the Position of the Altar which Abraham Built Between Bethel and Ai', *PEFQS* 4 (1869), pp. 123-26.

Wiseman, D.J., 'A Fragmentary Inscription of Tiglath-Pileser III from Nimrud', *Iraq* 18 (1956), pp. 117-29.

Wolff, Hans W., *Hosea. A Commentary on the Book of the Prophet Hosea*, Hermeneia; Philadelphia: Fortress, 1974.

Woudstra, M., *The Book of Joshua*, Grand Rapids: Eerdmans, 1981.

Wright, G. Ernest, *Isaiah*, LBC; London: SCM, 1964.

Zevit, Ziony, 'The Problem of Ai', *BAR* 11/2 (1985), pp. 58-79.

INDEXES

INDEX OF BIBLICAL REFERENCES

INDEX OF AUTHORS

JOURNAL FOR THE STUDY OF THE OLD TESTAMENT
Supplement Series